To Brent

Best wishes,
Jack Sheehan

Dear Brent —
I hope you enjoy
the book —
Deana L. Bennett

Forgotten Man

Other titles by Jack Sheehan
Skin City
Quiet Kingmaker of Las Vegas
Class of '47
Buried Lies
Embedded Balls
The Players: The Men Who Made Las Vegas
Above Las Vegas
Chicken Soup for the Golfer's Soul

Forgotten Man

How Circus Circus's Bill Bennett
Brought Middle America to Las Vegas

JACK SHEEHAN

STEPHENS PRESS • LAS VEGAS, NEVADA

Editor: Geoff Schumacher
Designer: Sue Campbell
Publishing Coordinator: Stacey Fott

Cataloging in Publication

Sheehan, Jack.
Forgotten man : how Circus Circus's Bill Bennett brought
middle America to Las Vegas / Jack Sheehan.

244 p. : photos ; 23 cm.

ISBN: 1-935043-32-3
ISBN-13: 978-1-935043-32-4

The life of Bill Bennett, owner of the Circus Circus Hotel and Casino in
Las Vegas, Nevada, is told through the recollections of his family, friends,
and business associates.

1. Bennett, William Gordon. 2. Las Vegas (Nev.)—History. I. Title.

338.092 [92] dc22 2010 2010931655

STEPHENS PRESS, LLC
A Stephens Media Company

PO Box 1600
Las Vegas, NV 89106
www.stephenspress.com

Printed in Hong Kong

Contents

Introduction

DIANA BENNETT TELLS A CHARACTER-REVEALING STORY ABOUT HER FATHER, BILL, FROM when he was a boy growing up in Glendale, Arizona.

As a slowly emerging but still rural suburb of Phoenix, Glendale in the 1930s had a full-time population of just five thousand and didn't offer a lot in the way of youthful recreation. But there was a series of irrigation canals running through the farmlands, and it didn't take long for country kids with fertile imaginations to devise a method of hooking a ski rope to the back of a pickup truck and driving like moonshiners along the canal banks with a water-skier in tow.

Most of the kids in the neighborhood were older than Bill, and they quickly got proficient at the daredevil maneuvers, but they weren't about to share their strategies with the younger ones. No one had told Bill, just thirteen at the time, that along the canal route were occasional low bridges, and that a skier had to let go of the tow-rope handle well in advance of a bridge to avoid being decapitated.

When the first low bridge appeared, young Bill let go too late, spun out to duck under it, and was carried miles down the rapid waters of the canal before he made his way to the bank. The older kids laughed and poked fun as they urged him to ride back with them in the pickup, but he was so angry he walked the entire eighteen miles home.

Bill Bennett had to learn that lesson on his own, the hard way, which would establish a consistent pattern in his later life as a businessman. Young Bennett didn't have a role model in his home or neighborhood, nor did he have a particularly sophisticated education in the Glendale school system. He was one of those rare youths who was too smart for public school studies. It bored him. But he did have a strong work ethic, one that would set a high bar for the thousands of men and women who would come to work under his direction.

In his many stop-offs on the way to the *Forbes* magazine list of the 400 Wealthiest Americans, Bennett would make his share of mistakes, but he would seldom if ever repeat those mistakes. As importantly, he studied strategies in each business endeavor he tackled that would help him overcome his deficiencies and fill in his gaps. With an innate intelligence that showed up in every challenge he undertook, and a steely determination to prove he was better than his middle-class upbringing, Bennett would become one of the dozen most influential men in the evolution of Las Vegas from a mid-sized quirky town to a place *Time* magazine called "the last great western American city."

WILLIAM GORDON BENNETT WASN'T MUCH FOR FORMAL EDUCATION, PRECISELY BECAUSE THE pace of classroom learning was too slow and there was a bustling world out there waiting for him. Upon graduation from Glendale High, he enrolled in only one year of community college before his restless nature got the better of him.

Like his Glendale High School classmate Marty Robbins, who would go on to a legendary career as a country singer, with huge hits like "El Paso" and "Devil Woman," Bill Bennett sensed early on that he had what it took to conquer a universe beyond Arizona's borders. So he dropped out and enlisted in the U.S. Navy to fight near the end of World War II. Marty Robbins joined up the same time as Bill, not even bothering to get his high school diploma.

When Bill took the initial pilot's examination to join the service, he scored so high that the test administrators thought he must have cheated. They'd never seen an exam with so few wrong answers. So they made him take an oral test, and he scored even higher on that.

He had a few close calls as a pilot, including once crashing his plane into a pineapple field in Hawaii, but he was able to leave the Navy otherwise unharmed. The discipline he learned in his military stint would stay with him throughout his career, and his sense of patriotism and love of country only grew stronger.

Returning to Arizona after his service, Bill worked for a short time in construction, then found employment in a Phoenix furniture store. Business at the store was slow in those first months, primarily because the owner, shopworn from years of running the business, hadn't kept up with modern furniture trends. His inventory was badly outdated.

The postwar years were a time of upward mobility in America, and the growing families of the baby boom era were conscious of keeping up with current styles. Optimism ran high during that period, and with the Great Conflict behind us, the baby boomer generation felt entitled to enjoy the finer things in life, like large television sets, hi-fi sound systems, and the latest home furnishing designs.

Bill Bennett read all the current catalogues, and he sensed an untapped market in a city with the fastest-growing population in the country. Within a year, Bennett was able to buy out his boss, and several years later owned the most successful chain of furniture stores in the area.

Bill had a pleasant way with customers, always seeking their opinions about their tastes and buying habits, and he was a good listener. His easy manner, and an ability to adjust to changing trends, allowed him to move inventory as fast as it was displayed on the showroom floor. At six-foot two, well dressed and with distinguished good looks, Bennett radiated success, and customers who dealt with him appreciated his ability to listen to their purchasing appetites and find the items they wanted.

By his mid-thirties, Bennett seemed to have it all. He was married to the beautiful Bobbie, a former winner of the Miss Arizona pageant, with three children, Diana and Bill Allen Bennett, from Bobbie, and a stepdaughter Lynn from Bobbie's brief marriage as a teenager. He was already a millionaire, from his expanding furniture store chain and co-ownership of a tropical-themed bar and restaurant that was a rising hot spot in Phoenix. And he was a near-scratch golfer, winning amateur tournaments at the prestigious Phoenix Country Club, the longtime hangout of esteemed Arizona A-listers like Barry Goldwater and residential and real estate magnate Del Webb, who owned the New York Yankees. Webb would play a pivotal role in Bennett's life a few years later.

But by the beginning of the 1960s, when Bill was in his mid-thirties, several cracks were forming in this idyllic portrait. His ten-year marriage was troubled, and he was rumored to be dating an eighteen-year-old girl who was the daughter of his personal secretary.

This tryst was likely the cause of a separation from wife Bobbie while their kids were still in grade school. Bill's daughter, Diana, who says of her father that "he was my rock, he was the world to me," was so distressed by her parents' separation that she couldn't hold down food and needed prescription medicine to get to sleep at night and again to get going in the morning.

"I couldn't stand not having him living with us," Diana says. "With his long work hours, we were very limited in the times we would see my dad, and my mother was obviously very unhappy during that time."

Her father's sense of decorum kicked in, and after nine months living apart from the family he resolved to patch things up in his marriage. Bill moved back home.

Around this same time, Bobbie Bennett was diagnosed with a faulty heart valve. The prognosis was not good. Surgical techniques to repair her heart — methods that are used frequently today — hadn't yet been introduced, so she was advised merely to take things slow. That was not easy for Bobbie, as she was an active tennis player and the upcoming star of the country club's musical production of *South Pacific*.

Bill suggested they take a vacation to Acapulco, where he and Bobbie had enjoyed their honeymoon thirteen years before. He thought perhaps romantic surroundings would help them reignite the fire. But her heart apparently gave out while there. Bobbie Bennett died in her sleep at age thirty-two, leaving Bill widowed with their three children.

The loss of his wife was just the beginning of a string of unfortunate events for Bennett. Because her death had occurred so suddenly, and he had not prepared a legal will for Bobbie, he was hit with having to pay Arizona's large estate taxes.

Bill had also made a mistake in turning over the reins of the furniture chain to his older brother Bob, who was not an astute businessman. Bill had always felt protective of Bob, in large part because his brother had experienced a troubled childhood and had been effectively disowned early on by their father, Jack, a complicated man with a hair-trigger temper. The void was so great between Jack Bennett and his older son that he banished him from the family home at a young age, forcing him to live with his grandmother.

No one in the family can cite any viable reasons for Jack Bennett effectively disowning his oldest child, but it's clear that Bill was determined to fill this paternal void, so he watched out for his brother throughout his life, offering him employment whenever the need arose.

In the first years working for his kid brother at the furniture store, Bob had done a competent job, so Bill ceded more and more control to him as his personal life fell into disarray. But Bob gradually got in over his head. By the best recollection of family members, Bob allegedly forged some loan documents and made some other tactical errors in running the furniture stores. Compounding his money problems, Bill's large investment in a friend's financial company went south due to mismanagement.

Although his professional career was in jeopardy, Bill was finding happiness outside of work. Two years after his wife's sudden death, Bennett married again, to Lynn Hummel, the teenager he'd been dating during his separation from Bobbie. It's apparent in hindsight that the embers still burned between Bill and Lynn, all through the period of attempted reconciliation with Bobbie. Some nine months after her death, on a return home from college, Lynn reconnected with Bill at an office Christmas party.

They dated steadily from that time on, and were wed in a quickie ceremony in Las Vegas, just days after Lynn turned twenty-one. Bill was seventeen years her senior. The ceremony was conducted at the quaint and historic Little Church of the West.

Few could have foreseen that the chapel the new couple chose would one day years later be relocated to a plot of land that sat in the middle of a vast stretch of Strip acreage owned by the megacompany Circus Circus Enterprises. And that Bill Bennett would have absolutely everything to do with that eventuality.

To the surprise of most of the family's circle of friends, instead of the three Bennett children resenting the young woman who had replaced their mother in the family home, and at a time that she was just a few years older than they, the kids took to Lynn Hummel immediately. Diana Bennett, just thirteen when she met her father's new sweetheart for the first time, said she was so taken by the vivacious young beauty that she developed a "girl crush" on her.

"She was the cutest thing you've ever seen," Diana says, "with a nineteen-inch waist and an outgoing personality that made you like her instantly. Within weeks of coming into our lives she became like my big sister, and she was able to give me all sorts of advice about boys and fashion and all those things that young girls care about. Looking back, it's amazing how she was able to fit in so smoothly to a difficult situation."

Lynn Lucia, Bill's stepdaughter, who at just five years younger than Lynn Hummel was the closest in age to this new woman in the house, says, "I was a snotty kid, and I used to yell things out in the grocery store, like 'Yo, Mom, do we need any tomatoes?' I did it just to get a reaction from people wondering how this young woman could be my mom. But I grew to love her. She was good to me."

Al Hummel, Lynn Bennett's younger brother by seventeen months, says that when his sister married Bill Bennett it was a happy time for their family.

"I think there's a good chance that our mother was in love with Mr. Bennett, too," Al says. "I mean, come on. He was handsome and smart and successful. Many women were attracted to him. So while there might have been a hint of jealousy from my mother when Lynn married him, she felt good that her daughter had married well."

Any outsiders who might have rushed to the assumption that this young woman had latched on to Bill Bennett for his money would be disproved in the coming months and years as he experienced his financial freefall. He was married for just over a year to his new bride when he was forced to declare bankruptcy in Arizona. Liens were put on his stores and even his home, and bill collectors hounded him relentlessly.

Bennett's son Bill Allen Bennett recalls an evening when three different bill collectors and lien holders made their way to the family's front door.

"After they'd left, my father took all their papers and just threw them up in the air and laughed like crazy," he says. "I could tell he wasn't going to let them keep him down too long."

The new Mrs. Bennett stayed the course without hesitation, doing her very best in the role of surrogate mother. Without hesitation, months later she even accepted a low-paying job as a casino clerk when her husband was given an opportunity to enter the gaming world.

BILL BENNETT SOMETIMES USED THE GOLFER'S TERM "MULLIGAN" TO DESCRIBE THE SECOND-chance opportunity given him in 1964 by L.C. Jacobson, who was the president of Del Webb's Nevada gaming interests. The Webb Corporation owned the Sahara Tahoe in the northern part of the state, and the Mint Hotel in downtown Las Vegas and the Sahara hotel-casino on the Las Vegas Strip. Jacobson knew Bennett from Bill's occasional gambling visits to Las Vegas at a time when his business fortunes in Phoenix were on the rise, and he understood that Bennett was an exceptionally bright and capable businessman who had merely run into some bad luck in Arizona. L.C. offered him a job as a casino host at the Lake Tahoe property.

While some might have looked at the gaming offer as a setback, especially considering that Bill would occasionally be tending to the hospitality needs of former business peers in Phoenix, he seized the opportunity wholeheartedly. Although Bennett had been just a casual gambler himself, he immersed himself in the casino games like never before. He studied players' strategies for blackjack, craps, and roulette, and became so proficient at betting strategies that weeks after taking his new job he would be reprimanded by his new bosses in Tahoe for offering too much good advice to gamblers.

While by all accounts Bill and Lynn, whom he had by this time nicknamed Sam (in part because his stepdaughter was also named Lynn), made the transition from hot and arid Phoenix to the mountain country of Northern Nevada relatively smoothly, it would not be as easy for the children. Diana, just sixteen at the time of the move and fully engaged in school activities and sorting out boyfriends, was miserable at having been jerked out of her large high school in Arizona and forced to adjust to a much smaller school in a cold and icy climate that required a snowplow to get out of their driveway. She recalls wearing slick-soled flat shoes to her first day of school in Tahoe, and slipping on the ice and cutting up her legs in full view of her new classmates.

Diana's three-years-younger brother Bill had asthma, and he was beginning to be plagued with what would turn into a life-long battle with depression. The older girl Lynn, the stepdaughter who had never felt loved or wanted by the man who married her mother, was just out of high school when the move north was made. She elected to fly the coop entirely; she ran off to Texas and married a rodeo cowboy.

The Tahoe venture turned out to be a short-lived but important first step in Bill Bennett's new career. He regarded the opportunity as a temporary stop on a rise through the ranks of the gambling industry. He sensed immediately upon entering the casino world that he could quickly out-hustle and out-think most of the old-time gamblers and second-chance scufflers who populated the executive ranks of Nevada casinos. He spent his daytime hours hosting customers, paying close attention to their wants and needs, and his evenings learning the operations of other departments in the hotel. Bill was a business owner at heart, not merely a pit boss or a glad hander, and although he didn't verbalize his aspirations to others, he sensed early on that one day he would run his own gambling operation.

It didn't take long for the Webb Corporation to recognize a rising star, and within a year Bennett was transferred from Lake Tahoe to the Mint Hotel in Las Vegas, where he took on the job of assistant general manager.

Once he had gotten his feet wet in gaming, by all accounts Bill never gave a moment's thought to leaving the industry or returning to Arizona. Years later he would tell one of his key executives, Glenn Schaeffer, "I had to go to Nevada to reinvent myself, because it wouldn't have happened in Phoenix. That city was dead . . . the whole state of Arizona was a death to me."

Within a year of his assignment to Las Vegas, Bennett was the Mint's general manager, and in his second year there the property made $9 million in net profit. The following year the profit numbers doubled to just under $20 million, a staggering total in the 1960s for a hotel-casino located downtown, an area that had always been viewed as the ugly stepsister to the more glamorous Strip. Like a triple-A baseball player who bats .390 in the minors, it was only a matter of time before Bennett would be playing in the major leagues.

By 1969 Bill was running all three Webb properties in Nevada, including the Sahara Hotel at the Strip's north edge. To rise from a gaming novice to the company's key executive in five short years was a feat that caught the attention of everyone in the gambling industry, in particular E. Parry Thomas, the Valley Bank of Nevada president who would become a key component to Bennett's biggest "promotion" some five years later.

As Las Vegas resort developer Steve Wynn said, in an interview this writer conducted for a biography on Thomas, "In the 1960s, Parry Thomas was Eeney, Meeny, and there was no Mo. Anyone who wanted to expand a gaming operation, or enter the big-time world of Las Vegas hotel-casinos, needed to get the blessing of Parry."

Thomas had several meetings with Bennett in the late '60s and early '70s, discussing different buying opportunities that existed for a bright executive with revolutionary ideas about how best to run a gambling property. But it would take some time to find the right fit financially.

Bill Bennett noticed in his years with Del Webb that his company had done a good job hiring and training bright young managers, but too often and too soon they left to become stars in other organizations. He felt the reason for the talent drain was a poor pay structure, one that was salary based with few incentives or bonuses for outstanding performance. In his own case he didn't receive a pay raise when the Sahara Hotel was also put under his management, and he received no appreciable bonuses for taking the company from a losing position to earning significant profit. Promotions and greater authority were nice perks, but they didn't put food on the table. If Bill ever got a chance to run his own operation, he determined things would be done differently.

He got that opportunity after he met Bill Pennington, who like himself was a war veteran, a patriot, and an entrepreneur. Bennett and Pennington were the same age, both sharp as could be, both men's men, and both extremely focused on making truckloads of money. Pennington had made significant profits for the time, selling lucrative oil leases and hitting one gushing oil well in Northern Nevada.

At the point of their meeting, around 1968, Pennington had built a sizable slot machine route that leased machines to casinos throughout Nevada. His slots were a clear notch above conventional machines of the day as they had built into them a random-number generator that prevented slot cheaters and "mechanics" from figuring out a pattern of payoffs. Once a slot pattern could be deciphered, a good mechanic could figure out a way to have a machine hit jackpots at regular intervals.

After purchasing more than one hundred previously rigged slot machines out of a Reno warehouse — illegal equipment that had been seized by the Nevada Control Board — Pennington installed the new random-number mechanisms in them, and he was off and running. With his outgoing personality and sales ability, he built a slot route that spread quickly throughout the state.

The two Bills became fast friends, and they saw in each other the means to up their stakes in the world of legal gambling. Pennington initially had more money than Bennett, and a more sophisticated understanding of the powerful lure of slot machines to the average weekend gambler. He understood that the middle wage earner was more attracted to a game where he didn't have to expend a lot of knowledge or brain power. The games of craps and blackjack require gamblers to make decisions, and possess a decent understanding of numbers and calculations. Slot machines were no-brainers, and someone losing on them could always blame bad luck. If a gambler lost at table games, the common perception was that he had only himself to blame.

Bennett's wide range of skills neatly filled in Pennington's blanks. He had the management expertise to run a large casino, and he had a sharp eye for young talent. He was highly confident in his own capabilities. He didn't have a shade of doubt that he could assemble a winning operational team and run a hotel-casino as well as or better than anyone in the business. In a short period of time, and after several long and sometimes heated negotiations, they merged their goals and Pennington made the bold decision to let Bennett become a fifty percent owner in his slot machine company, called Western Equities. Their common goal from day one was to find and purchase their own casino.

Soon after forming the partnership, Bennett told Pennington that within five years after buying their first casino property they would make enough money to own hotels in both Las Vegas and Reno. That way, Pennington could spend most of his time up north, where he was more at home. The challenge was to find the right place to buy.

They looked first at the Space-Needle-shaped Landmark, which was then owned by Howard Hughes and brokered by Parry Thomas who, as noted, financed nearly all of the Strip resort transactions during that period. But the Landmark deal didn't work out, nor did their interest in purchasing the Four Queens Hotel, which sat on the most active corner of Glitter Gulch in downtown Las Vegas. Bennett would tell associates in later years that one of his biggest breaks in business was not being able to purchase either of those properties.

Finally, in 1974, Thomas steered them toward the troubled Circus Circus, which had opened six years before under the hand of a colorful and controversial entrepreneur named Jay Sarno.

Sarno had built the dazzling Caesars Palace to much acclaim in 1966 and had then parlayed his Caesars' profits into an unlikely and bold second property two miles to the north. By the early 1970s Circus Circus was hemorrhaging money badly, and the Nevada Gaming Control Board let it be known in industry circles that qualified new owners would be welcomed.

Sarno couldn't have been more different from the man who would take over his beleaguered property, either in temperament or style. Jay was a character straight out of a Damon Runyon short story. He thought of himself as a skilled huckster and a modern-day P.T. Barnum, and he frequently dressed as a ringmaster in publicity photos for his new hotel, which featured live circus acts performing above the gaming floor and at one time even a flying elephant on bungee cords passing overhead.

The hotel had achieved a degree of infamy in its early years when *Rolling Stone* writer Hunter S. Thompson famously penned the following words in his classic gonzo journalistic novel, *Fear and Loathing in Las Vegas*:

"The Circus Circus is what the whole hep world would be doing on Saturday night if the Nazis had won the war. This is the sixth Reich. The ground floor is full of gambling tables, like all the other casinos . . . but the place is about four stories high, in the style of a circus tent, and all manner of strange County Fair/Polish Carnival madness is going on up in this space."

The place was by any standard an odd curiosity sitting in the middle of the neon-flashing Strip, and many wondered whether Sarno's wildly imaginative creative side hadn't totally blinded him from the realities of making money.

There were myriad questions asked by tourists who stared at the byzantine structure, which was dramatically different from anything else on the river of neon comprising the Las Vegas Strip. One of the most frequent was:

Why name a place twice? A lounge comedian who performed up the street at the Silver Slipper joked that it was because Sarno stuttered.

Another question frequently asked was: Why would anyone build a family attraction in a city that catered almost exclusively to adult behaviors, with nude shows up and down the Strip, gambling and drinking encouraged, prostitution tolerated if not outright legal, and open-liquor container laws off the books? Who in the world would want to expose their children to all of that?

As gifted as Sarno was as a designer who could put form to concept and create a themed environment that would draw interested crowds and gawkers, he was a woefully poor businessman. And he had a number of vices, in particular gambling and women, that interrupted any business momentum he might achieve.

Sarno had actually opened Circus Circus without any hotel rooms because his money had run out during construction, and in the first year he charged admission merely to enter the casino: two dollars for tourists and one dollar for locals. But more damning to his long-term chances for success was that to finance construction of his hotel he had gone to Teamsters Union boss Jimmy Hoffa and one of his top lieutenants, Allen Dorfman, to get capital from the union's pension fund.

The Teamster money came encumbered with several jagged strings attached, in particular Dorfman's insistence that certain shady tenants from Chicago be allowed to run gift shops and concessions at Circus Circus. The most notorious of these shop owners was Anthony Spilotro, the mob's designated enforcer in Las Vegas, who was years later immortalized by actor Joe Pesci in the movie *Casino*. [*Pesci played the character who put a man's head in a vice and cranked it until his eyes popped out of the sockets, a crime that Spilotro actually committed. Spilotro had more than one nickname, including "Tony the Ant" and "Ice-Pick Tony," and a former Clark County sheriff estimated that he personally killed more than twenty people during his time in Nevada.*]

Once Bennett and Pennington struck a deal to lease Circus Circus, with a promise to purchase, included in the agreement was a clause allowing Sarno to live in the elaborate penthouse he had constructed as his private playpen. Sources say Sarno embarrassed Bennett on more than one occasion by strolling through the casino in only his bathrobe, and shouting out to Bennett, "Hi, Billy," as he dabbled with plans to build another of his dream projects, which he called Grandissimo.

It would be an understatement to say that Bennett and Pennington were taking a huge risk to invest their hard-earned money in a place as encumbered by baggage as Circus Circus carried six years into its existence. It was the equivalent of betting all their cash that they'd hit a blackjack on their first hand. But the hotel did have a good central location on the Strip, near the heavy action at the time, and underscoring it all was the unbridled optimism of the two war veterans with successful business backgrounds.

"There were several reasons we agreed to make the loan to Bill Bennett," said Parry Thomas, in a late 2009 interview from his horse farm in Sun Valley, Idaho.

"L.C. Jacobson of the Del Webb Company was a friend of mine from back in the 1950s, and our bank had financed the Sahara Tahoe, where Bill Bennett had broken in and done a good job. And I knew he had done an outstanding job in his years managing the Mint in Las Vegas. Bennett was without question a good operator, and if anyone could turn Circus Circus into a winner, we thought he might be the guy to do it. He and Bill Pennington had some strong cash flow from their slot routes, and that was what gave us the confidence to give them the loan."

After the painful lesson he'd learned in the furniture business by allowing others to run his affairs, Bennett's focus rarely strayed from business in the first years after he and Pennington took over. He exuded the confidence of a man who'd been in gaming all his life, and he made smart choices in bringing in young and talented executives to run the hotel's various departments. Bill Pennington was a fixture on the Circus Circus property in those first years, and while he wisely deferred to Bennett in most major operating decisions, there's no question that his own successes in other high-risk ventures made him a valuable ally in key marketing decisions.

In personality, the two men were very different. One former woman employee described Pennington as "the kind of man you felt like hugging when you met him."

Of Bennett, she said, "You had instant respect for him. He was stately, and you could tell instantly he was intelligent, but you would never have thought of hugging him. There was a certain distance about him. He wasn't cold, but he was a far cry from being warm."

While the two Bills fed off each other's individual energies and talents in those first years, the relationship between the two would grow icy in the 1980s, and they kept a respectful distance from each other from then on. Rumors about some arguments in their personal lives still exist today, but privately it was known that Bennett didn't want Pennington overly involved in the operations of their properties, particularly those in Southern Nevada. For his part, close associates say that Pennington felt resentment that he was kept at arm's length in a company that would never have gotten off the ground without his total involvement.

In later years, as he chose to travel frequently and enjoy the riches that Circus Circus afforded him, Pennington occasionally chided Bennett for working so hard. He often encouraged his business partner to spend more leisure time with his wife, children, and grandchildren. But adjectives like familial or affectionate would never be applied to Bill Bennett. Of foremost importance to him was working hard and devising strategies to build his empire. He did have his hobbies, particularly building remote control airplanes and boats in a workshop behind his home, and he did take wonderful vacations on his yachts, but Bennett's mind never strayed far from business and the day-to-day performance of his Nevada properties.

THE AERIAL ACTS AND ANIMAL PERFORMERS THAT HAD BEEN SUCH A DISTRACTION TO MANY gamblers at Circus Circus in the Sarno era were kept at the hotel in the first years after the takeover to carry out the theme, but the midway and carnival games popular with the children of the primarily mom-and-pop clientele were removed to a separate floor, where they remain today.

While Bennett and Pennington understood the importance of having attractions to draw customers inside, they knew that gambling, and in particular the slot machines which had provided the capital to acquire Circus Circus, were the key to their long-term success.

One of the first to get walking papers was the elephant. No longer would a crap-shooter have to worry about Dumbo crapping-out from fifty feet above the green felt tables. [*Diana Bennett recalls that the carpeting at the*

*time of the takeover from Sarno had an elephant-dung pattern, so that any
voluminous mishaps would be less obvious before they were cleaned up.*]

From his years growing up in a rural area, Bennett understood the wants
and needs of the folks who lunched at McDonald's and shopped at Wal-
Mart. While most Strip hotels in the 1970s did everything in their power
to entice high-rollers to their tables, Bennett extended his arms to weekend
travelers who were accustomed to living, and gambling, on a budget.

He enjoyed strolling through the casino, picking up loose papers on the
floor, attending to the most minor details. He often stopped and introduced
himself to customers, and asked them what they liked and didn't like about
their stay in his hotel. In his conversations with Parry Thomas, Bennett
had heard from the banker what so many other gaming operators had been
told but had sometimes ignored. A key to a hefty bottom line in the casino
business was full hotel rooms, the more the better.

One of Bennett's first key moves, mere days after moving into his executive office, was to bring in a dragstrip owner and marketing whiz he had
known in Phoenix, Mel Larson. Larson was in town for a brief stay in 1974,
meeting with hotel executives and selling closed-circuit television viewing
rights to the Indianapolis 500, when he got word from a third party that
Bennett wanted to meet him at Circus Circus.

The two had first met years before when they occupied nearby offices in
the Del Webb building in Phoenix. They renewed their friendship years
later when Larson, a skilled race-car driver, drove in the Mint 400 off-road
race at a time when Bennett was running the hotel. Bennett had been so
impressed with Larson's knowledge of auto racing that he put him in charge
of promoting the race.

When Larson showed up at Circus Circus on a Saturday night to meet
Bennett, he had no idea that his friend had just purchased the hotel. He
assumed Bill was just staying in a guest room. Mel picked up an in-house
phone and was told to report to the executive offices.

There was Bill Bennett, seated behind a big desk. When he told Larson
that he and Pennington had just bought the place, Mel was stunned.

"I thought Circus Circus was kind of a joke of a property," Larson said in
a 2009 interview. "And I knew Bennett was a prim and proper kind of guy.
He was as different from Jay Sarno as two people could be. It just seemed

like a very odd fit to me. I asked him why they had bought the place, and he simply said, 'I think we can make some money here.'"

Bennett hired Larson on the spot and told him to attend an executive meeting that very night in the showroom. Mel was instructed to report to work full time on Monday morning, just thirty-six hours later.

"I was still living in Phoenix with my fiancée, Marilyn, whom I married shortly thereafter, and I owned a home there," Larson says. "And I was being told that I would be starting my new job in two days. Obviously, Mr. Bennett had a sense of urgency to get things going. He told me not to worry about housing for a while, that I would be staying at the hotel. He also gave me one very clear description of my job: 'Keep the rooms full.'"

Larson did that by employing every marketing strategy he could dream up, including billboards scattered near and far proclaiming cheap rooms —nearly always under $20 a night — and peppering radio ads over the Interstate 15 freeway drive from Los Angeles to Las Vegas. Larson understood that while rich people in Southern California flew into Vegas, Joe Six-Pack drove his car.

When there were no rooms available, Larson had well-trained clerks placed at the front desk who would refer turned-away customers to other hotels, get them reservations, and then give the overflow patrons discount coupons so they would return and gamble at Circus Circus. Those types of courtesies fostered loyalty in customers, many who felt they were treated better at Circus than at other Strip hotels that were always on the lookout for high-rollers.

Less than four months after Larson signed on, Bennett rewarded him with a bonus check equal to his annual salary.

Twenty years after his abrupt hiring in 1974, Larson retired from Circus Circus a millionaire dozens of times over.

The pattern of finding good people, hiring them on the spot, and giving them performance bonuses and stock options worked wonderfully well for Bennett over the next twenty years. Key executives like Mike Ensign, Bill Paulos, Mike Sloan, and Glenn Schaeffer, among a group that was sometimes referred to as the "Young Turks," would lead Circus Circus to a stature in the late 1980s as the world's most respected gaming company, and would make them all wealthy beyond their wildest dreams.

❧

Bill Bennett was a complicated man, brilliant without question, extremely hard working, disciplined, a man whose professional demeanor, administrative abilities, and laser-sharp intelligence earned him immediate respect from all those who worked closely with him. In interview after interview with prominent executives who worked at his side, comments like, "I really loved the man," and "I owe any success I have to him" were heard repeatedly.

But Bennett had a hard time emotionally connecting with people, particularly those closest to him, and despite the counter evidence of occasional romantic letters to the girl who became his wife and remained at his side until his death forty years later, he had a tough time uttering the word "love," even to his children.

He had no meaningful relationship with the stepdaughter who came into his home when she was an infant. As an adult Lynn Lucia gathered the courage to once tell Bill that she had always loved him growing up, despite the fact they didn't get along. He point blank told her he had never loved her. Never one to tell white lies, Bennett was rigid with employees about ever giving him anything but the unvarnished truth.

"He had a sniffer like a beagle," Glenn Schaeffer says. "The stupidest thing you could ever do was to try to give Mr. Bennett a half-truth, or attempt an explanation for something you weren't dead certain about."

"Mr. Bennett was the best listener I've ever known," says Circus Circus's longtime legal counsel Mike Sloan. "Sometimes you'd find yourself continuing to talk when he would be silent for a long time, but that was always a mistake, because he listened to every word you said. If you weren't careful, you'd hang yourself by going on too long."

"He was the last man on Earth you'd ever want to bullshit," says Bill Paulos, one of the few top executives who was able to leave the employ of Bill Bennett on good terms. "If he thought you were blabbing your gums just to give him a satisfactory answer, or that you were dodging the painful truth for any reason, he would crucify you. You learned to measure every word before it left your mouth when you were talking to him."

An executive in the slot department at Circus Circus once complained to Bennett that he didn't have enough to do in his job, that he wanted more responsibilities. "I'll give you something else to do," Bennett replied. "Go look for a new job. You're fired."

Bennett never did give his daughter Diana her due in the gaming industry, although by the accounts of several other key Circus Circus executives she was deserving of a top management position long before she was given that opportunity. And that was presented not by her father but by Clyde Turner, who Bennett had chosen at a late stage of his career as his heir apparent.

Bennett's relationship with his only son, who bore his father's first name but not the middle, was strained from the time the boy was in his early teens. The two didn't see each other for the last ten years of Bill Bennett's life, although Bill Allen Bennett did attend his father's funeral in 2002. The son was also left a generous sum in his father's will, even though he had been told repeatedly through the years that he was officially disowned and would be cut out of the estate.

Diana Bennett says that for her entire life she yearned to hear the words "I love you" from her father. But she would have to wait until a year before his death, at a point when he was hospitalized and in constant pain, to enjoy that privilege. One day as she was casually leaving his room to get him lunch, she parted with her oft-repeated sentiment, "I love you, Daddy."

Her dad shocked her by responding: "Diana, you have no idea how much I love you."

She says she was so surprised and overcome by this long-awaited declaration that she nearly dropped to her knees in the hallway.

IN REPEATED INTERVIEWS I'VE DONE THROUGH THE YEARS WITH TITANS IN THE GAMING industry, when they are asked to list the top movers and shakers in Las Vegas, the names Steve Wynn, Kirk Kerkorian, Howard Hughes, and Parry Thomas come up nearly every time. Only rarely have I heard the name Bill Bennett in these conversations.

Yet from his and Bill Pennington's takeover of the Circus Circus in 1974, up until the 1990 opening of the Excalibur (which, with four thousand rooms, became the largest hotel in the world, and was totally paid off in less than five years), and the three-years-later opening of the pyramid-shaped Luxor, no one individual pushed the envelope further, nor did any do a better job marketing Las Vegas to the masses of people earning annual incomes under one hundred thousand dollars.

One can surmise that the reason Bennett has not gotten his due is because the last chapter of his life was bleak. Those who worked most closely with him during the glory years had either been exiled or fired by the time he purchased the Sahara Hotel as a parting shot in 1995.

The main cause of the rifts was Bennett's failing health. He was beset by circulation problems in his legs, caused possibly from years of indulging his passion for constructing model airplanes and inhaling glues and paints that hadn't adequately been tested for toxicity. As the discomfort mounted, which eventually would lead to the amputations of toes, then feet, then both legs, he tried to ignore the pain and continue a hectic sixteen-hour-a-day work schedule, even as plans continued in the early 1990s to complete the grandest accomplishment of his career, the Luxor, in 1993.

The resort instantly became a worldwide attraction, was featured on the cover of *Time* magazine, and should have put an exclamation point on a wonderful career. But insiders knew that behind the sloping pyramid walls all was not well.

Bennett was overmedicating himself to numb the pain, sometimes taking as many as thirty to forty Percocets in a day, and drinking far more than his two-cocktail norm. His performance at a stockholders' meeting in June 1994 was termed by the *Wall Street Journal* a disaster, and at a board of directors' meeting immediately following that same day, Bennett sealed his own demise when he urged the board to fire two of his key people. He demanded the ouster of Clyde Turner, whom he had promised would replace him as chairman of the board, and his loyal longtime counsel Mike Sloan, whose savvy advice and political connections had vastly increased the company's muscle in the Nevada Legislature and on Capitol Hill.

Less than a year later, to the anguish of everyone involved, Bennett was forced out of the company he had built into the most respected gaming organization on Wall Street.

Although that would have been a natural time to relax, enjoy leisurely vacations on his 100-foot yacht with wife, Lynn, and their friends and family, and take better care of his health, pride and paranoia took hold. Bill Bennett had no intention of leaving the battlefield on his shield.

He attempted a takeover of the Hacienda Hotel, knowing his former company was planning to buy the property and use the land to build another resort. He would soon learn that legally he was forbidden to do this, because he had signed a noncompete agreement with Circus Circus when he left. So he started to look at other opportunities to get back in the game.

He eventually purchased the Sahara Hotel, the property he'd once managed for Del Webb, in late 1995, for $193 million. His clear intent was to go after the same grind market he had controlled completely in his heyday with Circus Circus. But by then the pain in his legs had gotten worse, as had the paranoia.

Bennett's Young Turks had gone on to greener pastures with other companies, or stayed with Circus Circus as it merged with another Strip power and evolved into the Mandalay Bay Resort Group. He still had his loyal inner circle of relatives: daughter Diana, nephew Scott Menke, and brother-in-law Al Hummel, who at various times took management positions at the Sahara. But eventually he fired all of them. According to Menke, the reason was because they were aware of Bennett's tendency to medicate and drink too much and they were protective of his welfare.

For a man who was used to controlling his environment totally, having people around with that insider knowledge was just too much of an intrusion.

Bill Bennett didn't keep a lot of male friends. Nearly every relationship he had was business oriented. It is known he spoke frequently with Ralph Engelstad, the Imperial Palace owner with whom he'd partnered in building the $200 million Las Vegas Motor Speedway. In Engelstad he had a kindred spirit, another self-made man who had worked his way up from a middle-class background, and who knew and appreciated the struggles of forty-hour-a-week wage earners. They both had a soft spot for those less advantaged. While Bennett had been exceedingly generous to union workers, and paid for their meals during the nearly seven-year Culinary Union strike on the Strip, Engelstad was known to have hired more disabled employees than any executive in the industry.

"I think one of the bonds between my father and Bill Bennett was that they could trust that neither was trying to gain anything from the other beyond companionship and shared wisdom," says Kris Engelstad McGarry,

Ralph's only child. With her mother, Betty, and other trusted advisers of her father's, Kris now runs the Engelstad Family Foundation, which has given tens of millions of dollars to local charities.

"When a person achieves the wealth those two men did, they are conscious of the fact that nearly every person they come in contact with has an agenda, or some monetary or business-related incentive to pursue the relationship," Kris says. "Dad and Mr. Bennett were on equal footing, and I think a real trust developed out of that."

If indeed local history has neglected to give Bill Bennett his due because he exited the stage on a sour note, that is a shame. The pain he experienced in the last decade of his life should be an adequate explanation for most misjudgments he made, or bridges that he burned.

Historians might look instead at the empire he created, which started with one failing property on the edge of bankruptcy and grew into more than half a dozen thriving resorts and hotel-casinos that have now been absorbed into the giant MGM Resorts, a company that holds the fate of Las Vegas's future firmly in its hands as we enter a challenging new decade.

The kid from Glendale who made it on his own and developed a previously untapped market of customers from the largest demographic of all — the middle class — was by any measure one of the most important figures in Las Vegas history. Without his contributions, Las Vegas would be a vastly different and less complete entertainment Mecca today.

It is hoped that this compilation of research and memories will contribute to the eradication of Bill Bennett's reputation as a Forgotten Man.

— Jack Sheehan

CHAPTER 1

The Early Years

Diana Bennett

DAD WAS BORN ON NOVEMBER 16, 1924, IN GLENDALE, ARIZONA. HE DIDN'T TALK about his childhood a lot, but I've gotten quite a bit of information from my Aunt Betty Spitler, who still lives in Glendale. My dad's father, Jack, was not a particularly successful man, and he was an angry man.

Dad had two older siblings, my uncle Bob, the oldest, and Aunt Betty, who later married Clarence Spitler. They lived in a small house in Glendale that had a guest house attached to it, where my grandfather's mother lived.

For reasons I don't know or understand, my grandfather Jack Bennett hated his oldest son Bob, my uncle Robert Bennett, and made him live from the time he was eleven years old with his grandmother in the guesthouse. My dad never talked about that, but my Aunt Betty did, and you had to wonder what Uncle Bob did to be banished like that. Aunt Betty said she never really understood the relationship, but if her older brother simply walked into the main house, their dad would go into a rage. From what I understand, my grandfather did like his other two children, my Aunt Betty and my dad, Bill.

Betty Spitler (age 86)

MY BROTHER BOB WAS FOUR OR FIVE YEARS OLDER THAN ME. I THINK HE WAS FIVE WHEN I was born. He didn't live with us. My grandmother lived on an acre of ground next door to us in Glendale, and my father thought that Bob needed to live over there where Grandma lived, because she was all by herself. He didn't go with us on vacations and things like that. It was very unfair.

I don't really know why Dad treated Bob like that but I have a theory that it was partly because Bob was born when my dad was away fighting in

World War I, and so the bonding that normally takes place when a child is born never occurred. That's just a guess, but whatever it was it kind of mushroomed as the years went on and Bob couldn't do anything right. My dad would get after him just for doing things that his friends were doing, like going out for the football team. Dad would give him a good whipping for getting involved in normal school things like that, instead of coming home and doing chores.

Linda Christie (Betty's daughter, age 66)
MY GRANDFATHER, WHO EVERYONE CALLED JACK, DIED YOUNG, AT AGE FORTY-SEVEN. I WAS just a year old and Mom was only about twenty-one when he died.

Betty Spitler
HE HAD A CEREBRAL HEMORRHAGE AND DIED WITHIN A MATTER OF FOUR OR FIVE HOURS.

Linda Christie
THAT WAS BEFORE THEY HAD HIGH BLOOD PRESSURE MEDICINE.

Diana Bennett
EVEN BEFORE I WAS BORN, I THINK MY DAD WAS IN HIS LATE TEENS, AND WHAT I WAS TOLD was that my grandfather went into a rage about something and was outside the house screaming, literally chasing the kids out of the house as he was screaming at them, and he had a massive stroke and died right then and there.

Betty Spitler
MY FATHER'S BIRTH NAME WAS ALLEN MALCOLM BENNETT, BUT EVERYONE CALLED HIM JACK. He had a cotton gin in Peoria, Arizona. It was called the Bennett Brothers Gin. We lived in Peoria for a time, and he ran the cotton gin and they'd pick the cotton and bring it in in big trucks. Then they had this suction thing, and they'd suck it up into the mechanism that takes the seeds out of it. Then they would store the seed.

One time they had a fire in the seed house and one fellow got burned really bad. I remember that, because it was so awful. My dad also went out and inspected crops. He took loans from an outfit in Phoenix until the crops came in, and then he'd pay off the loans. We did pretty well. I'd say we were upper middle class for that area, because the place was pretty poor otherwise.

My mother's name was Marjorie. She was both a housewife and worked outside the home. She had to travel every morning to the Peoria cotton gin. They had a big scale there and they'd pull the trailer behind a pickup and park it on the scale, and of course they knew the weight of the trailer and they subtracted that from the total weight. From that they could determine the weight of the cotton that was being brought in to be ginned. Mother had to be up there at five o'clock in the morning to start that. During cotton harvesting season, during the spring and summer, she worked forty hours a week. I guess Dad died right around the end of World War II (1944). I was about twenty-one and Bill was nineteen or twenty.

Diana Bennett

WHAT I REMEMBER HEARING WAS THAT MY GRANDFATHER KIND OF DRIFTED FROM JOB TO JOB, mainly in construction. I guess it's something of a family mystery why he hated his firstborn son, Bob, but I know he liked my Aunt Betty and he liked my dad.

My grandmother . . . she was a little different. She was a businesswoman, and she held full-time jobs back in a time when women didn't always hold jobs. Marjorie Bennett was not what you would call a homemaker. She cooked, but only as infrequently as she could. My Aunt Betty took over the cooking for their family, and when I was growing up you always went to Aunt Betty Spitler's house for family dinners because she cooked beautifully. She *had* to learn how to cook, because her mother wasn't going to.

But after her husband Jack died, Marjorie was able to keep the family living pretty well, because she was independent anyway, and Uncle Bob was working, and not long after high school my dad went into the Navy and became a Navy pilot.

I always heard Dad and Aunt Betty had a great time growing up in Glendale, because it was kind of out in the middle of nowhere and there was a lot of room to play and have adventures. Glendale is a small-town suburb of Phoenix, but far enough away from the big city before the population exploded that it retained that small-town feel. They had a bunch of canals around Glendale [*which irrigated the fields*] and Aunt Betty would talk about how they would hook a rope to the back of a truck and water-ski on the canals. My dad was the youngest of all these kids that were hanging around and he didn't know all the tricks. The first time they let him ski on the canal with them, they didn't tell him that they would keep coming to bridges and that he needed to let go of the rope well before they reached the bridge. And of course he held on too long and spun out and the water carried him miles away.

Dad had a real temper, and he was so mad he wouldn't talk to any of the other kids and he ended up walking home. I was told he walked all the way home. Took him about five hours. That story was repeated many times when I was a girl.

Betty Spitler

I WAS A TOMBOY AS A LITTLE GIRL, SO I PLAYED OUTSIDE A LOT WITH BILL. WE HAD A whole acre of ground at our place and one time Bill was determined to make a cave, so he dug deep down into the ground. But when my dad saw it he made him fill it in, because sometimes kids got buried in those caves. In the summers, we played a lot in the irrigation ditches and the canals, which wasn't a very good idea. We'd climb up into tall trees and jump into the canals.

My mother lived long after my dad died. She had a long life.

Linda Christie

I'VE GOT MY GRANDMOTHER'S OBITUARY HERE. [*LINDA OPENS ONE OF MANY SCRAP-books she's kept. She's a professional at assembling scrapbooks, and thus was helpful in checking dates and facts for this book. She reads the obituary.*]

It says, "Marjorie Dean, 97, died on December 19, 1995, at Life Care Center of North Glendale. She was born in Tulare, California, and came to Arizona in 1911, setting in Miami, Arizona, where she was the first graduate of Miami High School, and the only member of the first graduating class. . . . She worked along with her late husband, Jack, for the Bennett Brothers' Gin in Peoria. She is survived by sons Robert Bennett of Mesa, William Bennett of Las Vegas, and Betty Spitler of Glendale, plus five grandchildren, ten great grandchildren, and one great-great grandchild."

Betty Spitler

IT'S GOOD THAT MOTHER GOT TO SEE BILL'S GREAT SUCCESS IN LIFE. SHE SPENT A LOT OF time in Las Vegas when he was running the Circus Circus.

Linda Christie

WE HAVE MOTHER'S YEARBOOK FROM GLENDALE HIGH SCHOOL, WHEN SHE WAS A SENIOR and Uncle Bill was a junior. Glendale High is where they went to school, where I went to school, and where my children went to school. Bill was in the letterman's club.

Betty Spitler

BILL PLAYED FOOTBALL. HE WAS ABOUT SIX FOOT ONE, BUT SLENDER. HE WASN'T A PARticularly good student. I don't think he was all that fond of school. I had pretty good grades, better than Bill. It certainly wasn't that he was dumb. He just wasn't trying or putting himself into his schoolwork the way he should have. I can't say that I thought about it much one way or another, but I certainly wouldn't have guessed he would become as successful in business as he did.

Diana Bennett

AFTER DAD GRADUATED HIGH SCHOOL HE TOOK SOME COLLEGE COURSES AT THE LOCAL COLLEGE in Phoenix. I think it was the community college. Then he went into the service. It was 1943, the country was at war, and he joined the Navy. The story goes that he took the test to become a Navy pilot, and it was a written exam and he scored so high they accused him of cheating. So they made him come back and take an oral exam, which he again passed with something like the highest scores they had ever seen. So he got into the pilot program without a college degree, which was extraordinary.

When my dad got out of the Navy, he did a little work with Del Webb in construction for a while, which is when he met Mr. Webb, and then he went into the furniture business. Dad started with one store and then added more and it became Trader's Furniture Stores. And he eventually took in Uncle Bob as a partner.

He married my mother in 1948. Mom's maiden name was Barbara Pullins, and she was a beautiful woman. Earlier, she had entered the Miss Arizona pageant, which was a preliminary to Miss America, and she won, which earned her the right to go to Atlantic City. But her father, Bert Pullins, who was the community pharmacist in Glendale, wouldn't let her go. He thought it would be a bad experience for her, and so she missed out on that marvelous opportunity. My mother's parents eventually divorced, and I know her mother Doris, my grandmother, was an alcoholic. I remember my dad saying he hated to go over to their house because there was a lot of tension there.

My mother was married briefly to an Army man, Colonel Urpschot, but that marriage lasted only one year. They had one child, my sister Lynn. It was odd because my dad didn't adopt Lynn after he married my mother, even though Lynn was just an infant. My mother wouldn't let him. She told him right from the beginning that Lynn was *her* child, not his, and that she would do all the disciplining and raise Lynn herself.

I think that has partly contributed to Lynn's having a difficult life. Neither of my parents was particularly affectionate anyway. They were both reticent about showing open affection, and so Lynn never really had that true father figure in her life that's so important, because her biological father basically disappeared from her life after the divorce.

Lynn Lucia (stepdaughter)

MY NAME ALL THROUGH SCHOOL WAS LYNN BENNETT. I DID NOT FIND OUT THAT I WAS NOT adopted by Bill Bennett until I was an adult and went for secret clearance when I worked at a company called General Dynamics.

My biological father was Jerry Urpschot. He was in the Air Force, and he and my mother, Barbara, who many people called Bobbie, got divorced when I was less than a year old. I never knew my biological father at all. I met him once after my mom died. I went to visit him in New Orleans, when he was a retired major. He was a nice man, but he was a stranger to me.

Really the only thing he did to acknowledge that he had a daughter with my mom was to send me porcelain dolls from different countries that he picked up in his travels with the service. It was a pretty special collection. To be safe, my mom had put the dolls up on a shelf in a closet way up high so we couldn't play with them. They were only for looking at. She said when I was older I would appreciate the value of them. One day a little neighborhood boy came over and he wanted to see them and he climbed up and pulled on the shelf and they all smashed to smithereens. I was only about seven or eight at the time.

I remember Mom spent the entire day crying in the closet, picking up the pieces, trying to find even one that wasn't broken or could be glued back together. But she couldn't find a single one. They were all beyond repair.

That was the only sign that my biological father had any care for me —
those dolls. And then they got shattered. Maybe there's a symbol in that.

Mom married Bill Bennett shortly after the divorce. I don't know whether she was involved with him while she was still married to my biological
father, but I've always thought so. But that's nothing more than a suspicion.

Bill Allen Bennett (son)

MY EARLIEST MEMORIES ARE OF LIVING ON SIXTH STREET IN PHOENIX. I WAS BORN IN
1951. I am two and a half years younger than Diana, whom I've always loved
and respected very much. She's got a brilliant mind for business, like my dad.

I'm not Bill Bennett Jr. My father was William Gordon Bennett, and
I'm William Allen Bennett.

We moved to Phoenix when my father was building his furniture empire.
Here is the story he told me. He was quite intoxicated at the time. He
was old school, you know, and he liked to drink. At any rate, the story he
told me about his start in business was that when he got out of the Navy
and was looking for a job he went into a furniture store in Glendale and
they needed some help. The business was struggling. My dad started to get
things on track, and he was given a lot of responsibility. As Dad told it, after
a few months the owner said to hell with it and walked out of the store and
told my dad to run it. The owner didn't return for a few months, and when
he did return the store had been repainted, there was a new sign out front,
and the business was making money.

The inventory in the store was all wrong originally, so my dad held a
parking lot sale and got rid of all the old stuff that wasn't selling, and with
the revenue he purchased more modern furniture that people wanted. He
made a thriving business out of it. The owner decided to give my dad half
of what was in the business's bank account at that point, and my dad used
that money to go about a block away and open another store. Within a
matter of months he put the guy out of business. Now that was the story
that came right from my dad's mouth, although like I said he'd had a few
drinks when he told it to me.

Lynn Lucia

WE LIVED ON A DEAD-END STREET IN PHOENIX, AND WE HAD OUR OWN LITTLE CLIQUE OF
kids. Our next-door neighbors were the Clevelands. The boy was Tommy
and the girl was Linda. Why I remember their names when so much of my

youth is a total fog, I can't tell you. I have major blackouts about a lot of that time, which I'll explain later. But Linda Cleveland and my sister Diana were the same age and they used to get in fights. Then Tommy, who was my age and two years older than Diana, would come over and beat up Diana for beating up Linda. So I'd have to stand up for Diana because she was too little, and Tommy would then beat the crap out of me. I used to beg Diana to quit fighting with Linda so I could keep from having to fight Tommy.

Tommy joined the service and I know he was killed as a young man. It might have been in Vietnam or an airplane crash or something.

Diana Bennett

Tommy Cleveland joined the Navy and was going into the JAG program. He was attending law school at Arizona State. During the summer, he was on assignment in San Diego and was flying in a helicopter off the coast when their helicopter had a malfunction and went down in the ocean. Everyone on board was killed. It was very sad.

Tommy was actually a bully when we were kids but he grew into a kind and handsome man. At his sister's wedding, we connected and were actually communicating back and forth the summer of his death. I still talk to his sister Linda about once a year or so.

Lynn Lucia

As I recall, Diana and Tommy reconnected when he was in the service and they went out on some dates, right before he was killed.

Diana Bennett

My dad's original family — my grandmother and my aunt and uncle and my mom's dad — they all continued to live in Glendale, and they supported themselves and did fine, but we moved to Phoenix when he had the furniture store. I just remember Dad became successful very quickly. I recall we were the first house on the street to have a color television. That was huge. And then we had the very first TV with a remote control, which at that time was just this big long cord that had an attachment to it.

Bill Allen Bennett

My dad took me to the factory once, after he started a furniture-making business. It was called Western Classics. He gave me a big speech about how to shake a person's hand, and look them in the eye. He was grooming me at the time in proper behavior. He was a good representative of, what do they call it? America's Best Generation, or something like that.

Diana Bennett

I DON'T THINK MY MOTHER IN THOSE EARLY YEARS OF THEIR MARRIAGE WAS DYING TO BE A liberated woman. In the 1950s she was very much into just being a housewife, although we had a housekeeper, and she enjoyed having lunch at the country club and playing tennis at the country club. Our family belonged to the Phoenix Country Club, which was a very old-school, old-money club. My dad was a good golfer when I was growing up, capable of shooting even par. I think he even won the club championship one year.

Lynn Lucia

ONE OF MY LASTING MEMORIES OF MY MOTHER WAS WATCHING HER IN HER BIKINI, DANCING and singing to the song, "I'm gonna wash that man right out of my hair," from *South Pacific*. She had won that lead part in a presentation at the Phoenix Country Club. It was either the whole musical or a talent show, and she had the Mitzi Gaynor part, and she would practice her routines in front of Diana and me. She was a beautiful woman, with a great shape. I just worshipped the ground she walked on.

Diana Bennett

IN THOSE YEARS MY MOM HAD A GOOD LIFE, BUT SHE WAS A VERY HIGH-STRUNG INDIVIDUAL, prone to terrible migraine headaches. I remember she would lock herself up in her room for days at a time.

I never saw a lot of affection between my mother and my father. I always felt very close to my dad when I was growing up. He loved little girls, period. He just wasn't one to verbalize it, nor was my mother. As a result I've always gone overboard with affection. My poor kids have to suffer through hugs and kisses, because I missed that so much as a kid, and I know how important that is.

My dad was soft spoken, but he had an air about him that was intimidating. When I was growing up, my friends would always ask if my dad was home before they would come over to the house, because if he was there, they didn't want to come. It's not that he ever yelled or disciplined me in front of them. He wasn't that scary kind of dad, but he just had this air about him that was off-putting until you got to know him.

Later on, in the workplace, when he was with his employees he was just the opposite. He knew the names of all the waitresses in the coffee shop, and he knew if they had a child that was sick, and he truly cared.

My brother and I have discussed this many times, the fact that in many ways he showed more concern about a waitress and her problems than he did his own children. That was just one of the many ironies about my father. He was a complicated man.

Lynn Lucia

I WAS SO SELF-ABSORBED AS A CHILD, BEING OVERWEIGHT AND HAVING KIDS ALWAYS MAKING fun of me, that I wasn't really tuned into the relationship between my mother and my stepdad. The doctor kept telling my mother that I just had baby fat, because it was affecting me emotionally.

I'd hear all the taunts at school, "Fatty, Fatty two by four. . . ." And nicknames like Chub-ette, or Heavy Load. It was miserable.

I do remember one day when I came home from school and Mom was in the living room, sitting Indian-style on the floor in the middle of the room, listening to a Judy Garland record, and she was just sobbing. I asked her what was wrong, and she brushed it off and said, "I'll be fine. I'll be fine. Just go on." So I left the room.

So in hindsight it was clear that she was having problems, but despite that she didn't ignore me and my problems. One day I came home from an exceptionally bad day at school, and point blank told my mom I was going to kill myself. She knew I was serious. I had actually contemplated it for some time. You know when you're young you don't realize suicide is a forever kind of thing. All you know is that you want the pain to end.

Mom took me to the doctor and they discussed a diet that would help me lose the weight. From then on she served me dinner before everyone else. I would get a hamburger patty, a sliced tomato, and cottage cheese. I remember that meal quite clearly. Then Mom would send me outside to play with the other kids. It worked because by the time I was an adolescent I had lost the weight and a lot of the teasing stopped.

Here's a story that tells you how I liked to play victim. Horses have always been the love of my life. Don't know how it first started, but I've been a horse-girl ever since I can remember. So this one Christmas, all I wanted was a horse. And I guess Diana expressed an interest in horses, too, probably because I talked about them so much. So Mom bought Diana this inexpensive, pretty young mare that had a little colt that came with her. And she bought her a Mexican-type saddle that had a lot of silver gauchos and trinkets all over it.

Mom bought me a registered quarter-horse and a used Toots Mansfield saddle, which is a very high-quality saddle, but it had been used.

In my infinite self-pitying wisdom, I went out to look at the horses on Christmas Day. Now mine was lying under a tree, and Diana's was running through the pasture with this little baby behind it, and then under the tree was this beautiful, flashy saddle with turquoise on it, next to my older saddle, which was used. Naturally, I thought I had been ripped off, when actually I had received the far better horse and the better saddle because my mother knew I was more passionate about my love of horses. But when you're as self-absorbed as I was growing up, you find ways to play the victim, and that was just one example.

Overall, Diana and I had a good relationship, but we weren't real tight as kids. We certainly never had a bad relationship. When we would get mad at each other, we would tear each other's room apart. I would go in her room, and she would go in mine, and we'd tear the sheets off the bed and pull all the clothes out of the drawers and throw them around the room. Then when all that anger was spent, we would go back to our respective rooms and clean 'em up. Which got to be a lesson in controlling your anger.

I guess in hindsight Mom and my stepdad were having problems during that time, but I was so self-absorbed in my own sadness that I wasn't really in tune with their situation.

Diana Bennett

I REMEMBER AS A CHILD — AND I'M SURE MY DAD KNEW WHAT I WAS DOING — I WOULD pretend to fall asleep on the floor or the couch, because that way I could get him to pick me up and carry me to bed. And I just treasured those times because that was when I felt the closest to him.

I don't know whether his behavior was due to his father being such a violent man, or what it was, but when he would get angry at you he would talk in this very, very quiet voice, so you would almost have to lean in to be chastised. He would say things like, "Well, you handled that situation about as gracefully as an elephant stepping on eggshells."

Dad never once laid a hand on me, but he could make you feel about two inches tall without ever raising his voice.

While that outward show of affection was never there, my father always made me feel safe and secure. Now, I don't think you're going to get that same sense of him from my sister or my brother.

If I got in trouble with my mom, which I did often because I was a tomboy, and if the neighbor boy was picking on my brother, I'd go stick up for him. Then I could count on my dad to take me to his store as a way of keeping me out of my mother's hair. I'm sure I did a lot of those things intentionally so I could spend more quality time with him.

I got less attention from my mom than the other two kids, because my sister Lynn, who looked more like my mother, had a little bit of a weight problem. So Mom would take her to modeling classes and do these things to help her control her weight. And my brother Bill, who we called Willie, was born with asthma, and he was always fairly sick, so he got a lot of attention for that.

I was this skinny, scrawny tomboy with straight hair that the nanny used to braid in two long pigtails that stuck out from the side of my head, until one day my sister cut them off. The nanny had mentioned one time that we needed to be afraid that the Indians were going to come and take me off because I had these long braids, and it scared my sister so much that she cut off my hair to prevent that from happening.

Bill Allen Bennett

WHEN I WAS FOURTEEN I WOKE UP ONE MORNING AND THERE WAS SOMETHING REALLY WRONG with me. I didn't know what it was for a long time, but then I finally had it diagnosed as chronic depression. I've had it all my life. It's been diagnosed by a variety of doctors. I had a lengthy psychological exam and computer testing and it all came back to that. I've tried many anti-depressants but nothing has ever worked. In fact, I think a couple of those medications did some damage.

Chronic depression is so misunderstood, sort of like Lou Gehrig's disease. My father didn't understand it at all. He'd say, "Oh, you've just gotta kick yourself in the rear-end."

My father looked at my depression as a character flaw. Well, it's not like that. I mean, you can no more make depression go away by kicking yourself in the rear-end than you can multiple sclerosis. But nobody understood it at the time, so it led to some problems. I became the black sheep of the family, so I buried myself in music because I found that by playing music I could achieve a level similar to meditation, where my depression would go away while I was playing, you know.

I grew my hair long, like other guys who played music, and initially that didn't cause too many problems, but it did later on.

Diana Bennett

WHEN MY DAD WOULD TAKE ME TO WORK WITH HIM, THAT'S WHAT STARTED MY KNOWING that I was going to work my whole life. I was never somebody who thought that I was going to get married and have kids and just be a stay-at-home mom. I always knew from those early days that I wanted to work. I just loved going to work with my dad. We'd be in the furniture store and we'd talk about where the refrigerators should be placed and things like that. He valued my opinions. He would never just sit me down with the secretary to keep me out of his hair. I was involved in some of the decision making, and it made me feel important.

He often worked fourteen to sixteen hours a day, and I remember many times his coming home from work just as we were going to bed. I don't think Mom liked that too much.

While she was into the country club scene during the week, my father would play cards and golf on the weekends. I think he looked at golf as just another adjunct to his business, because the guys he played with at the club would often become customers of the store. He understood the networking value of the country club.

He eventually got in with some partners and they opened up a restaurant called The Islands, on Seventh Street in Phoenix. He then spent a lot of time after work at the restaurant, and it became our favorite place to go as kids because it had a neat Polynesian theme and was very tropical.

[*Barbara "Bobbie" Bennett died suddenly in 1961, while she and Bill were in Acapulco.*]

Betty Spitler

IT WAS SUCH A SHOCK. BARBARA DIED SO SUDDENLY. AS I RECALL SHE WENT TO BED AND was complaining that she didn't feel good, and she kind of regurgitated and couldn't swallow and choked. Diana was just twelve years old when she lost her mother.

Diana Bennett

MY MOTHER HAD A CONGENITAL HEART DEFECT, AND SHE HAD STARTED PLAYING TOURNAMENT tennis at the country club, and the exercise weakened this hole in her heart. One of the doctors told my dad that she was dying and there was nothing he could do but make the rest of her life as happy as he could. So he took her back to Acapulco where they had their honeymoon, and she died in her sleep. Her death happened only about six weeks after the diagnosis. He hadn't told any of us about her condition, so her death came as a complete shock. She was just thirty-two years old.

Linda Christie

I GRADUATED FROM HIGH SCHOOL IN 1961 AND I HAD GONE DOWN TO START AT THE University of Arizona that year and remember how shocked I was at the news. I came up for the funeral and Uncle Bill lent me Aunt Barbara's pink convertible to drive back to college.

Diana Bennett

I REMEMBER THE EXACT CIRCUMSTANCES OF LEARNING ABOUT HER DEATH. MY SISTER AND I were in my parents' bedroom, where we weren't supposed to be, and we had two friends with us. My sister's friend was Priscilla, and my friend was Trudy. We were sitting on the bed and we were listening to this Bobby Darin song, "Somewhere, across the sea . . ." That song was on the radio as my dad walked into the room. My parents weren't due back for another seven days and I remember my heart kind of falling, thinking, Oh, we're in trouble now, because we weren't supposed to be in their bedroom.

Dad looked at Priscilla and Trudy and quietly asked them to leave the room. They left, and he said, "Girls, I have to tell you that your mom passed away yesterday."

My sister said, "Oh, my God," and I said "Oh, my God."

Neither one of us knew how to process this news. My sister was fourteen and I was twelve. My brother was already asleep — he was nine — and my dad had to tell him separately.

Lynn Lucia

MY MEMORY MIGHT BE PRETTY BAD FROM THOSE YEARS, BUT I REMEMBER THAT DAY QUITE clearly. Dad took us into their bedroom and sat us down, and he was very, very gentle as he said, "I have something to tell you. Your mom passed away."

I remember looking at Diana, and her looking at me, and I just went into a state of disbelief. I zoned out.

When Diana left the room, Dad asked to speak to me privately. And that was about the first and only time he was ever nice to me. He said, "I will try to be a good father. I know we haven't had a good relationship, but I'll try to do better and I'll try to build a bridge. . . ."

I just said, "Okay."

I remember that he said that, but I was really not hearing him because I had just heard that my mother was dead. She died on the Ides of March, March 15, 1961.

Diana Bennett

THE WAY IT HAPPENED, ACCORDING TO MY DAD, WAS THAT MY MOTHER DIED LYING RIGHT NEXT to him. Literally, she had her cigarette in her hand. They were talking, and she just stopped talking, and so he thought she'd fallen asleep. And in the morning she was in the same position. The cigarette had just burned down to her fingers.

I believe today that she had a PFO, a patent foramen ovale, which is a hole or weak area of the heart. When she got into her late twenties or early thirties, she started playing tennis very actively. It is the assumption that the physical exertion further weakened that area of her heart. I remember one night she woke up screaming in the house and my dad rushed her to the hospital. She was there for a couple of days. We were told she had a bleeding ulcer, but actually the doctor told my father that the weakened area had broken through and that there was an actual hole between the two halves of her heart.

Today, they could easily repair the valve or leak, but they didn't have that advancement then. The doctor told my father that she had only a few months to live and that he should take her home and keep her as immobile as possible.

He decided not to tell anyone and took her back to Mexico. She died in her sleep there. It took almost two weeks to get her body back from Mexico to Phoenix, and I don't believe an autopsy was performed because the doctors knew what was going to kill her.

Immediately after that it turned into a zoo around our house, because, well, when my dad decided to do something, he just did it without much hesitation. One of the first things he did was get all of her stuff out of the bedroom, so it wouldn't stir memories for us kids. He also wanted to sell the house right away and move us to a new house, so that we wouldn't be surrounded by all those memories of Mom.

Several of her country club friends came over to the house, and I can remember them going through her clothes and her furs and her jewelry and trying things on. My sister was a basket case, so she just took to her room and stayed to herself. We tried to contact her father, and when we reached him his response to my dad was that he'd remarried, he had his own family, that he didn't even know his biological daughter, and that she was my dad's to take care of. So Dad had that responsibility thrust on him — this child that he'd never adopted but would continue to raise.

Thinking back, I don't remember my sister's biological father ever visiting her even once. He was a career military man and he used to send her porcelain dolls from wherever he was in the world, so she developed a wonderful doll collection, but that's all she had of him.

So when our mom died, Lynn lost the only real parent she'd ever had. I think she wanted to be close to my dad, but she never really was, and I don't think she knows to this day — or until she reads this — that her real dad said he didn't want anything to do with her.

As I said, there were all sorts of complications in getting my mother's body back from Mexico, and a few days after I'd gotten the news, I was very upset with the women picking through her clothes and jewelry. I just decided to go to my friend Sydney's house. I basically ran away from home. I walked eleven miles to get there, and when I arrived Sydney's mom called my dad and told him I was there.

He said, "How did she get there?"

And she said, "She walked. And I think you need to let her stay here a few days because she's pretty upset with everything that is going on."

Then we had the funeral and I remember having to wear this pink ruffled dress, because it was the last dress my mom had bought for me. It was to be for Easter, which was a few weeks off. My mom always wanted me to be girly, but I just never was, and I remember how upset I was having to wear this god-awful pink dress to my mother's funeral. I thought I should be in black, so that was just wrong.

I remember my dad cried during the funeral, and I hadn't seen that before. It was a huge service, and there were hundreds of floral arrangements along the walls and outside the church from friends and business associates of my dad's and country club people. To this day, I hate gladiolas because there were so many of them, and I always associate that flower with the funeral.

After the dust had settled a little, my mom's friends would come over to the house and take Lynn and me shopping, and try to fill in a little, and my dad hired a full-time housekeeper and we moved to a new house. He threw himself completely into his work.

Lynn Lucia

I REMEMBER ASKING MY DAD TO SEE MOM AT THE FUNERAL HOME, TO SAY GOODBYE. BUT he wouldn't allow it. Which turned out to be a blessing, because I don't have a bad memory of her lying in a casket. I just have the memory of this beautiful woman dancing and singing for Diana and me as she practiced to be in the show at the country club. And that's a wonderful memory.

One of my biggest regrets from that period of time after Mom died was that I wasn't there more emotionally for Diana and Willie. I was the oldest child in the household, and I certainly could have done more to comfort them, but I was gone, off in my own little cocoon of self-pity.

[In 1963, a series of setbacks befell Bill Bennett's furniture business and he was forced to declare bankruptcy. It was a stunning setback for him, almost overnight going from a millionaire and business leader in Phoenix to having to start over. Again, the family has different takes on what happened.]

Linda Christie

IT WAS MY UNDERSTANDING THAT UNCLE BOB MANAGED THE DISCOUNT FURNITURE STORE FOR Uncle Bill. And as I recall there was some discussion of Uncle Bob having caused the problem that led to the bankruptcy.

Betty Spitler
I KNOW THAT BILL AND BOB WERE AT ODDS AT THAT POINT. I KNOW THEY WEREN'T GETTING along — I guess you'd put it that way. But I don't recall exactly what happened to cause that.

Diana Bennett
MY DAD HAD STARTED THIS BEAUTIFUL FURNITURE STORE ON CENTRAL STREET IN DOWNTOWN Phoenix and it sold really high-end stuff. It was a really pretty store. And he had a factory and was making furniture and that's when I'd go to the stores with him. I learned how to gold-leaf furniture during this time.

Phoenix was really developing at that point in time and these huge high-rises were being built. This boom period had started even before my mom died.

And then when she died, it was discovered that she didn't have a will. And Arizona is tough on taxes, so my dad had to pay estate taxes on half of his own estate, because my parents had never set up any kind of will or trust or anything. So that was part of the problem. Also, cars parked at his furniture store were being damaged by things falling on the cars from the adjacent high-rises that were under construction, and they came after my dad for that money.

And then as I understood it my uncle Bob ran the furniture stores into the ground and creditors were coming after my dad for money. With all that going on, he had to file for bankruptcy.

Al Hummel
I MET MR. BENNETT WHEN I WAS ABOUT TEN YEARS OLD. MY MOTHER, ELEANOR HUMMEL, worked for him as his secretary at the furniture store. She even started this time-payment plan for customers, and this was back when they didn't have these kinds of financial arrangements. It was probably his idea, but she ran it for him.

My older sister Lynn, who would become Mr. Bennett's wife some time later, was about eleven or twelve when she first met him.

I would go to the YMCA in the summer, because there was nothing else to do in Phoenix for a kid, and then I would take a bus down Central Avenue to the furniture store to meet my mom. I ended up working for him as a teenager, at Trader's Furniture. I worked in the warehouse, doing odd jobs. I married young, still as a teenager, and I worked in his high-end furniture factory, Western Classics, then I moved on. I spent eighteen years working for the Otis Elevator Company, in San Francisco and L.A. I even worked on the World Trade Center in New York as that was being built, in 1970 and '71, when there was a situation with the union.

My sister married Mr. Bennett in 1963, when I was just nineteen or twenty, so he became my brother-in-law at that point, but we never had that kind of relationship. I always called him Mr. Bennett, never Bill, and he never asked me to call him Bill. I just had so much respect for him. He was an idol to me. He was smooth-talking, a genius at business, and it seemed like anything he did he mastered. He was really something.

He always told me that the main thing he found in business, especially later on when he got in the hotel and casino business, was that the most important thing was for him to hire people he could trust.

Although I was working for the elevator company for all those years, I threw my name in the hat as someone he could trust who would always protect his interests, if only to protect my sister's interests, whatever the situation might be.

My mother and father were divorced in about 1950, when I was just in the first grade, and Mother was single when she went to work for Mr. Bennett. I didn't know anything about his first marriage, but I do know that he was always kidding around with my sister when she was at the furniture store. But it was under the eye of my mother, so there was nothing too out of line. I'm sure he watched his P's and Q's.

To tell you the truth, my mother was probably in love with Mr. Bennett, too. Most women were. I mean, come on, he was handsome, smart as they come, and so when my sister married him there was probably a touch of jealousy for my mother, but it was a happy occasion. She had the comfort of knowing her daughter had married well.

Bill Allen Bennett

I HAVE SOME MEMORY OF WHEN THE BANKRUPTCY WENT DOWN. I WAS PROBABLY ONLY ABOUT ten or eleven years old at the time. One night the doorbell rang at the house, and I answered it, and there was a man with some official papers to deliver to my father, and he was served.

He looked through the papers, and I could tell it wasn't good news. I remember I felt worried for him. Dad kicked back in his easy chair, and the TV was on but he had muted the sound with this big remote control we had, with the cable connected to it.

Then ding-dong, the bell rings again, and here comes another person with papers. And then one or two more. Dad just threw them all up in the air and gave this huge belly laugh. And he told me that night, because he could tell that I was worried, that he had made some furniture for Del Webb, and that Mr. Webb liked him and told him if he ever needed help, or needed a job, to get a hold of him.

So I think having that to fall back on probably eased some of his worries during that difficult time.

Diana Bennett

BEFORE ALL THE STUFF WITH THE FURNITURE STORE HAPPENED, I SHOULD GO BACK A BIT. My parents had separated when I was in the fifth grade, in 1959, and that separation lasted for about nine months. Dad moved out of the house and he would come and visit my brother and me about once a week. I was really miserable when that separation occurred. I couldn't sleep. I couldn't eat. My mother was giving me pills to go to sleep, and pills for me to get up to go to school. I was closer then to my dad than my mom. He was my rock. I was just devastated during that time that they were split up.

In all honesty, I think my dad had been seeing Lynn Hummel, who he nicknamed Sam, at the time. That is most likely what caused the separation of my parents. And Sam was just eighteen years old at the time, and my dad was around thirty-five.

I think in hindsight my parents ended the separation and got back together because of me. About that time Sam went away to college. I think she and my dad realized that their relationship was upsetting to everyone and was not going to work, and so she went off to school, and Dad and Mom got back together to try and make it work.

I didn't know it at the time, but my father and Sam started dating again right after Mom died. I was just so lonely then, and Dad was never at home. We had a woman named Bea and a man named Arnold who were our caretakers. He took care of the yard and the pool, and she took care of us. My sister Lynn had her group of friends, and I had my group, but I was still really lonely.

Lynn Lucia

I HAD NO IDEA THAT MOM AND BILL WERE EVER SEPARATED. IS THAT STRANGE, OR WHAT? I was just living in my own little isolated world in those years, and although that probably happened I wasn't aware of it. I know that sounds unbelievable that I wouldn't know about it, but it's true.

Diana Bennett

ONE DAY, PROBABLY A YEAR AFTER MOM DIED, LIKE IN 1962, DAD CAME HOME AND HE said, "I have somebody I want you to meet."

He had Sam with him. Unbeknownst to me, everybody who knew they were a couple had been telling Sam that she was going to have a problem with me, because I was the closest of the kids to my dad, and Sam was just seven years older than me. And how could this young woman replace my mother, and all those sorts of things.

Well, the day he brought her to the house, in walks this drop-dead gorgeous young woman. She's got her hair in a ponytail, and she had on these little white short-shorts, and her waist was tiny. Rather than having an attitude about her, I think I got a female crush on her from the moment I saw her. I know that sounds funny, but I liked her immediately. I remember I was preparing for a talent show at school at the time, and I did a dance for her that very first day.

It is totally politically incorrect in hindsight, but two of my friends and I were going to dance to the song, "Way down upon the Swanee River . . ." and we were going to do it in black face. Don't ask me why we thought that was okay to do, but we did. I had these pantaloons and a stupid little blouse for the routine, and I put it on and danced for her right there. She got a big kick out of it and went home and told everybody that she wasn't going to have any problems with me. I think she sensed the same thing that I did, and that was we were going to get along just fine.

I have more than a strong suspicion that my dad's relationship with Sam never died out, even when he reunited with my mom. I have the book from my mother's funeral, and Sam signed the book. She was there. And there are letters Dad wrote to her when she was away at college, at Northern Arizona University in Flagstaff. She wasn't much of a student, more of a party girl.

Supposedly, they got together when she came back to Phoenix from college. The story Dad and Sam told me was that when she came home for college at Christmas, which would have been nine months after Mom died, she brought her then-boyfriend to my dad's office party. Sam was the daughter of my Dad's longtime secretary, Eleanor Hummel, so that complicated things even further. Anyway, in the middle of this party the boyfriend got mad at Sam for something. Apparently, he was way out of line, and my dad escorted him out of the party and told him he was no longer welcome. And then Dad asked Sam to dance, and he told her if that was the kind of guy she was looking for, she was in trouble. He told her she needed to go for someone much better than that. I think the relationship just grew from there.

The truth of the matter is that theirs was the one really great love story that I've ever known. They loved each other madly. She was the one person that he showed affection to. He was outwardly affectionate towards her.

Understand, after Mom died he was considered this handsome and eligible guy in Phoenix, very successful in business, so when he married Sam the perception was that she was a gold-digger. Here she was just twenty-one, and he was thirty-eight. They were married in Las Vegas at the Little Church of the West, on April 3, 1963, just three days after she turned twenty-one.

But that theory about her proved wrong when it was only a matter of a few months later that my dad's business went bankrupt and he had to start all over. He lost everything. They even took Sam's diamond engagement ring. They left her with only the band, and Dad borrowed money from friends so he could buy back her engagement ring. If she'd been a gold-digger, she could have split right then, but she hung in there and did whatever she could over the next few years until they were back on their feet.

Linda Christie

I KNOW BILL'S STEPDAUGHTER LYNN HAD TROUBLE WITH SAM COMING INTO THE HOME. HERE Sam was twenty years old or something like that, and never had kids, and here she is trying to raise these kids. And high school kids besides. Lynn was just five years younger than Sam, and Lynn's mother had never let Uncle Bill chastise her or discipline her, you know, so there was never a lot of love lost between Uncle Bill and Lynn. So Lynn was already probably at a rebellious stage in her life, and to suddenly lose her mother who was her lynchpin in life, whom she was very close to, had to be very difficult.

Also, Uncle Bill had a thing about weight. He was always critical of over-weight people. He liked his women thin. I remember he said to me once, "Linda, you have the Bennett butt," which was not exactly a compliment. Lynn was chubby, certainly not obese, but then here comes Sam into the house as slender as can be with a model's figure.

Lynn Lucia

MY FIRST IMPRESSION WHEN DAD BROUGHT SAM TO THE HOUSE WAS THAT I THOUGHT SHE was perky. Of course I didn't like her, but it had nothing to do with her personally. I wasn't going to like whoever was brought in to take my mother's place. Sam was very pretty and just five years older than me, so of course I had an attitude about her. I used to love to call her Mom when we'd be in a store, just to embarrass her in front of other customers. "Yo, Mom, you need any tomatoes?"

People would give us a funny look, which was exactly what I was shooting for.

Diana Bennett

OH, WE HAD A GREAT TIME WITH SAM, PLAYING OFF THE IDEA THAT SHE WAS OUR REAL mom. The first summer after Dad and Sam were married we went to Mission Beach, and we told everyone that she was in fact our real mother and that we came to the beach because Sam had a very specialized diet of sea-weed salads that she ate during the summer, and that she ate only fresh cactus when we were back in Arizona in the winter. That was why she was so youthful and attractive. It's amazing how many people fell for that line.

Of course any guy that would give my sister or me a second look would forget about us the minute they looked at Sam. She was gorgeous. I still have her wedding dress, and her waist was so small that no one in our family can fit into it.

Lynn Lucia

AT HOME I CALLED HER SAM. HER REAL NAME WAS LYNN, SAME AS MINE, AND DAD HAD given her that nickname early on, so we all just called her Sam. The only thing that bothered me about her was that my mother was gone and she was there. It wasn't *her* problem. It was *my* problem. But I grew to love Sam. She was always good to me.

Diana Bennett

THE REASON WE CALLED HER SAM WAS BECAUSE WHEN THEY WERE DATING THEY WENT OUT on one of my dad's motorcycles, one of his many toys, and they were having a picnic under a tree and he took out his knife and carved a heart in the tree. He wrote, "Bill loves . . ." and she was all excited that he was going to write Lynn, and then he carved "Sam" as a joke.

He called her Sam from that day on. It was easier for the family to call her that, because my sister was Lynn and we couldn't have a Big Lynn or Little Lynn, because while my stepmother was older, she was smaller than my sister.

Dad called her Sam until the day he died. Her family on the other side continued to call her Lynn, but anybody in Las Vegas that became good friends with her after marrying my dad called her Sam.

Bill Allen Bennett

I DON'T KNOW THE EXACT TIMING OF THIS, BUT AFTER THE FURNITURE BUSINESS WENT bankrupt, I remember my stepmother was worried about how she was going to pay the bills. Dad must have already talked with Del Webb's people, because soon after the stores were gone he was running off to Las Vegas to gamble. He had gotten stacks of books on how to count cards, how to beat the system at blackjack, things like that.

I remember him coming home in the winter, and back in those days the casinos paid off with real silver dollars — this was in the early and middle 1960s, and he'd tear open a big bag of a hundred silver dollars and throw them in the swimming pool and all of us kids would jump in the pool late at night and scramble along the bottom for those dollars.

I recall he had this big stack of books he was reading about casino gambling. Whenever my father wanted to know how to do something, he'd read everything he could get his hands on, and the amazing thing was he was able to remember it all.

Diana Bennett

IT WAS L.C. JACOBSON, WHO WAS A TOP EXECUTIVE WITH DEL WEBB'S HOTEL COMPANY, who made Dad the direct offer to work for them. He told Dad that he had all the components of a casino executive, that he was good looking, that he understood gaming, and that he would make a good casino host. They said they could place him at the Sahara Tahoe, a Webb property, and they could teach Sam how to be a cage cashier. So that was a real life-changing moment for our family and for me. We bought this tiny little house up on the top of the Kingsbury Grade at Lake Tahoe, near Stateline.

Bill Allen Bennett

WE WENT FROM HAVING THIS NICE BIG HOUSE IN PHOENIX TO THIS MUCH SMALLER HOUSE at Lake Tahoe. And I remember for the first few months we were worried about the creditors coming up there and taking our TV set from us. I was either twelve or thirteen when we moved up there, and I have to say I loved it. I was at an age where I had all the benefits of snow without the downside. I didn't have to drive in it, and I didn't have to go to work in it. If the bus couldn't make it to school, I got the day off. The Kingsbury Grade is on top of a mountain at an elevation of over ten thousand feet. It's basically the crater rim of Lake Tahoe, which was carved out by a glacier, and we were living on one of the highest spots up there.

I loved it up there until I got sick. I woke up one day and I had symptoms like the flu. I was achy all over. Depression hurts physically, although I didn't know at the time that's what it was. My first sense was that I had lost something that I wouldn't get back. It was like whatever it is that makes us happy and gives us the energy to thrive and strive had been ripped from me. I tried to explain this to Diana. I remember telling her that I was moody like a pregnant woman and not feeling well at all. I didn't want to go to school, but my stepmother Sam was a pretty strict disciplinarian and she wouldn't let me stay out of school for very long.

I found out real quick that people don't understand depression, and they definitely don't want to hear about the doom and gloom that goes with it. So I started acting like everything was fine. I just decided to take it one minute at a time, one day at a time, and try to act as normal as I could. But the depression affected everything I did from that point on. The truth of it was that I was kind of a mean, bratty kid before the depression hit, but when it came on it really humbled me.

I tried to explain it to my father once or twice. He said it was just a character flaw.

Diana Bennett

I WAS SIXTEEN WHEN WE MOVED UP THERE, RIGHT AT THE BEGINNING OF MY JUNIOR YEAR of high school. And I was hating it and making sure everyone knew how much I was hating it.

My dad had flown up to Tahoe early and rented this tiny house and he'd started work at the Sahara Tahoe, so it was up to the three of us to make the move from Scottsdale up there.

My sister Lynn had been very active in the rodeos in Scottsdale — in fact, she was Miss Prada del Sol or something, the queen of some rodeo — and she met a rodeo clown and they got married right away and moved to Texas. She couldn't wait to get out of Arizona and start a new life. I couldn't blame her. Lynn didn't like Sam much, and although she was part of the family, she had never been that close to my dad, as I said. She actually wrote these letters anonymously to my dad saying that this woman had only married him for his money and stuff like that. We later traced it back to my sister as the one who composed the letters. So Lynn never made the move to Lake Tahoe with us.

It was up to Sam and me and my brother to make the move, and arrange for the moving van to load up the few things we had left, because the bankruptcy hadn't left us with much. The rules were that they allowed everyone a bed, and one living-room set, and some personal belongings, and that was about it.

The car we had to drive up there was a little Mustang convertible Dad had bought for Sam, hardly the ideal vehicle for a move like that. Especially considering we had two cats and a dog with us.

So we're on this excursion from Phoenix to Lake Tahoe, which is about fifteen hours, and just as we're crossing the border from Kingman, Arizona, to Nevada, we hear this clunk and we look back and our transmission or some other important car part is sitting on the highway.

We hitched a ride with a trucker back to Kingman, where we managed to find a hotel that allowed us to keep the animals. It was right by the railroad tracks, noisy as can be, and we stayed there for three days. That's how long it took to repair the car.

We then made it to Las Vegas before we blew a tire, and we got ripped off by some mechanic there. I don't remember where we stayed, but it was near Fremont Street downtown.

From there we made it to Ely or Elko, where we ended up pretty much in the red-light district. I know it was in an area we had no business being. I just remember there were a whole lot of flashing lights. We called Dad and he said we couldn't stay there, that we needed to keep driving until we got to Lake Tahoe.

Remember, I'm sixteen at the time, and I've been pulled out of Arcadia High School, a large school which I loved, with two thousand students. So I'm going to a place where I'm gonna be the new kid in a small school. I'm distinctly unhappy. The whole way, as all these car problems and everything kept happening, I am telling my stepmother that we are having these predicaments because God does not want us to make this move.

"God wants us to go back to Phoenix," I said more than once.

When we finally got to Tahoe, we had to drive up the back of Kingsbury Grade. At that time it was a one-lane highway, period. So if two cars were coming in opposite directions, one had to pull off the side of the road. And this is with three people and three animals in a Mustang.

Finally, we get there and we pull up to this little house. Our house in Phoenix was probably four thousand square feet, and this place is about eight or nine hundred square feet.

It was in that house that I learned that heat does not know how to come around a corner. You walked through the front door into a small living room, and there was a doorway and a kitchen. And there was a wall heater between the kitchen and the living room. And then there was a hall where my Dad and Sam's bedroom and my brother's bedroom were. And there was a heater in the hallway between their two rooms. Then you went around the corner, and there was a bathroom and my bedroom. No wall heater. Nothing.

We had been there about a week or so when we got the first snow. Now I'd been raised in Arizona, and I had no tolerance for the cold. I couldn't get out of bed when I woke up, with absolutely no heat coming around that corner. I said someone has to get me an electric blanket. I was told we didn't have enough money for one. We basically had nothing right then.

We didn't even have trash service. Two or three days a week we put our trash cans in the back seat of the Mustang and drove to the city dump. The snow plows also didn't come all the way up the hill to our rented house. My dad really liked it when I dated guys who had snow plows on the front of their cars or trucks. That's how he decided whether my date was a good guy or a bad guy. If the guy had a snow plow, Dad liked him. If he didn't . . . hmmm, not so much.

I enrolled immediately in George Whittell High School. It had an entire student population of about two hundred, roughly ten percent of Arcadia High. It was a beautiful school, I will say. It had this glass front looking out over South Lake Tahoe. The view was so beautiful I wondered how anyone got any work done there.

I remember we got out of the car that first day and I had on a pair of little patent leather flats, because that's what I always wore. I had them in every color. And I'm walking on ice and woops! . . . I go right down and slide like thirty feet on the sidewalk. And everybody is looking out from these glass classrooms and they see the whole thing.

We had to wear dresses to school then, so with my pratfall I just shredded my legs and there's blood dripping down. How about that for a graceful entrance? I went into the restroom and washed off the blood and that kind of started my reputation at that school as a klutz.

It actually helped me fit right in because the other students and I could laugh about it, and surprisingly, despite how unhappy I had been about making the move to Lake Tahoe, I very quickly fit right in with the other kids. Because it was such a small school, you could find your place in a lot of different activities. I actually went to cheerleader tryouts and made the squad, even though I was like the worst cheerleader in the world. I also got involved in school council and became editor of the yearbook. And I maintained my reputation for clumsiness because I was always falling down in the middle of things. Grace was never my middle name.

Meantime, Dad was a casino host on swing shift, and my stepmother was a cage cashier on the same shift.

Lynn Lucia

I STARTED DATING A RODEO CLOWN NAMED TOM LUCIA MY SENIOR YEAR OF HIGH SCHOOL and we got married right after graduation. It's a fair statement to say I took the first chance I had to get away from that household.

The Bennett family moved to Tahoe, and I stayed in Phoenix for a while, because my husband was off following the rodeo and we were just starting out and he couldn't afford for me to travel with him. So I lived with his mother, which as you can imagine was not an ideal situation. Years later we had two wonderful sons, T.J., who is now thirty-seven, and Josh, who is thirty-five.

The marriage lasted ten years. Tommy Lucia is still rodeoing. He is pretty famous. He has a dog and a monkey which ride on horseback, and he has performed many times at the National Finals Rodeo in Las Vegas.

Bill Allen Bennett

DAD ONCE TOLD ME THIS STORY ABOUT HOW HE ROSE THROUGH THE RANKS IN THE CASINO business. In his position as casino host at the Sahara Tahoe, of course it was his job to make certain he got high-rollers to the gaming tables and kept them happy.

What his job description did not include was teaching gamblers how to beat the house. But he knew how to count cards, he'd gambled a lot himself, and he'd read every book he could find on blackjack. With his good customers, he was actually helping them learn how to count cards and how to win. In a sense he was helping them beat his own casino. He had also worked with all the dealers on how to protect the game from cheaters, so he was basically helping everyone. But because he was helping gamblers win, the casino manager went to Del Webb and complained about what Dad was doing. Webb's response was something like, "Well, Bennett obviously knows more about the casino business than you do."

Shortly thereafter he made my dad the casino manager. Dad jumped into that job wholeheartedly, and he started using basic business practices, like forecasting and making projections and doing things nobody had bothered to do in the casino business up to that point.

Not long after that he became general manager of the property, and the hotel started making money like it never had before.

It wasn't long after that that Del Webb praised my father for turning things around up there, and asked him to go to downtown Las Vegas and try to turn around the Mint Hotel.

Diana Bennett

I REMEMBER DAD SET UP A BLACKJACK TABLE IN THE GARAGE AT THAT FIRST HOUSE IN TAHOE, and he taught himself all about dealing. He would have my brother and I play the hands. Dad just had an insatiable curiosity about the game, and how he might catch cheating. He wanted that firsthand knowledge of how all the games worked, because I'm sure he knew even then that his future was going to be in the gambling business.

Although I was getting along fine at Whittell High School, the situation at home was hectic. They dumped way too much work on me. Because my dad and stepmom were working swing shift, they would get home after my brother and I were in bed, they would have a meal, and then leave the dishes for me. So I would have to get Bill and myself ready for school, clean up the kitchen from their mess the night before, and then when I'd get home from school in the afternoon clean the house so it was looking good when they got home from work. This is in addition to my homework, cheerleading activities, and everything else.

My stepmom had employed a housekeeper from when she first married Dad, and with our financial limitations all of a sudden that role was just thrust on me.

When it came time to buy my cheerleading uniform, which was twenty-five or thirty dollars, I was told we couldn't afford it. It cost something like thirty bucks. So I got a job at a local Sprouse-Reitz store, a five-and-dime place. I would take my brother to a neighbor's house so they would watch him and then I could go to work for a four-hour shift. I picked up some extra money that way, but I ended up making my own uniform.

One day this all came to a boil and I had a huge fight with my stepmom. I explained to her in very direct terms that I was carrying far more responsibility than I should have had. It was one of only two big fights I ever had with her.

That was one of the times Dad used the line, "You're about as subtle as an elephant walking on eggshells." But he understood my point.

He said, "Sam and I are both working really hard, and our lives have changed, and we just didn't appreciate how much we changed your life as well."

So the pressure lessened after that. Our family was not one that fought a lot. When we had a situation like that, we talked things out. We really did.

At the end of my junior year, we bought a house down by the lake, far down the hill from the ridge where we'd needed a snow plow. You could actually walk to the lake. I was thinking life was really good once again. Then about six weeks later, in August, Dad told us he was being promoted to assistant general manager of the Mint in Las Vegas.

I did my typical teenage angst routine and said I wasn't going.

My dad said, "What are you talking about?"

I said, "No way. You moved me once, I had to get totally re-established, and now I'm on the student council at school, I'm editor of the yearbook, and I'm a cheerleader. I've made new friends and I want to have a great senior year. I don't want to transfer to a new big school in Las Vegas where I'm going to be a big nothing."

Believe it or not, he and Sam understood my argument. They realized that it would be unfair to move me like that again. My brother wasn't as entrenched in school as I was. I think he was a ninth-grader when they moved.

One of the girls on my cheerleading squad named Patty asked her parents if I could stay with her family for the school year, and my dad agreed to pay them for my board and room. Dad was getting a good pay raise to go to the Mint, but we were still watching every dime, so I knew I couldn't go to Las Vegas until Christmas break. There wouldn't be any flying back and forth to visit.

What I didn't know when I accepted my friend Patty's offer was that her father was an alcoholic who went on these two- and three-day binges. Patty and I would have to go searching through the bars and taverns of Tahoe to find him when he'd been gone for several days.

Also, her father was a hunter, and as far as having meat on the table, we'd only eat what he would kill. So I had to learn to skin a deer, and pluck all the feathers out of a duck or goose. If that wasn't bad enough, Patty's mom and dad would have these horrible screaming fights all night long, probably brought on by his drinking. I was sharing a room with Patty, who'd grown up her whole life with this going on, but to me it was intolerable. My grades started to suffer.

I was still cheerleading and working on the yearbook, but it was a miserable situation. I called my parents and they said wait until I came home at Christmas and we could talk about it then.

Finally, Christmas break came, and although I had a driver's license I didn't have a car, so Dad found some friends who drove me down. I didn't get a car until I went to college in Arizona.

I was dreading the first meeting with Dad because I knew my high school had sent him a notice slip that I was making a D in physics. I had always gotten very nearly straight A's, and that's what he expected. So I knew I was going to be in big trouble when I got to Las Vegas. I remember the moment well. I had on a yellow-and-white wool skirt and a yellow cardigan sweater. I had used a big safety pin to hold up the skirt because I had lost so much weight. I was 5' 6" and weighed about 105.

The car took me to the Mint, and they paged my dad to come down to valet parking to get me. He came out, and he literally had that pink slip in his hand that said I was failing physics. My first thought was, Oh my God: he has the notice in his hand.

But he took one look at me and the clothes just hanging off me and he just opened up his arms. He crumpled the slip in his hand and I came running into his arms. He said, "I think it's time for you to come home."

I said, "Yes," and I started crying. I never went back to Tahoe.

I finished my senior year at Western High School in Las Vegas. It was a rough school, but I made a couple of good friends and I had boyfriends. As I had imagined, I was a nobody at the school, and I didn't even get to go to my senior prom because the guy I was dating had asked somebody else early in the year and that girl hadn't found a new boyfriend. Here, I'd been the junior prom queen in Lake Tahoe, and I didn't even get to go to my senior prom in Las Vegas. But I was home, and that was the most important thing.

Dad was the assistant general manager of the Mint for one year, and then they promoted him to general manager. He was just so good at every job he had that it didn't take him long to get those promotions.

CHAPTER 2
Vegas or Bust

Diana Bennett

IT WAS AN IMPORTANT PROMOTION FOR DAD WHEN HE WAS MADE ASSISTANT GENERAL manager of the Mint in 1966. My guess is his salary went from about thirty grand a year at the Sahara Tahoe to around fifty at the Mint. And the new position meant that my stepmom, who was making a little over minimum wage working in the casino cage in Tahoe, didn't have to work anymore.

The Mint was right next door to the Horseshoe in downtown Las Vegas, and a helpful occurrence from that time is that my dad became friends with Benny Binion. Everyone knows that Benny was about the smartest guy in the gaming business when it came to understanding customers and what worked and what didn't work in a casino.

You could barely walk into the Horseshoe without bumping into a slot machine. Benny taught Dad about all the pay tables for slot machines, and he explained why you put the nickel machines in the front of the casino, because they're always busy and that activity draws people in.

Dad learned from Benny that you treat a slot floor like you do a grocery store or furniture store, with the loss leader items up front and the more essential items in the back. It's why the milk and eggs and bread are always in the back of the grocery store, so you have to pass by all the aisles to get to them.

Benny taught my dad about end-cap machines, which have a higher hold percentage than other slot machines. It's the same principle as in a grocery store, where they have potato chip displays and doughnuts at the end of an aisle, and the impulse is to grab them and put them in your basket. People will be walking through a casino and impulsively play a machine on the end of a row, even though those machines will have a much higher hold-ratio, like 12 percent. Those end-cap bets are all based on impulse, and so your machines that pay off the least frequently are placed there.

I think the reason Benny was so generous with my dad in sharing that information is because he saw in him someone who was truly interested in learning a lot, and I don't think Benny felt the Mint was a threat to the Horseshoe. Binion's drew some of the highest rollers in the world, while the Mint was more of a grind joint.

The Mint did have a few good customers, but things were so different then. I mean, there were actually times when my dad went into the pit and dealt cards to good customers. You certainly wouldn't see that happen today.

I recall this one big customer the Mint had, whose wife had a huge diamond ring on her finger. Everybody just stopped and waited on him when he came in, and they even allowed him to walk into the pit if he felt like it. What I didn't notice right off was that if you looked closely at this woman's ring, you could see the carbon in it.

I started working at the Mint in the summer of 1967, after I graduated from Western High School and before going to Arizona State. I would fill in for secretaries on their summer vacations. I had good typing skills and I could take shorthand, so that worked out well, and eventually I got to work in other departments as well.

Billy Conn

I STARTED WORKING AT THE MINT SOMETIME IN 1967. I HAD JUST COME BACK FROM MY time in the service, and I started at the bottom and worked my way up. I'd worked for the Del Webb Company previously at the Thunderbird, as a busboy and then a waiter, and then I went to Vietnam and I came back and worked at the Mint. Mr. Bennett was the assistant general manager and then the general manager and that's where I first met him.

I started as a head waiter at the Mint, then became the banquet manager and then the catering manager. Eventually, they put a big buffet in on the mezzanine and closed their catering department and banquet rooms, and I moved over to the Sahara Space Center as the banquet manager over there. By then Mr. Bennett was in charge of that hotel as well for Del Webb.

I had instant respect for Mr. Bennett as my boss, and I think he also saw something in me. I was a young man, twenty-one years old, a Vietnam veteran, and probably more likely *not* to succeed than the other way around. I had grown up with six different stepfathers, and I got in fights nearly every day as a kid, and found my share of trouble, but I had a strong work ethic.

I guess it was just my destiny to be a fighter, because although I never met my biological father, his name was Conn and his brother was the great champion boxer Billy Conn, and I was named for him.

[*A former light-heavyweight world champion, Billy Conn gave up his crown to challenge world heavyweight champion Joe Louis in May 1941. Going to round thirteen of a scheduled fifteen-rounder, Conn was leading on all the judges' cards when he made what he called "the biggest mistake of my life." Rather than continuing to score points with boxing skill, he went for the knockout and instead was knocked out by Louis. Both fighters went into service during World War II, and in the much-anticipated rematch in June 1946, in the first-ever televised championship bout from Yankee Stadium, Louis won again with an eighth-round knockout.*]

When I was in school the kids would tell their dad they had a friend named Billy Conn, and the dads would say "Billy Conn is a great fighter," so they'd come back to school and I'd start fighting. I don't know whether I was actually angry as a kid or what, but all these stepdads that would come into our home would try to show that they were disciplinarians, and they were all gonna make me toe the line. I wouldn't put up with it, and if they hit me, I'd hit 'em back.

My mom was in Las Vegas for twenty years, and then I didn't see her for twenty years, and then she passed away from Alzheimer's. It was her choice to live the way that she did, and I loved her, because you only have one mother, but she chose one lifestyle and I chose another, and that's that.

Anyway, Mr. Bennett loved his employees and he paid close attention to them, both their strengths and their weaknesses, and he gained a real trust in me early on to take on a variety of assignments.

The respect I felt from him was one of the most important things in my life, and I was definitely closer to him than any of the men my mother chose to bring into her life.

He thought as much of his everyday employees on the floor as he did his top executives. He just identified with hard-working people who gave the extra effort, and he appreciated that they had more to offer than just the forty-hour work week. That's why there was always an employee suggestion box, and why he would go out of his way to compliment an employee, whether it was a waitress or someone who cleaned the restrooms, when they were doing a good job.

Because I was in catering and special events, I was in Mr. Bennett's home all the time. I handled all his personal functions or gatherings, whether it was Thanksgiving or Christmas. Even stuff like laying down a bet on a horse, or taking a case of whiskey or hors d'oeuvres or something for his wife Sam or the family, he trusted me to be his liaison.

Because he was a military veteran himself, a true patriot, I think he probably identified me as someone that had served our country, and that was a part of the invisible fiber that connected us.

I didn't meet Diana, and start that chapter of our lives, until about nine years after I started working for Mr. Bennett.

Bill Allen Bennett

MY DAD COULD BE TREMENDOUSLY GENEROUS TO STRANGERS, AND AT THE SAME TIME TURN his back on family members in need. There's a story that shows you one side of him. It was when we were in Las Vegas, during the time he was working at the Mint, and we were out on Ann Road in North Las Vegas flying model airplanes, which is something he and I really enjoyed doing together when I was younger.

We found a little strip of asphalt where we could fly our planes without being disturbed. I was probably fifteen or sixteen. We had brought out a cooler and we had our beverages and cold cuts and bread and stuff to make sandwiches. It was just him and me. Suddenly a carpool of foreign people pulled up. I think they were from India or Pakistan, and because this was Las Vegas they got the idea that we were putting on some kind of show, or that we were staging an event that charged admission.

They actually pulled out money and tried to pay my dad for watching us fly these planes, but of course he wouldn't take their money and he tried to explain that they could watch for free, that we were just having fun out there. They still didn't understand, because when we stopped flying and decided to make lunch they lined up and waited to get food at the back of our vehicle.

Again, Dad tried to explain that we weren't selling meals, and they didn't understand. They seemed disappointed in the menu we had to offer. I started to explain the situation to them and I instantly got that look from my dad. I knew that look, and I knew the penalty I would pay for continuing to open my mouth because I'd done it a time or two in the past. So I just shut up.

I remember Dad was using an airplane propeller to spread the mayonnaise and mustard, and the people must have thought that was pretty strange. But Dad got a big kick out of doing this for them, and on that particular day they all got lunch and he and I didn't eat a thing. There he was just getting the biggest charge out of helping these people who were delighted to be getting a free show.

Then there was the other side to his personality: Years later, I was divorced and living on the east side of town in a Winnebago with no heat, no power, and no air conditioning, and working as a graveyard-shift clerk at a 7-Eleven store in a district that was known as a center for methamphetamine use. That period of time was about as low as I'd ever been. I put in a call to my dad, and I couldn't get him to help me out. It wasn't until I got behind on some child-support payments, and my picture went up in the post office, that I got a response. This was during a time in the early '90s when America was on the rampage against deadbeat dads, and I got a call from Diana. She said, "The police don't want to arrest you, but they will if they find you, and they are definitely going to find you. So we gotta do something, you know."

A meeting was set up and this was actually the last time I saw my father. I didn't see him once in the last ten years of his life. And I went in and his attorney, John McManus, was there, and he told me I was as good as dead with this warrant hanging over me. So my father put up the money to get the back child support taken care of.

At the time I told my father that I needed to go into a hospital for depression. So I went into one of these hospitals here in town where I was once again diagnosed as being chronically depressed. They put me on antidepressants, but it didn't help much.

Billy Conn

I HAD A BRIEF MARRIAGE BEFORE DIANA. I WAS INVOLVED WITH A GIRL, AND I CAME HOME on leave just before I went to Vietnam, and we got married. I came back from Vietnam and four days after I returned I found a letter in her car from another guy, and it was obvious there was someone else in the picture. Some time after that we got divorced. But she had gotten pregnant, and then after we were apart she had our daughter, Toni. She's forty now.

I was at Circus Circus one morning early in 1976. It was around the time when the Culinary Union went on strike and the strikers closed down the Strip. I had gotten up early one morning and gone to the butcher shop to pan bacon, taking it out of the cases and putting it on pans and into the oven. This good-looking gal came in and I was introduced to her as Diana — no last name was given — and told that she would do whatever we needed to help out, so we started panning bacon together. We started to have a relationship right away.

I remember looking at Diana and I saw something special. Not just a pretty gal, because I'd been single awhile and I'd had a lot of girlfriends, but in the end I saw someone who could be the mother of my children, and I'd never seen that in a woman before. Even though I was married before, and had a daughter, that was a quickie thing I'd done as a young man, and not knowing what would happen in the war and all that. The whole time I was married to that girl I was in Vietnam, so we didn't have much of a chance to make it work.

The way the word got out of the bag that I was dating Diana Bennett was pretty funny. One night I was sitting at the bar at Circus Circus with Mr. Bennett and Joe Hulsey, who was the entertainment director, and I'd had too much to drink and couldn't drive. Joe offered to drive me home.

We got in my Suburban with Joe at the wheel. I probably shouldn't admit this, but I had a .41 Smith and Wesson in the car, and I got on my knees, on the floorboard, and as we drove by the famous old Stardust sign — the one that's now in the neon boneyard museum — I shot a hole in it. You can find that sign today, and that bullet hole is still there.

Joe must have hit me about twenty times to get me to stop, but I was pretty crazy and real drunk. He kept asking for directions to my house, but when we got to where I'd directed him, he got a confused look, because it was an apartment complex.

We walked up to the door of this apartment, Joe knocked, and when Diana Bennett answered the door, Joe said, "Oh my God! We're all getting fired."

I was feeling pretty sick, but Diana took me in, and she told Joe it was okay, that she'd take care of me. Obviously, shortly after that night the story got out that we were in a relationship.

Diana Bennett

LIFE HAS ITS UPS AND DOWNS AND ONE OF THE DOWN PERIODS WAS WHEN, UNFORTUNATELY, my marriage to my two sons' father, Billy Conn, fell apart after eleven years. My husband had some personal issues that caused the breakup.

When I first met him he was the catering manager at Circus Circus. He was a hard worker, very smart, and he worked his way through the ranks. He kept getting promoted, and the unfair perception was that he got those promotions because he was married to Bill Bennett's daughter, which wasn't the case. He worked for them and deserved them. He ended up as the general manager of Silver City, but somewhere in that period of time he developed some problems, and he eventually had to quit. With his issues, which I'd prefer not to discuss, he had gotten to the point where he thought he could come in and do the job in one hour that others would take nine hours to do.

I confronted him about these issues, and he eventually left. It was not a good period. I was getting calls at home from some scary characters telling me Billy owed them money. I wouldn't pay them, and I had to call every credit agency and tell them to cancel the credit. I was about sixty thousand dollars in debt, with four children in the house: my three and my about-to-be ex-husband's daughter Toni from his previous marriage. She chose to live with us instead of her mother. Toni was just fourteen or fifteen at the time, which is a tough stretch for any kid. I talked to Toni's mother and told her I couldn't keep her with us, and so that situation turned pretty ugly also. So it was just a really bad time for everyone.

Although I had no money, I did have some Circus Circus stock, and in the divorce my husband was going to get half of that, so I asked Dad if I could pledge my Circus stock and would he loan me some money. I was unemployed with all the responsibilities of being a full-time mom at the time. I didn't know what I was going to do.

He said, "No, I think you need to go out and find out what the real world is all about. I don't feel like I can loan you the money."

I was devastated. I told him, "I *am* living in the real world. The real world is being unemployed with three kids to feed and sixty thousand dollars in debt."

The very next day I met with Burton Cohen, who was the president of the Desert Inn. I had worked with him at the Flamingo. And in the afternoon I met with Mike Ensign, who was at the Pioneer Club.

Burton said, "Come back and see me on Monday and I will have a job for you."

When I met with Mike Ensign later that day he hired me on the spot. He was running both the Pioneer and the Gold Strike south of Las Vegas, and he toured me through both properties and made me the marketing director that very day. As fate would have it, the headline in Monday's newspaper read, "Burton Cohen resigns from the Desert Inn." So God was looking after me on that one.

When Mike Ensign hired me, I was making only $400 a week, but it was a blessing. I called Dad and told him, "Don't worry about it. I got a job and I'm gonna sell my house and get a smaller house."

In the meantime, my stepmother Sam had spoken to him about my situation. And Dad surprised me and said, "I'm going to give you a hundred thousand dollars so you can make a down payment on a new house, but you should know I'm going to give a hundred thousand to your brother as well, because I can't give that money to you without also giving it to him."

I think it was a combination of both things — Sam's talking to him and my going out and getting a job on my own — that gave him a change of heart. My getting that job was a way of saying to him, I don't need you. I'll make it on my own.

I know he really appreciated the independence I showed. If you didn't ask for things from him, he was very likely to volunteer them. He always appreciated and expected you to do things for yourself. As a kid I was allowed to set my own curfew, but I could not break it by a minute or I was in big trouble. There was a standard, and you had to live up to it.

I remember my brother didn't show up on time for a flight to Arizona for my grandmother's ninetieth birthday, so he missed the party. If it was wheels up at quarter to six, you had better be there by five-thirty ready to go. My dad's plane would take off right on the minute, no matter who you were.

Bill Allen Bennett

It was during these first years in Las Vegas, around 1968 and '69, that my father would come home from work, put on this jumpsuit that he liked to wear, and he'd have a few martinis and loosen up and he'd tell me stories and ask me questions. He was very concerned about the cultural revolution that was going on in America at the time, and the reactions of so many young people to the Vietnam War.

I was into my music then and I had long hair and we would talk about hippies. This was in the days that I refer to as B.C. , which was Before Charlie, and the Manson murders that took place in the summer of 1969. Before Charlie, hippies were becoming socially acceptable, and the good guys in the movies were often young people with long hair, and they were typically cast in a pretty good light. I mean, look at the Woodstock Festival. You've never seen that many people get together with so much joy and so little violence. There were some amazing things going on Before Charlie.

But after the Manson murders happened, my father, you know, all of a sudden was all over my case. I could do nothing right.

The cultural revolution scared him a little bit. That fact that young people were so up in arms about the war and President Nixon scared him, and the increase in drug use scared him. I'm not talking about marijuana, and I'm not talking about alcohol. But LSD and hallucinogenic drugs . . . there was some really dangerous stuff, too. Before there were methamphetamines there were amphetamines . . . speed . . . and even the hippies said, "Speed kills."

I remember telling my dad, and this was Before Charlie, of course, that a lot of what the hippies were proposing made sense, especially when it came to the environment and all this toxic stuff we were putting in the air. The hippie movement was against all the industrialization. They were wanting to go back to a simpler way of life, you know. It wasn't communistic, because that meant losing freedom, and hippies were all about having more freedom. I really believed in the cultural revolution and most of what it stood for. But there was no reasoning with my father about that topic after the Manson murders, because he didn't want to hear anything about that. He just became so against anything that had to do with music and long hair and that whole scene. And there I was, right in the middle of it . . . a musician with long hair who smoked pot.

It's too bad, because the Monterey Pop Festival was a beautiful thing, and Woodstock was a beautiful thing, and then After Charlie the concerts weren't peaceful anymore. That's when the Hell's Angels started becoming bodyguards for the Rolling Stones and people were getting stabbed and the violence increased.

My dad was pragmatic enough not to have a problem with hotel customers who had long hair. That was no big deal to him as long as they had money to spend. I was pretty young, but I can remember back to when he was at the Sahara Tahoe, and he had an assistant GM who had long hair and was a hippie, and Dad was bragging about his hippie executive and how he was doing such a great job. It's important to understand, he was not anti-hippie until After Charlie.

Diana Bennett

I RECALL ONCE SITTING AROUND THE DINNER TABLE WHEN BILL WAS AROUND FIFTEEN OR sixteen. He was saying that he wanted to leave the house, get on a motorcycle and just drive around the country. It was when the movie *Easy Rider* was popular and that seemed like a romantic thing to do. He said he didn't care about finishing school and he didn't think that he needed a formal education to lead a full life. When he was asked about how he could afford the gas and food to make this trip, he said he would find a way and that he'd live off the land.

As Bill was talking about this, I clearly remember him eating a t-bone, and I made a smart-ass comment, something to the effect of, "It's easy to say that when you have a roof over your head and all the food you want, like that huge steak."

I didn't really think about the possibility of his struggling with depression at the time. I suppose I viewed it as a lack of drive or work ethic.

Bill Allen Bennett

IT ACTUALLY DIDN'T TAKE ME TOO LONG TO UNDERSTAND THAT WITH MY CHRONIC DEPRESSION and with an authoritarian father, that I was never going to be able to please him. I'll explain how I first knew that. It's because my sister Diana — and no one could ever ask for a better, more considerate sister, she's just a super person — would sometimes be in a room with my father, and I'd see her leave the room in tears, despite the fact that her grades were good, her performance was good, her attitude was good. Yet my father just never seemed to have anything good to say about her. I knew from seeing that at a young age that I didn't have a chance of ever living up to his expectations.

I was just nine years old when my mother died, and he would say things to me like, "Well, your mother was messing around a lot, you know."

I have no idea whether that was true or not, but it hurt me to hear that. There was definitely a mean streak in him that would come out from time to time. My father disowned me many times. The first time I recall was when I was just fifteen years old, and he and Sam went out of town and trusted me to be on my own in Las Vegas. Well, I borrowed the car and wrecked it. I didn't even have my driver's license yet. And he told me he was disowning me and taking me out of his will.

I said, "Fine, I don't ever want to gain anything from your death."

There were a lot of ups and downs in our relationship, but there were good times, too. I think my fondest memories of him were as a little boy in Phoenix working with him in our model airplane shop at the house. He would help me build the planes, and I actually got pretty good at it, but every bit of our conversation would be on the task at hand. There was no small talk. All of our exchanges were about what we would have to do next to build the model plane.

Billy Conn

OF ALL THE GREAT THINGS THAT BILL BENNETT DID — AND I LOVED HIM DEARLY AND HE was my mentor — he missed the most important link of life, and that was a close bond with his family.

No one knows but those of us in the family how much his children and grandchildren missed that affection and warmth. My wife Diana, who I loved with all my heart, wanted to please her dad so much, and she just couldn't do it.

I could be a psychoanalyst of that situation because I saw the tears and the pain that her disconnect with him caused.

It was never that he was mean to Diana, nothing like that, but he never appreciated or acknowledged how smart she was.

None of us are perfect, but we want perfect lives for our loved ones, and so I was there to see how badly that lack of connection hurt.

Diana Bennett

IN THE LATE 1960S, AROUND THE TIME OF THE MANSON MURDERS, I WAS LIVING AT HOME and working as a secretary at the Flamingo Hotel. I can see the back wall of my brother's bedroom even now. It had this black psychedelic wallpaper. Bill was having a tough time in high school, at Western High, and he almost didn't graduate. I still have the program from his graduation day and his name is the last one listed, even though the names of the graduates were listed alphabetically. That's because they had printed the original programs without his name, and then added it at the last minute. Only because my dad went to the high school and got permission for Bill to take further tests and pull his grades up.

I certainly remember the Manson murders vividly, just because they were so horrible. Maybe I just wasn't around when Bill and my father had those conversations, but I never remember talking to my brother about Charles Manson, nor my father, even though I had good conversations with both of them about other topics. I find it very interesting that Bill places so much importance on that.

My father didn't have a lot of love for long-haired guys either before or after the Manson murders. I remember one long-haired guy I dated in high school, and my dad said about him, "If you're gonna marry a guy like that, you might as well take a gun to your head right now."

I was in college in the late 1960s, during the Haight-Ashbury Summer of Love and Woodstock period, but I was kind of a goody-two-shoes back then. I was certainly not part of the love-in movement. I was a member of an Air Force auxiliary that was a community volunteer group and drill team. Our function, I guess, was to be part of a group of 'pretty-girls-in-uniforms' symbol for the Air Force and ROTC to parade around. I was so very innocent that when I was approached one day by a group of "Make Love, Not War" protesters blocking me from entering the ROTC building, I was amazed that they would find anything I was doing as a promotion of the Vietnam War effort and in conflict with their desire for peace.

I guess I tried in so many words to tell them that, when one of them bonked me on the head with a peace-sign placard. It was their way of indicating that they not only disagreed with my position, but found me rather dense as well. The arrival of some Air Force personnel saved me from further physical damage and loss of personal pride, although I still carry to this day the scar from that assault by a "peace-lover."

That incident was just one of many incidents at Arizona State that led me to believe that I was not getting out of the university experience everything I'd hoped for, and that I should go to work instead to feel like I was accomplishing something.

Shifting gears, I do think Bill's depression is real. When we lived at Lake Tahoe, he and I were very close because my parents worked swing shift, and Bill and I were on our own. I cooked all his meals and helped clean up after him, so we were together a lot. He never spoke to me of depression at that age, when he was thirteen or fourteen. I remember him doing okay in school, nothing great.

What was different is that Bill never had highs or lows. Nothing ever gave him great joy, and nothing made him really mad. He was always on this even plane, and it just broke my heart because nothing ever made him really happy, and naturally as his big sister I wanted him to be happy. I found it sad that he never had highs or lows. That continued through most of his life.

When Bill fell in love with Mary and got married, I thought that might change things, but it didn't really. That was in the mid-'70s, when he was working at Slots A Fun and he was in his early twenties. I certainly didn't see any evidence that my father gave up on Bill after the Manson murders, although there apparently was some sort of emotional shift that I wasn't aware of.

Lynn Lucia

I WAS LIVING IN TEXAS WITH OUR NEWBORN SON, T.J., AND MY HUSBAND, TOM, AND I wanted to buy this tiny little farmhouse. This was when my stepdad was at the Mint. It took all the courage I had to make the call, but I phoned Dad in Las Vegas and asked him if I could borrow three thousand dollars as a down payment.

He said yes. I was actually surprised that he agreed to do it. He said he needed an IOU to be notarized that said I owed him that money, and that as soon as he received that he would send the money to me. Well, we had that done immediately, and I sent the document off.

We waited and waited and the closing on the farmhouse was about to fall through, and, what do you know, he never sent the money.

So Tom called his best friend, Johnny Tatum, and told him that we were in a real jam. Johnny said, "The money's in the mail tomorrow. No problem."

And Tom asked him if he wanted an IOU, and Johnny said, "No, of course not. We're friends."

The money came and it was paid back within the first year or two.

I called Dad to tell him what had happened, and when his secretary, whose name I believe was Nancy, answered the phone, she asked who was calling and I said Lynn Lucia.

She said, "How do you know Mr. Bennett?"

I said, "I'm his daughter."

And she said, "No you're not. He has only one daughter and that's Diana Bennett."

Of course, I'm already hurt by the fact that he never sent the money he'd promised, so this is insult to injury.

I said, "Actually, he does have another daughter and I wish you'd just get him on the line for me, please."

He got on the phone, and I said, "I just wanted to tell you that I never received the money that you said you'd send, even though you have an IOU that says I owe you three thousand dollars. I just called to tell you that I will never ask you for another penny till the day I die."

And I never did.

He said, "I'm sorry you feel that way."

And that was that.

Years later we patched things up, but needless to say you never forget moments like that one. Here was my father demanding an IOU, and then breaking his promise to send the money, while a good friend was more than happy to send the money the next day with no questions asked.

While I'm on the subject, I wrote Dad a letter one time. I'd watched some silly show on television about people who spent their whole lives misunderstanding other people. And at the end, these people take the time to talk to one another and clear the air and try to figure out where the misunderstanding occurred. Anyway, this TV show really affected me, so I sat down and wrote my dad a letter and I told him that I had tried my whole life to impress him. In it I said I knew he didn't like the fact that I was overweight, that he didn't like the fact that I was unattractive, and that I knew he never thought anything I did was good or right. I said that despite all my efforts to impress him, I had never accomplished it. And I said that I knew definitely that he didn't love me because he told me once point blank. And that I sort of understood that, because Mom would never let him scold me or whatever.

But I went on to say that I wanted him to know that I had loved him my whole life, and although I could never meet his expectations, that I had tried hard to be what he wanted me to be. And I sent the letter before I chickened out and ripped it up.

I got a letter back shortly thereafter, and I still have it. He wrote something like, "I know you think the way you're feeling is your true feelings, but the truth of the matter is we never much liked each other."

So there he was discounting what I'd worked so hard to get the nerve to put in writing, you know. But he went on to say that we could always be friends. And he signed it, "Love, Bill."

I circled that "Love, Bill" a couple of times, and I remember saying out loud, "See, he *does* love me! Right here in this letter, it says so!"

Nancy Gambardella

I WORKED AS A SECRETARY FOR MR. BENNETT FOR EIGHTEEN YEARS IN ALL. I STARTED IN April 1984 at Circus Circus Enterprises, worked until 1994, and then joined him again in August 1995 and worked for him at Bennett Industries and the Sahara Hotel until just after his passing.

I don't like the term "secretary." To me it's like "housewife" in that it minimizes the responsibility of those roles. I had broad responsibilities, and in addition to the desk work I handled a lot of his personal stuff, the bills, made sure taxes were paid on time, and more.

I distinctly remember Lynn Lucia calling and identifying herself as his daughter and my telling her that he had only one daughter. I didn't know she existed until that day. Mr. Bennett didn't discuss his personal life around the office. He was a quiet man, like the John Wayne movie.

Diana Bennett

I WORKED TWO SUMMERS AT THE MINT WHILE MY DAD WAS THERE, AFTER MY SENIOR YEAR in high school and between my freshman and sophomore years at Arizona State.

I started out with English education as my major. I thought I was going to be a schoolteacher, and I really wanted to teach high school, but my college counselor said, "You can't teach high school. The boys will just eat you alive."

My first English instructor in college, who was going to be my teacher for all four years in one way or another, asked us to write a story about an event in our life that changed us forever. I wrote about the death of my mother. She then informed us that the entire semester would be spent writing and rewriting that story. I know it was a good exercise, and would have been a good learning experience had I written about something that I would have cared to analyze and reanalyze. Instead, having to revisit the saddest moment of my life time and again, I was miserable.

So then I decided I would teach elementary school and I did some student teaching in Arizona. I ended up buying shoes and clothes for all these poor little kids that I was teaching. I got too emotionally involved with them and their situations. So, okay, I realized that I couldn't do that either.

Then I switched to business education, and I thought I could do that. Eventually I dropped the education altogether and my last semester of college was just pure business. But I found that I missed the hotels, and the energy of working in that environment. By that time the hotel business had gotten in my blood.

I came home during Easter break of my sophomore year and my grades were really good at the time, and I showed my dad how well I was doing. I told him I didn't want to go back to school after my sophomore year. I didn't want him to think I was a quitter who was dropping out because I wasn't doing well.

Dropping out of college is the biggest regret I now have, because I wish I'd gotten an MBA and a law degree. But back then I don't think my dad thought I was ever going to really accomplish a whole lot of anything.

Shortly after I informed him that I was quitting school to go to work in the hotel business, he bought me my first car. It was a red, 1969 Mustang. I took that as a sign of his approval.

Dad was at the Mint just two years, first as assistant general manager, and then as general manager. He was then promoted to general manager of the Sahara Hotel, and in a relatively short period of time he became head of all three of Del Webb's Nevada gaming properties. That all happened in a period of five years. He was just so good at his job almost immediately after getting into gaming. There was no stopping him. He was just a shining star in that field.

I remember that my first job at the Mint was not as a secretary, but as a lifeguard. I was the assistant lifeguard and Brock Thompson, who was the son of Earl Thompson, the Mint's general manager when we first came to Las Vegas, was the main lifeguard. So naturally I got to do all the wonderful chores like cleaning the bathrooms. Brock was the one who sat up on the lifeguard chair watching the water and acting cool.

One day a couple came to the pool and requested a cocktail. It was only around ten in the morning, and we didn't start beverage service until eleven. So I told these people I was sorry, but the cocktail waitress wouldn't be at the pool for another hour.

Brock says, in a stern voice, "Go get them a drink!"

I'm like, "I can't do that. I'm only eighteen years old."

Now Brock is standing on the lifeguard stand and I'm standing below and in front of him, and he kicks me right in the chest. I went rolling back, and he yells, "I said go get them a drink!"

So I went down to the service bar that was for the Top of the Mint restaurant and asked the bartender for two Bloody Marys.

The bartender says, "Are you crazy? You can't order drinks!" And he calls over the bar manager, who comes raving and screaming at me, and I had put a shirt on over my bathing suit to go down there, and I opened up my shirt to explain what happened and showed him this big bruise of a footprint from Brock kicking me.

So the manager says, "I'm taking you home."

He obviously recognized that this was not a good situation with Brock's dad being the general manager and mine being the assistant general manager. In the meantime, somehow it had gotten back to my dad that I had tried to buy drinks. So the bar manager takes me home, and as we pull up to the house my dad is just leaving, and he stops the car and gets out and is just livid because when he hears the story he sees our liquor license in danger, our gaming license in danger, all that kind of stuff. And he starts to yell at me, and I remember the bar manager saying, "Mr. Bennett, let Diana go in the house and let me speak to you."

The bar manager told the whole story, and so that ended my brief career as a lifeguard. Obviously, they should have fired Brock, but his dad was the GM so that wasn't going to happen.

I got hired the very next Monday as a secretary, so it worked out all right.

[The relationship between Bill Bennett and Bill Pennington started out in Las Vegas around 1969, when Bennett was general manager of the Mint Hotel, and Pennington was a Northern Nevada businessman parlaying a small fortune he'd made in oil leases and ownership of one lucrative oil well into the slot-machine business.

The two men were a lot alike, in that both were entrepreneurial, ambitious, and patriotic. Both had been bomber pilots during World War II, Bennett with the Navy and Pennington the Air Force. They were less than a year apart in age, and both were men's men with innate leadership qualities. By all accounts, they struck up a quick friendship over their common interests, and both soon realized that they filled in each other's blanks. Pennington was more outgoing, the kind of a person that one female employee said "you just naturally wanted to hug," while Bennett was more aloof and cerebral, but both had enjoyed a taste of business success and were eager for more.

When Pennington heard about several hundred illegal blackjack machines that had been seized and warehoused by Nevada Gaming Control because they contained cheating devices, he purchased them at a bargain price and had some engineers from his company, Western Equities, install random generators, which allowed the machines to issue cards randomly. Previous to this innovation, slot machines issued cards in some sort of predictable pattern, which could eventually be deciphered by savvy gamblers who would then figure out how to beat the machines.

These were the exact type of machines that casinos were looking for — relatively cheat-proof — and when Bennett realized the potential that these ma-

chines would have for the ever-expanding casino industry, and how in Pennington he had found a kindred spirit who wanted to attain much greater success and the wealth that would come with it, he proposed they form a partnership.

Pennington was so impressed with Bennett's management skills and his vision for the future, that in a short time he agreed to give Bennett fifty percent ownership in Western Equities. Early on, the men had agreed that a near-term business goal was to buy and operate a Las Vegas casino. That was where the real money was to be made, argued Bennett, who was convinced that in the next few years someone would develop a better blackjack machine than the ones they were leasing and selling.

As with many high-level business partnerships, the Bennett-Pennington alliance would hit many snags down the road, but their early friendship and ambition, and the partnership they formed, would turn both of them into Nevada business legends and forever change the face of the gaming and hospitality industries in Las Vegas, Reno, and Laughlin.]

Bill Allen Bennett

After his job at the Sahara in Las Vegas, my dad partnered up with Bill Pennington from Reno. Mr. Pennington knew about this warehouse that was full of the slot machines which had been confiscated by the Gaming Control Board, because the people that built them didn't set them up legally. They weren't truly random machines, and when this was discovered they were confiscated. The percentage of payoffs on them was way too high, and so there was this whole warehouse full of machines that were for sale at a cheap price. Bill Pennington was the one that found them. I would say there were close to a few hundred machines.

My recollection was that Dad met Bill Pennington when he was working at the Mint. At least he made his acquaintance then.

My impression of Mr. Pennington was a merry, Santa Claus kind of nice guy, very cheerful. He was not nearly as good a businessman as my father, and in a way was something of an opportunist. He got something started that made him vastly wealthy, a multi-multimillionaire, but Dad did most of the work.

Pennington said that all they had to do was make these machines truly random and they would have something. And I guess he found the engineers who figured out how to do that. For instance, the machines originally had 2-to-1 payouts on blackjack, instead of the normal 1.5-to-1. So Pennington and my dad had them pay 2-to-1 on blackjack, because you can't split a quarter and pay thirty-seven and a half cents, and that would entice more people to play them.

Once the machines were set right, they became very popular. They came in two-player and four-player versions. They weren't single, stand-alone machines. They handled quarters and dollars, and I believe we even had some set up for fifty-cent pieces. Those machines made so much money it was unbelievable. It was those machines that bankrolled and eventually led to the ability to buy Circus Circus.

I worked as a pick-up man and driver for the Pennington and Bennett company, which had that slot route. We leased those machines to casinos and they made money hand over fist. I was the drop man, and I carried a large amount of cash as I made my rounds. Every day I would go to the casinos and notify the slot manager that I was there. The floor manager would have security come, and we would take the money from the machines in bags, take it to the count room, count it, and then we would do the split. It was usually a 60–40 split, with the casino taking the sixty percent, and we'd pay the license fees and all that.

I was usually carrying between twenty and thirty thousand dollars in cash to the bank and depositing it. My job was to drive aggressively from one point to another and be unpredictable in my route. I was not armed with a weapon, even though I probably should have been.

Had someone been sizing me up, they might have thought, He's not a very big man, so I had to be extra cautious. But they would have had a hard time catching me because I was a good driver and I was very aware of the cars that might be following me.

My workdays usually ran six or seven hours. I would probably make a stop about every forty-five minutes. And I never lost a penny. I heard after I left the job that every drop man who worked for the company afterwards got robbed. I know the guy who followed me at the job got robbed, because I was the one who had recommended him. And the guy who followed him got held up as well.

But it was all that money from the slot route that provided the capital to buy Circus Circus, and the rest is history.

I worked for about two years for the Bennett and Pennington slot route, and then in excess of ten years at Circus Circus properties. I had worked up to general manager of Silver City when I was suddenly fired.

I was called over by my father's number two man, Rick Banis. He told me the numbers were dropping and that we were kind of going through a recession, and that he had been ordered to fire the general manager of the casino that had experienced the largest drop in revenue over the last year, and he said that happened to be Silver City. So he asked for my resignation.

I was in my middle thirties at the time. I didn't put up any resistance and I went over to my office and drew up my resignation papers. This happened, not coincidentally, the very day before my stock options were supposed to go into effect, which would have been worth a *lot* of money. It was the exact day before.

Then I got a call from another general manager and he said, "Bill, there was an auditing mistake. Your casino did not have the lowest drop in revenue. You're *not* fired!"

So I went back to Banis's office and I sat across from him and I had a big smile on my face. I said, "I guess the numbers were wrong, huh, Rick?"

He said, "Yeah, the numbers were wrong, but I talked to your father and we have a policy of never hiring back a general manager we have terminated."

So that was that. I think if it had been anyone but me, my father and the company would have been slapped with a lawsuit. But I would never sue anybody, especially my family.

Ben Speidel

BILL BENNETT, THE SON, WAS A GREAT FOOD AND BEVERAGE DIRECTOR FOR ME AT SLOTS-A-Fun. He was very well organized, and he would come up with good ideas. Some things didn't relate to what we were doing, but he definitely showed some intelligence.

I think sometimes he tried to emulate his dad. I remember we made an employee video once, and as Bill was filming his part he sort of changed his voice to sound more authoritative, and he held his fingertips together the way his dad did. I thought that was odd.

During the time he worked for me he got married to a cocktail waitress at our place named Mary. I remember Mr. Bennett called me up to confirm that Bill wanted to marry this girl. I told him that was my understanding.

He said, "Tell him if he marries her, he will not be in my will."

So I called Bill in and told him what his father said.

Bill said, "Ben, I'm not getting married for money. I'm getting married for love. I love Mary, and it doesn't matter what my father says."

I called Mr. Bennett and told him what Bill had said, and he asked me to send Bill to his office.

Bill went over there, and when he returned about forty minutes later he threw a check on my desk. It was made out to him for a hundred thousand dollars. His father obviously had softened after they had their conversation.

Some time after that we went to their wedding at the Little Church of the West. His dad and stepmom were there, so there apparently weren't any hard feelings. I remember Mr. Bennett walked over to me with a handful of rice at the end of the ceremony, and he just poured it into my pocket without saying a word.

Bill Alan Bennett

IT'S NOT EASY TO DESCRIBE MY RELATIONSHIP WITH MY FATHER AFTER I STOPPED WORKING for the company. Basically there wasn't a relationship. I had saved up some money and I had a family, and then after I lost my job, my wife wanted a divorce.

The money lasted for a couple of years. I bought a lot of musical toys, and within three or four years I was in pretty serious financial trouble. At my lowest point, I ended up living in a Winnebago with no heat, no air conditioning, and no power. [*he gives an uncomfortable laugh*] It was pretty pathetic. I finally got a job at the most dangerous 7-Eleven store in town. I worked the graveyard shift on East Lake Mead Boulevard, right by a trailer park that was called Heroin Heights. There were heavy heroin and methamphetamine users living there. You couldn't find a worse neighborhood, and the big surprise was that I was never held up there.

I might have called my dad a few times to ask for help, but I didn't hear back from him or his people until they put my picture up in the post office as a deadbeat dad. I owed child support, and at that point I was an embarrassment to the family.

My sister Diana, who was always the one to contact me about anything to do with the family or my dad, called me. I was living off the barter system at the time, teaching music to kids, and I found a couple of families that would let me live at their house and teach their kids music with the goal of forming a band. I had those kids doing gigs within six months. I always had a knack for music, and I could barter music instruction in exchange for food and lodging.

When Diana called she said that the family had to do something. The problem was taken care of, but that pretty much effectively ended my relationship with my father.

Diana Bennett

THE SLOT COMPANY WE WORKED FOR WAS CALLED P & B GAMING, WHICH I GUESS WAS under the umbrella of Western Equities. I worked there too, as a secretary. Bill was exactly right about the machines, which had been seized by Gaming Control because they were not exactly random generated.

An engineer was brought in to help re-program the machines, and they were then approved by Gaming Control. The company operated both in Las Vegas and Reno. It was about 1970. Dad was at the Sahara, or had just left the Sahara, when P & B Gaming got going. There was a slight overlap between his phasing out at the Sahara and joining Pennington full time. I know Dad didn't like being in the corporate office. He really liked running the joints, rather than telling other people how to run the joints.

His office with the slot company was on Industrial Road, with a warehouse in the back. As I recall, Bill Pennington put up the money to purchase the machines, and dad ran the Vegas side of things. Bill Pennington's sister Jackie ran the company in Reno. It actually was a very successful business and the revenue from that slot route did provide the down payment to get the lease on Circus Circus in 1974. They didn't actually purchase the hotel until about 1982.

When they bought that department store in Reno and opened Circus Circus Reno in 1978, I think it was to fulfill a promise to Bill Pennington that they would both have hotels to operate within five years of taking over the Circus Circus in Las Vegas. They made it in less than four.

The relationship between the two was fine for several years, but then it began to erode. You have to understand my father's respect for a work ethic. He worked all the time, and he expected his key people to work all the time. Pennington didn't have that work ethic. He always wanted to run Circus Circus Reno, and my father went along with that even though Bill Pennington was not a gaming guy.

As the company made more and more money, Pennington enjoyed his life more. He traveled a lot, played a lot of golf — which my dad had excelled in during the Arizona years but gave up as the demands of business took over — and he had a house in Palm Beach that he spent a lot of time at. Here they were equal partners, but my dad was working a lot harder than Pennington. I think some resentment crept in because of that. There were some personal situations that arose as well, that I'm not comfortable talking about, which further drove a wedge between them.

Lynn Lucia

I WAS ABOUT THIRTY-FOUR YEARS OLD, NOT TOO LONG AFTER I'D GOTTEN THAT LETTER FROM my dad that really hurt my feelings. I decided to shoot him back another letter and in it I wrote, "Okay, I know you don't believe me. I know you don't love me. That's okay, Dad. All I want you to know is that I loved you. I had to let you know. I loved you, I always did, and I always will."

And I signed it Lynn, and I added a P.S. that said I did not expect, nor did I want an answer to this letter. And I sent it off, and I did not get a response to it.

About a year later, Dad called me. And he'd never called me. He said, "Lynn, this is your dad."

And I thought, Oh, shit. What have I done now? I thought for sure the only reason he would call is that he was upset with me.

He said, "I just wanted to let you know that I put you in my will and you're going to be inheriting some money, and I thought I'd send you a small portion of what you're going to inherit."

He sent me a check for a hundred thousand dollars. Oh, what a shock that was. I won't pretend that I didn't love having that money. I bought my husband Joey a brand new truck and I bought some land with it. But more than the money was the thought that he would take the time to send it. It was a definitive sign that he cared about me. It was just so unexpected, and yet appreciated.

Glenn Schaeffer

I DIDN'T KNOW THERE WAS A STEPDAUGHTER, BUT THEN ON ONE OCCASION, IT MIGHT HAVE been Mr. Bennett's sixty-fifth birthday, around 1989, there was a gathering for him and there were three Bennett children there. I knew Diana, of course, and I'd met his son Bill before, but I had never heard of the third person in the room [*which was Lynn Lucia*].

I knew that he once sent her a sum of money, but I had just never heard of her before that day when all three children were there.

E. Parry Thomas

AFTER I GOT TO KNOW BILL BENNETT LATER ON, I LEARNED HOW HE AND BILL PENNINGTON had done very well with a slot route, and how they'd expanded it to where it became about the biggest in Nevada. They were placing slot machines in everything from gas stations to mini-marts and any other outlets they could find. They would pay the landlord a certain amount per machine, and they developed a helluva business. They got to where they could eventually cash out Circus Circus from Jay Sarno, and they turned that place into a true winner.

Circus Circus worked for their partnership mainly because Bill Bennett was a good operator and ran every department correctly.

Our bank [*Valley Bank of Nevada*] did a lot of loans with Bennett and Pennington together. We financed their slot route when that was really going well.

I recall Bill Bennett got into a debate one time with Henri Lewin at the Las Vegas Hilton about the value of conventions to our city. Bennett felt that conventioneers didn't gamble enough, and that too much emphasis was being placed, and too much money being spent, by the hotel association on bringing large conventions to Las Vegas. Of course, I think he was wrong on that score, because filling hotel rooms is about the most important thing we can do for our economy here. Bill Bennett certainly understood as well as anyone the importance of filling rooms, and he did a great job of it. I think his main beef was that he couldn't get convention-goers to make a bet in his casino.

There's a funny story about the first time I met Bill Bennett. Sometime in the 1960s, after our bank had arranged the financing to sell the Sahara Hotel to the Del Webb Corporation, there came an opportunity to purchase the Thunderbird Hotel, which was close by, separated only by a three hundred-acre parcel between the two. I called Del Webb and his president, L.C. Jacobson, and told them they ought to look at this deal. I met with L.C. in the penthouse of the Sahara, and he had two guys with him. One was sitting in on the meeting, and the other was serving drinks behind the bar. The guy who was serving drinks turned out to be Bill Bennett, but I didn't learn that until later. Bill was a bright young guy in their organization and they had him there to secretly listen in on the meeting.

Del Webb decided to buy the Thunderbird, and they brought a fine operator named Bud James up to run it. About six months later they moved Bud over to the Sahara, where over the years we became very good friends. Shortly thereafter, they sent Bill Bennett downtown to run the Mint. It's kind of funny that Bill Bennett, who years later was in *Forbes* magazine as one of the wealthiest men in America, was first introduced to me as a bartender.

Peter Thomas
THERE'S NO QUESTION THAT BILL BENNETT WAS A MAJOR PLAYER ON THE STRIP FOR TWENTY years. I think for sure he's in the top five most important figures in the history of the Las Vegas Strip. Steve Wynn and Kirk Kerkorian, of course, are in that top tier with him, but the list of men who did as much as Bennett did is pretty short.

I knew him at his peak, where he was a guy who came in and took a very interesting idea at Circus Circus, conceived by Jay Sarno, but which was not working. Bennett transformed that property into something very profitable.

Certainly one of the things Bennett did was to remove those circus acts from performing over the gambling pit. He put a roof over the pit, but kept the acts going, because he understood that gamblers didn't want to be distracted from the games, and yet the acts were a signature attraction for his place.

At Valley Bank we helped him with the expansion projects, where in typical Las Vegas fashion the last addition you put on your hotel raised your income enough to finance the next addition or expansion.

When Bennett got into using public debt in 1983, with the help of Mike Milken, we were then just his bank of depository, not a lending source.

I remember my dad and I used to have lunch with Bill Bennett every once in a while at his hotel, mainly as a social thing. It was always in the coffee shop because he didn't like leaving the property. He wanted to know what was going on up and down the Strip. I know he told my dad several times that he wished his son was like me. He never said that with me present, but Dad told me that later.

I also remember hearing from people how Bennett's daughter Diana was a very capable businesswoman, but that she would never be given the positions in her father's hotels that she deserved.

One thing I clearly remember my dad telling me was how Bill Bennett had to file for bankruptcy in his furniture business in Phoenix, and how after he made some money in Las Vegas he went back and paid everybody off that he'd owed money to. Even though he was legally released from that obligation, he paid them off. When you're a banker, that gives you the best feeling you could possibly have about a man's character.

Mel Larson

I MET BILL BENNETT IN PHOENIX. I WAS BORN AND RAISED IN MICHIGAN BUT THE AIR Force sent me to Phoenix and I loved it and stayed there when I got out. At the time I met Bill I had a PR office in the Del Webb Building. I knew Bill casually from parties, but we didn't become friends until later on. At the time I met him, Del Webb and Bill were friends, and both were golfers. Bill was a scratch golfer, I believe, at the time.

This was in the early and mid-'60s. Bill was in sort of the Del Webb league and I was just a PR guy and a race driver and all that stuff. I lost contact with him when he moved to Nevada.

I was doing the Indianapolis 500 closed-circuit TV broadcast in Las Vegas and Reno and Tucson from 1964 to 1971. I lost out on the Phoenix rights to somebody else, but I was going to Las Vegas every year on Memorial Day weekend to do the Indy.

I had the rights to closed circuit from the Indianapolis Speedway to show it in Nevada, but when I first came there I didn't really know anyone, I was just a Phoenix guy, and I wasn't getting much interest from anyone. As I was headed for the airport on that first trip to sell the rights, I drove by the Flamingo and on impulse I went in and asked for the director of public relations. I didn't know where else to start. His name was Dick Odessky.

Dick thought it was a good idea, but he said I would have to talk to a higher-up executive, who turned out to be one of these mob guys from Miami. His name escapes me now, but he was a bigshot. And after I explained to him what I was selling, he says, "Well, I see how you're going to get your money, but how do I get mine?"

He was looking for a kickback, of course, but I didn't want to acknowledge that. So I said, "Well, I'm going to get mine from selling my tickets and you're gonna get yours from the people who come to watch the race and then gamble and eat and buy drinks in your hotel."

I kind of just played dumb. Anyway, to my surprise, he says, "You've gotta deal."

That was my first big break in Las Vegas, but then over the next few years I got the Sahara Hotel and some others. Somewhere in the process I got involved with the Mint 400 off-road race as a driver, and then I helped with the promotion of the race when Bill Bennett was the general manager of the Mint. I guess he was impressed with the job I did on that. So that's how we first got together in Las Vegas. Bill had known that I was a race driver and did promotions and had a race track in Phoenix that I promoted.

So now it's 1974 and my wife, Marilyn, and I are staying at the Tropicana, working on the Indy 500 telecast, and I got a call from someone saying that Bill Bennett wanted to talk to me, and that I could find him at the Circus Circus.

We went over to Circus Circus and I remember I gave Marilyn a two-dollar bill to play the nickel slots, which was all she would play in those days, and I went to find Bill. I called the hotel operator and said I was supposed to meet Bill Bennett, but I didn't know where he was. And she says, "Well, he's up in the executive offices."

I go in there and Bill's sitting behind the desk, the very same desk that I have right here in my home now. I bought that desk from the hotel years later.

I said, "What the hell are you doing here?"

He said, "My partner and I bought this place."

Now Circus Circus at the time was kind of a joke, and he was this prim and proper professional businessman, and I was surprised to hear what he'd done. I asked him why they bought it.

He said, "Oh, I think we can make some money here."

Then he said, "We're having a dinner tonight for all our executives and their wives in the showroom, and I think you're the final key to our executive team. I want you to run all the advertising and public relations."

I had no idea when I went in to see him that he was looking for me to work for him. I was just puttering around with my promotions and my drag strip in those days, and I'd have good months and make some money, and then months where I wouldn't. It was a very up-and-down situation. I guess you could say that answering that phone call to go see Mr. Bennett was the smartest decision I ever made.

Diana Bennett

My dad always had a great eye for talent. He looked for smart, hard-working people who could fill specific roles in his executive organization, and he gave such generous bonuses that the word spread pretty quickly that Circus Circus was a great place to work.

Bill Paulos

Mr. Bennett was so generous with the bonuses that you felt like you were owned, okay. You could get upset with him, or feel like you were working too hard, and there were moments when I said, "I'm not gonna take this anymore. I could go to Caesars Palace or half a dozen other places."

There might have been more status tied to being a Caesars guy back around 1980, when I started working for him, but I knew the executives at Caesars or MGM weren't making half of what I was making, with the huge performance bonuses that we got at Circus. Besides that, I knew I was learning the business from the best, so those moments when you thought about quitting didn't last very long.

Mr. Bennett earned your loyalty through the respect you had for him as a businessman, and he also bought your loyalty with the incredible bonuses he paid out.

Mel Larson

It was a Saturday afternoon when out of the blue Bennett offered me this promotion job, with a fancy title of vice president of marketing. I asked him when he would want me to start if we reached an agreement. He said Monday morning.

Now my soon-to-be-wife is downstairs in the casino, I've got a house in Phoenix that I'll have to sell, and my head is spinning. I'll have to put Marilyn on the plane back by herself, and I've got no place to stay in Las Vegas.

"Don't worry about it," Bennett says. "You'll live in the hotel until you find something here."

He then asks what salary it would take for me to accept the position. I came up with a number that was pretty strong, like twenty-five hundred a month, which would be thirty grand a year. In those days that was decent money.

He says, "That's a little more than we were thinking about paying."

I thought, Uh-oh, there goes the job. But I also knew that Bill Bennett had a good business mind, and that he wouldn't have offered me the job if he didn't think I could handle it. Back then, I had fairly long hair, and so I came back at him with kind of a wiseguy response. I said, "For that salary I'll even cut my hair."

He stood up and shook my hand and said, "You've got a deal."

So I go downstairs and find Marilyn, and she says, "What was that all about?"

I was embarrassed to tell her I got a real job because I was more of a freelance wheeler-dealer. So I told her and she was shocked. She said, "You got a *job?*"

She was happy because it meant steady income for a change. So that night we went to the big dinner for the execs and their wives, and the next day I drove her to Phoenix, packed up some clothes, and flew back early Monday morning to report to work. I didn't have a car, but it was like Bennett said: We worked such long hours and I was living in the hotel and hardly ever left, so he was right, I didn't need a car.

When I think back on how quickly I made the decision to accept his offer, I realize it was one of the luckiest choices I ever made. I had no idea then how that decision would positively impact my life.

Diana Bennett

MY DAD HAD AN INCREDIBLE WORK ETHIC, AND HE HAD GREAT RESPECT FOR PEOPLE WHO worked as hard as he did. Conversely, if you were lazy, you'd get scratched off his list pretty quick. He also believed in giving terrific performance bonuses. He thought those people that made a company successful should all share in the benefits of that success.

Mel Larson
MY MAIN JOB DESCRIPTION WHEN I TOOK THE POSITION AT CIRCUS CIRCUS WAS TO KEEP the rooms filled with customers. Bennett wanted one hundred percent occupancy, and anything reasonable I could do to keep the hotel hopping I was going to do. And we did a great job of that right from the beginning.

My office was on the fourteenth floor of the hotel, close to Bennett's office. There was an open area between our offices, but if he needed me he would just yell "Mel!" and I could hear him.

It might have been the first time he called my name like that — I'd been working there about three months — and I go into his office and he writes something down on a piece of paper, wads it up, and throws it at me. So I just look at this wad on the floor, and he's looking at me and says, "Well, pick the goddamn thing up!"

I said, "Why should I pick it up? You're the one that threw it on the floor!"

We could talk good-naturedly like that. We had a pretty good relationship.

"Just pick the son of a bitch up, will you?" he says.

So I pick it up and I'm just holding this wad of paper.

"Well, open it up and read it," he says.

"You didn't tell me that," I say.

It just had a guy's name and a phone number. I just stared at it and read the name.

"Well, call the damn guy up," he says.

"You didn't tell me that," I say.

When I make the call it turns out the guy is a salesman over at Cashman Cadillac. He asks me what kind of car I'm driving.

I tell him I have a Cadillac convertible.

He asks what color.

I tell him blue.

He says, "We'll have a new one for you in three weeks."

I tell him I'm not buying a new Cadillac, that I'm happy with the one I've got.

He says, "You don't understand. Mr. Bennett's gonna give you one."

I say, "Oooh!"

So then a month or so later, as we continue to fill the hotel rooms week after week, I get a call from the comptroller, who asks me where I'm buying my gas. I tell him the location of the station that I was frequenting. And he tells me I have to buy my gas at this other station.

I say, "Don't tell me where the fuck I gotta buy my gas, for Chrissake."

He says, "Well, if you want the hotel to pay for all your gas, you have to buy at this particular station."

I say, "Oooh!"

And that was just the beginning of the bonuses. A few more months go by, I'm sitting at my desk, and I hear "Mel!" I go in and Bennett throws this envelope at me. It didn't have any weight to it, so it just fell to the floor.

"Pick it up," he says. And we go through the same charade about how he threw it so he should pick it up. When I finally open it, it was the largest personal check I'd seen in one lump. It was a bonus.

I'd only been there five or six months, so I figured this was just the month they chose to pay annual bonuses.

I said, "Wow, do I get one of these every year?"

"Dammit no," he says. "If you keep doing the job you've been doing, you get one of these every three months. And if you do even better, the checks will be bigger."

My salary, as I said, was thirty thousand a year. And that first bonus check was for thirty thousand. And as the months went along, the bonuses got bigger, because we kept that hotel full all the time.

Diana Bennett

WHEN DAD WAS LOOKING TO BUY HIS OWN PLACE, I KNOW HE TOOK A LOOK AT A LITTLE slot joint on the northwest corner of Sahara Avenue and Las Vegas Boulevard, just kitty-corner from the Sahara Hotel. [*The lot eventually became home to the world's largest gift store, where customers bought dice clocks, coffee mugs, T-shirts, and nearly every Las Vegas souvenir imaginable. Years later, when Bennett bought the Sahara Hotel, he also acquired that large parcel across the street.*] He was looking at buying that whole corner as a site for perhaps building a new hotel. But just up the street to the south, the Circus Circus had opened a few years before and was going miserably and was not going to make its next payroll.

Of course Jay Sarno had designed the hotel and owned it and he was a very creative person, but he was not a great businessman. There were no hotel rooms at Circus Circus when it opened, and he even charged admission to go into the casino. It was two bucks for tourists and one dollar for Nevada residents. They had elephant acts and other animals and the carpet actually had elephant dung imprinted on it. I guess that was so if the elephants left droppings as they were paraded through the casino, you wouldn't know if it was real or not (*laughing*).

The space above the craps pit was open to the trapeze acts, so if you were a serious gambler, you could be distracted by bodies flying overhead, and there were even occasions where the circus people would fall or land in the pit. Most of the people would rather watch the acts overhead than gamble, which was rather counterproductive to earning revenue.

[*No writer ever had more fun lobbing parodies and cynicism at the design of Circus Circus than gonzo journalist Hunter S. Thompson, who brought a certain level of immortality to the hotel with his classic book* Fear and Loathing in Las Vegas. *In a 2000 interview with author and historian Douglas Brinkley, Thompson made this comment:*

"Fear and Loathing in Las Vegas *was very good journalism. The assignment from Random House was to do the near impossible: to write a book about the 'Death of the American Dream,' which was the working title. I looked first for the answer at the Democratic National Convention in Chicago in 1968, but I didn't find it until 1971 at the Circus Circus Casino in Las Vegas.*"]

Mike Sloan

OF COURSE HUNTER THOMPSON WROTE THAT BOOK BEFORE BENNETT AND PENNINGTON TOOK over, but I don't think Mr. Bennett would have found anything critical of Circus Circus amusing. He took Circus Circus very seriously. He didn't like anybody belittling the franchise.

Diana Bennett

ANOTHER UNUSUAL ATTRACTION THEY HAD WHEN JAY SARNO OWNED THE CASINO WAS THE dancing chickens. You'd put a quarter in the machine and the chickens would dance. Of course the reason they'd dance was because the coin would activate a hot plate the chickens were on and they danced to avoid burning their feet. I guess PETA wasn't around back then. Animal rights people would have had a fit over that.

When my dad and Bill Pennington took over, all those things left.

Mel Larson

W̲ʜᴇɴ I ꜰɪʀsᴛ ᴍᴏᴠᴇᴅ ᴜᴘ ᴛᴏ Lᴀs Vᴇɢᴀs I ᴅɪᴅɴ'ᴛ ᴋɴᴏᴡ Jᴀʏ Sᴀʀɴᴏ ꜰʀᴏᴍ ɴᴏᴛʜɪɴ', ʙᴜᴛ I was living in the hotel and he had the big suite for a year or two. That was part of his deal with Bennett and Pennington. He was comped into that suite. He would have the hookers and cocktail waitresses and you name it up to that place.

Jay was sorta like Nero in Rome, but I loved him. I enjoyed him and he liked me. We sincerely enjoyed each other's company. He once took me for a drive in his Rolls-Royce, and he had me drive it, and then he asked me to stop so he could show me how to drive a Rolls. We were on Charleston Boulevard and he would anticipate the green lights and drive like a bat out of hell. He acted like he owned the world, you know. His attitude was, what are the peasants doing today?

I think Sarno and Bennett understood each other but they were as different as night and day. Bennett appreciated that Jay had created the place and got it up and going, but their personal and business styles couldn't have been more different. I think when I knew him Jay was happy to be getting steady money so he could pay off his golf debts, you know, because he was suckered by everybody on the golf course, and everyone knew it.

One time when he was planning his dream project that he never pulled off, the Grandissimo, he had some potential investors in from Houston and he asked me to get the helicopter fired up. I had arranged for a helipad to be put on the roof of the Circus Circus garage, and another one later on at the Excalibur. So anyway this Houston guy has a hooker with him and we get in the chopper and I get in the pilot's seat, and Jay says, "Where is the pilot gonna sit?"

I told him I was the pilot, and although he knew I owned the helicopter, Jay was shocked. "You know how to fly this?" he says.

"Of course," I said.

Jay was just never quite living in the real world.

I remember times when Jay would have something on his mind and he would come downstairs and run through the casino to find Bennett, and he'd say, "Billy, I have this idea."

Bennett would just cringe.

Another time Jay stopped by my office and asked me to come upstairs, because he had some Wall Street investors coming by, to look at his plans for the Grandissimo. He tells me they're going to give him a bunch of money to help build the place and he's all excited. So I go up there about thirty minutes before these people are scheduled to arrive. He has a little desk for a secretary just inside this suite, and when I get there Jay answers the door and there he is with short shorts, no shoes, and a robe on, and the fly is open on his shorts. His dong is bouncing around. He's bald and his toupee is lying on the coffee table.

In the room are these beautiful easels, and really elaborate renderings of the Grandissimo in gold frames. Must have been a dozen of these easels, and all in all there was about twenty thousand dollars of pizzazz. He explained to me what each one represented, almost as though he were doing a rehearsal for the big meeting about to take place.

About then, the bell rings outside the suite. His guests have arrived. I expected that he would have the secretary hold them outside while he got dressed in business attire and put on his toupee, but no, Jay goes and answers the door just the way he is.

So here are four guys in suits and ties, wearing vests, and looking like they're straight off Wall Street, and there he is pretty much exposed, barefoot, and he didn't even fasten his robe. He starts giving them the pitch on Grandissimo like he's totally oblivious to how he appears. I know they had to be shocked by it all. I know I was. I finally had to leave. It was just too weird for me.

But I've got to say, I really liked Jay Sarno. I got a kick out of him, and in that first year when I was living in the hotel and working all the time, I had the feeling I was the only friendly soul around that he liked being with. He would gamble like there was no tomorrow, and he lost his shirt, but he was a classic Las Vegas character. I have good memories of him.

David Schwartz (Sarno biographer)

MOST OF THE FINANCING FOR CIRCUS CIRCUS, WHEN IT OPENED IN 1968, OF COURSE CAME from Jimmy Hoffa and the Teamsters Pension Fund. There were a couple other smaller investors, but it was mainly Teamster money.

Jay Sarno certainly didn't plan in the beginning to open the casino without any hotel rooms, but he just didn't have the money. It was always in his plan to build rooms. He originally planned to locate the hotel just to the north of Caesars Palace, so he'd have the Roman Circus next to Caesars Palace. It was to be where the Forum Shops are today. But he eventually went farther north, on land I believe was owned by the Teamsters Union.

Having worked on writing a biography of Jay Sarno for a good year now, I can tell you that he is a hard guy to read. When he told people he was in serious debt and not doing well, I don't know if he was being truthful or not. So much of his behavior was an act that it's hard to separate what's authentic from what's fanciful.

I do know that when Sarno talked to Jimmy Hoffa, he talked like a truck driver, with real crude language. He even did that around other hotel executives, to create the impression he was a tough guy. But he really wasn't a tough guy. He had a temper, but I haven't found any evidence that he got physical with anyone.

In a capsule, Jay Sarno was a wildly inventive, completely uninhibited man, and the personification of Las Vegas in a lot of ways. He was a guy who came here for not just his second chance in life, but more like his third or fourth chance. He tried to reinvent himself and he accomplished that, and he made himself into a casino executive and tried to re-create the city in his own image. What he wanted out of life was gambling, women, food, and fun. He was out for sensory overload, and that's what he created in Caesars Palace and Circus.

He saw himself as the ringmaster, you know. In all the old publicity pictures from Circus Circus, the man posing as the ringmaster is Jay Sarno. He saw himself as this guy who was orchestrating all this pleasure for people. That was who he was.

There are all sorts of stories about how Jay Sarno died. We know it was in a suite at Caesars, and we know he had company. It's funny how the legend has grown. I've heard he was with two hookers. I've also heard there were four. What I heard from Jay's daughter September was that he met up with one of her girlfriends, and they went to Caesars and after a night of wining and dining, they went to a suite where he had a heart attack and died. That's probably the most reliable version out there.

Billy Conn

THERE'S DIFFERENT KINDS OF THINKERS. THERE'S PEOPLE THAT CAN TELL YOU WHAT'S WRONG with something, but they can't fix it. There's people who can tell you how to fix something and then show you how. Then there's big picture people who can oversee an entire operation and know how to put the moving parts together and make the whole thing work.

Bill Bennett was a lion tamer. He knew how to assemble a strong team of lions and keep them from tearing one another apart. He was brilliant at overseeing an entire company and keep the parts moving forward.

Jay Sarno was a dreamer and an idealist and a brilliant guy in his own way, but he couldn't run shit. He ran everything into the ground. He also had some problems with the mob.

Bill Bennett was an honest, ethical man, odd and eccentric for sure, but at his core he was a good man. And the smartest man you could ever meet.

I was always envious of Mike Ensign because he got to spend the most time of anyone with Bill Bennett, and from that he gained the most knowledge. You always learned something if you sat with Bill Bennett and listened carefully. He just had so much knowledge.

I remember Mr. Bennett telling me, "Billy, you should never let attorneys or accountants run your company. They are there to advise you and help you make decisions, but it's your company at the end of the day. You have to live with your decisions, but they don't. If your company fails, they can move on and find another job, but you are out of business.

It was kind of funny because later on he didn't follow his own creed, and look what happened.

Diana Bennett

MANY PEOPLE HAVE DESCRIBED MY STEPMOTHER LYNN — WHO WE ALL CALLED SAM BECAUSE it was my dad's nickname for her — the perfect wife of a casino owner, and really she was. I was always close to her from that very first day Dad brought her home and introduced her to us.

When he got that job at the Mint in Las Vegas, and they moved down here from Lake Tahoe, Sam didn't work at a conventional job. She was fully supportive of his career and filling in as the mother-slash-big sister to me and my brother.

I went off to college in 1967, and while Dad was doing well then, we were not at all what you would consider wealthy. Sam taught me to sew, and she and I made all my clothes when I went off to school. Her role, which she accepted without question, was to take care of him and take care of us. She was also involved in the community. I remember she was part of the women's auxiliary at the community hospital, but if she ever had any outside activity that conflicted with one of Dad's business trips, she would have to cancel it because he always wanted her to travel with him. So she found it really hard to have much of a life outside of what he did. And pretty much her friends were the wives of his friends. That was just how it was, not only for her but for other wives of bigwigs.

They weren't big socializers and didn't care much for the party scene. My dad felt he had to socialize enough all day long, and he didn't want to do it once he got home. He did enjoy going out to dinner, and the Golden Steer was his favorite place to go.

We did have a boat on Lake Mead for a while, but when we got to Las Vegas from Lake Tahoe, he really started getting back into building his model airplanes. My stepmother and I would do the painting on the planes, and we would paint the little pilots. I got into trouble one time when I painted a black pilot. He didn't find that humorous for some reason. Because Dad was very patriotic, a lot of the planes were painted in red, white, and blue.

Lynn Lucia

IT WAS SOMETIME IN THE LATE 1970S, WHEN I HAD DIVORCED MY FIRST HUSBAND TOM and had married Joey Ziemian, who was a police officer in Euless, Texas, that my stepmom Sam Bennett invited us to Las Vegas. I think it was some sort of peace offering on Dad and Sam's part. And he gave us a suite at Circus Circus that was to die for. We were even given a nice car to drive around while we were there. Joey thought we'd died and gone to heaven, and I was wondering what was going on here. I couldn't help wondering why this was happening.

I noticed people were bowing down to Dad, and that he had become a really big deal in Las Vegas. I think Dad really liked Joey and the feeling was mutual. I even remember going to dinner with Dad and Sam, and Diana had Billie Conn, who was her husband at the time. A few years later

Joey brought me an issue of *Forbes* magazine that listed Dad as one of the wealthiest men in the country, and that was pretty amazing.

When I think back, I have to say that yes, I did have a tough childhood, and I'm not sure I ever did work out all the issues from that. But I have to be fair about it. It's wasn't that bad. I was never hungry, nobody ever beat me, I was never sexually assaulted. So it could have been worse, no question about it.

Chapter 3

Right Place, Right Time

Michael Milken

IT WAS AROUND THE TIME THAT BILL BENNETT WAS RUNNING THE MINT HOTEL THAT I first met him.

When I think of him and what he accomplished it was like the American Dream. He was a person who ran a business for someone else and ends up being an owner in the business. Isn't that the dream of so many managers in our country, that they'll someday actually own their own business? Now he didn't end up owning the hotels he was managing, but he started as a middle manager, worked up to senior manager, then executive, and then bought his own hotel and ran it, and eventually built his own hotels.

Bill understood that human capital is a scarce resource, so he chose his executives and people who worked for him carefully, and rewarded them for their good work.

Mel Larson

BY GOLLY I THINK BILL BENNETT KNEW RIGHT FROM THE BEGINNING OF OPERATING CIRCUS Circus what he wanted to do with the place. And I was just lucky enough to be on his radar at the time and got the opportunity of a lifetime.

I was working on the public relations for the Mint 400 auto race when Mr. Bennett was the general manager at the Mint, and one day he and Norm Johnson, who started the race, were going over these charts and try-ing to figure out the different classes of racers. The scoring back then was complicated. There were three or four officials from the off-road sanctioning body there, and they were trying to figure out the winners, and I was just peeking over their shoulders to try and understand it. I knew quite a bit about racing and had raced in the Mint 400 a couple of times myself, and I could tell that Mr. Bennett had no idea what was going on.

I sort of butted in and offered my opinion, and then apologized for sticking my nose in things, but I gradually straightened out the mess. Once Mr. Bennett saw that I had a grasp of things, he started to walk away and he said, "You can have the son of a bitch."

After that evening he told me he was not going to host the race again unless I agreed to promote it. And I really think that moment had a lot to do with why he eventually hired me full time to do the marketing for Circus Circus.

It was clear to me right away, especially after seeing how generous Bennett's bonuses were, that my main job was to fill that hotel to capacity every single night. If I could do that, everything else would fall into place.

I came up with all kinds of tricky ways to advertise and promote the rooms. We offered fourteen-dollar-a-night rooms and promised to place people in other hotels if we couldn't handle them. That was a whole big package I created by making deals with the hotels located near us, like the Riviera and the Stardust, to take our overflow, and they then paid us a travel agent fee for getting them the customers.

I won't take credit for much but I will take all the credit for filling those rooms, because I spent a lot of time thinking about different strategies and figuring ways to beat the competition. We did a lot of radio advertising on the stations between Southern California and Las Vegas, because a lot of people head for Las Vegas on the spur of the moment and don't make their decision about where to stay until they get here. So if I could get these visitors' attention on the drive over, and inform them that we had the best packages in town, I knew I could capture a good number of them.

People would say to me, "What's your job?"

And I would say, "I'm a room-stuffer. I stuff people in the hotel rooms, I stuff them in the restrooms, I stuff 'em in the barrooms, I stuff 'em in the casino. I'm a room-stuffer."

We had 102 and 104 percent occupancy all through those first years. You wonder how we could do that. Well, in those first months before my wife moved up to Las Vegas from Phoenix, I would hang around the hotel at night and in the lobby, just observing the activity. We had sofas there, which hotels don't have anymore because they don't want to waste the space. I'd see people coming down to the front desk with their luggage and end up going out the front door and getting in a cab at seven or eight o'clock. They might have had a late flight, or lost money in the casino, or needed to get home early, whatever the reason.

So then I put on a late crew of maids and bellmen and so forth, and they'd inform the front desk that a room which had already been paid for had been vacated, and we'd get that room cleaned up and sell it again. That's how we'd get two payments for the same room. When you have such low room rates, people will leave early and not worry about it. But that's how we kept occupancy at over a hundred percent all through those years. We just paid close attention to our business.

Our rates were always under twenty dollars in those first years. We might jump to sixteen or eighteen dollars, but as long as we could keep them under twenty dollars, I knew we could fill the hotel every night. Mr. Bennett said to me one night, only half kidding, "Give the damn rooms away if you have to, but fill 'em."

Bill Paulos

It's 1980, and I've been at Circus Circus for just a couple of months. I had graduated from UNLV, in the first graduating class from the hotel department, and I was one of the only executives there who had gone to college, so of course they called me Schoolboy or College Boy. Obviously, times have changed in the gaming business because a lot of these guys who run places today have advanced degrees or MBAs.

I was the hotel director, and probably a little on the cocky side, and I'm sitting in a budget meeting. All the heads of departments had to turn in their budgets, but I hadn't been there long enough to turn one in. The rooms budget was always done by Mel Larson, because his job was to fill the rooms. Well, it's no secret he filled them by using the cheapest fuckin' rate around, all right? In those days, you'd go to Circus Circus, get a room for $14.95, eat cheaply at the biggest buffet in the world, and you'd live like a king for a couple days on a hundred bucks.

Now we're sitting here and Mike Ensign is in the front of the room running the meeting, and he says, "Mr. Bennett wants three million dollars more on the budget forecast."

Now understand that we were forecasting knowing that our bonuses were based upon this budget, but if you didn't hit your budget, you were in deep shit. So this is pretty serious stuff. Bennett took whatever he had to pay to the bank. That was the level. Everything above the overhead was fifteen percent for the management bonuses. Then he had a formula for those bonuses. Some were on the A bonus plan, others on the B plan.

I'll never forget when the company was going public in 1983, and one of the bankers said to Mr. Bennett, "Why do you give fifteen percent of your bottom line to your management?"

Bennett's answer was, "Because I get the other 85 percent." What a great answer that was: "Because I get the other 85 percent!"

So Ensign has thrown this three-million-dollar figure out there, and he starts going around the room asking the various managers what they can do. Tony Alamo, who was the casino manager, says, "I can't add anything to what we've got. That's all I can do." And the slot manager said the same thing, and another manager, who hadn't been there very long, says he can't do more, and Mel Larson says he's doing all he can do, filling the rooms every night.

Then Ensign looks at me and says, "College Boy, what do you think?"

And I had been playing with some numbers on a piece of paper as the meeting progressed, and I said, "I can give you three million dollars."

Everybody snapped their heads to look at me, wondering how the fuck is this guy coming up with this.

"It's really easy," I said. "Up the average room rate." I can't remember exactly what I said, but it was either two or four bucks a night. With the amount of rooms we had, which I think was twelve hundred at that time, and with ninety-two percent going to the bottom line, because we were one hundred percent occupancy, I had penciled it out as the meeting was going on.

You would have thought I was a fuckin' heretic. The other managers looked at me as if I were crazy. Mel Larson . . . shit . . . he could have pulled a gun out and shot me right there, because I was putting the burden of this on his head.

Just so they wouldn't think I was being flip, I said, "This is a piece of cake, fellas. You're gonna have no fuckin' problem hitting that number." And then to Mel I said, "Okay, let's have marketing do a little work for a change."

Oh, Mel and I were like oil and water for fifteen years. Obviously, we got along okay, and he was great at his job, but I was always a rather outspoken fella and I thought that was something we could do, so I gave my opinion.

Mr. Bennett said that I had a great idea, but he also told me I was risking my job on that decision.

I felt that the difference between charging $14.95 and $19.95 was absolutely zero. There was no big difference in the consumer's mind. It's still under twenty bucks. When we got to that twenty break, that was gonna be a big one.

I mean, if occupancy suddenly fell to ninety-five percent, it just meant we had to go out and sell our butts off and get another five percent. And then we could give Mel Larson all the credit in the world because he knew all the little things to do that didn't cost a lot of money, like bombard the highway radio stations.

I think that moment improved my standing with Mr. Bennett, and after that he would ask my opinion about a lot of other things. He was, I thought, incredibly intelligent. And very logical. He was also fairly street smart, and you don't normally get that whole package in an executive. You get one or the other. See, I was a street smart guy, and not very intelligent [*laughing*].

Mike Sloan

I FIRST MET BILL BENNETT WHEN HE AND BILL PENNINGTON CAME IN FRONT OF THE GAMING Control Board in the mid-'70s. I was deputy attorney for the Nevada Gaming Commission, and so I met them in that setting.

Another time Parry Thomas and I went to see Mr. Bennett to try to get him to bid on buying the Aladdin. Parry was close to Ed Torres, and the Torres Family Trust owned half of the Aladdin with Wayne Newton. They went bankrupt, so they were trying to sell the place.

It wasn't long after that that Elias Ghanem, who was a very good friend of mine, called and said, "You know, Richard Bunker is going to be working at Circus Circus, in charge of doing all the government stuff, and would you think about the possibility of going to work for Mr. Bennett?"

My first response was, No, I don't think so. But I did have a lot of experience in the gaming sector. You know, I had represented Ed Torres, I had represented Morris Shenker when he owned the Dunes, I'd done some work for Moe Dalitz [*who built the Desert Inn and owned other gaming properties*], and I had built a huge gaming practice.

Eventually I called Richard Bunker and we talked a little bit. I then went out and talked to Bill Bennett, and I learned that everyone referred to him as Mr. Bennett. Before that day he and I had been more informal — it was just Bill and Mike — but that day I addressed him as Mr. Bennett. He did not make me the dollar offer that Richard had led me to believe he would make. So that made the decision to turn down the offer easy. Back then money was more important to me than power. I had no idea at that first meeting what kind of power went with the job, but the money wasn't right, so I just asked him to let me think about it.

I got back to Richard and told him it was an easy decision, that I was going to turn it down. This was in 1985, and Circus Circus had gone public two years before and Bennett didn't offer me any stock, and that was the key part of the ballgame.

Before I had a chance to call Mr. Bennett, I assume Richard got to him first, because Bennett called me and said, "I've been thinking about this. I think I made a mistake. Why don't we pay you [*this much*], and we'll give you [*this many*] shares of stock."

I said, "Fine. Deal."

I got what I wanted, and I'd already been told they had a great bonus system, where you got a salary of X and a bonus that was equal to your salary, or better.

Here was one thing that everyone should know about Bill Bennett: He paid people better than any casino executive in town. They used to put in our bonus a note that said something like, "This is your bonus. Do not discuss the amount of this bonus with anyone. It's between us."

They had a formula for these bonuses. Rick Banis knew the formula, and of course Bennett knew the formula, and maybe Glenn Schaeffer knew the formula. You'd open that envelope and your heart would stop beating, it was so much money. I mean I took so seriously that directive not to discuss the amount of the bonus that I wouldn't discuss it with my wife, or my preacher if I had one.

I used to tease Terry Lanni at Caesars Palace, telling him that I worked at Circus so I could afford to hang out at Caesars.

Some years later, John Giovenco offered me a job to be the president of the Las Vegas Hilton, and I told him, "John, I can't take the cut in pay. Besides, I know what I'm doing over here and I wouldn't have the foggiest if I went over to your place."

I'm sure he and others wondered how the general counsel at Circus, which was my position, could be making more than the president of Caesars Palace. But that's how it was. Eventually, the salaries up and down the Strip went up because of Circus's pay scale. Bill Bennett was an exceptionally generous man.

When he took the company public, he gave stock options way down below what is normal in the executive ranks. I mean, there were even operational people, like the woman who ran the casino cage, who got options. He had many of those people on the bonus system too.

For a lot of years, he allowed his top executives to use the private planes that he and Pennington bought. They had a G-2 and a G-4, and he'd let us use them. He was a remarkable guy when it came to rewarding his employees.

Bill Paulos

NOT TOO LONG AFTER I WAS HIRED BY MR. BENNETT, HE WAS BUYING THIS HOTEL CALLED the Edgewater down in Laughlin, Nevada. And he was negotiating to go into partnership with the guy who used to have the Landmark, Bill Morris. They called him Wildcat Morris. It was in September of '83, I think.

Mike Ensign told me the story that Mr. Bennett had offered the job of general manager of the Edgewater to this guy I graduated with from UNLV. No point in using his name. It was a definite promotion for the guy. But when the job was offered to him, he told Bennett, "I'll let you know tomorrow. I've gotta go home and talk to my wife."

Well, that was the wrong fuckin' answer. The offer was pulled.

So they offer the job to me and I accept it. So now I gotta go tell my family that they're going to Laughlin. Well, guess what? My family ain't goin'. Try asking kids if they'd rather live in Las Vegas or Laughlin. Not a question they have trouble answering.

So I go down there and I'm commuting every week, but let me say that Laughlin was the greatest learning experience in my life history, because down there I had a full casino to run and we were going to start building another one, the Colorado Belle.

Mel Larson

YOU KNOW WHEN BENNETT FIRST OFFERED ME THE JOB AT CIRCUS CIRCUS, I HAD NO IDEA how much money I was going to make. He asked how much I needed and I threw out a number, but I knew I was going to take the job regardless. I would have been happy with a couple hundred-dollar raise every now and then. But when he threw that first bonus check to me, I mean what the hell. And he didn't have to do that. And he did that with so many others.

Like everyone who got bonuses, I was instructed not to tell anybody about it, or that would be the last bonus I ever got. Well, with a check that large, thirty thousand dollars, I couldn't hide it from my wife, Marilyn, so I asked him one day if he would object to my telling her about it. He thought for a long minute and said, "Well, if you absolutely have to, I guess it's okay. But only your wife. No one else."

Mike Sloan

WITH THE MONEY WE WERE PAID, THERE WAS INTENSE LOYALTY TO MR. BENNETT. HE EARNED your respect in a lot of ways, but you were always on edge with him because you didn't know exactly what he was gonna throw at you. You'd get a buzz on your phone and you'd go to his office and he might be on the phone with someone and you wouldn't have the foggiest notion what kind of problem had to be addressed.

He hated it if you told him that you didn't know the answer to a question. Both Don Ashworth and Richard Bunker had warned me: Don't ever say "I don't know," or "I'm working on it," or "I'm looking into it." He hated to hear that.

I remember one time early on when I didn't have the answer to a question and I said, "Mr. Bennett, I really don't know the answer to that."

He said, "What do you mean you don't know? Both Richard [Bunker] and Don [Ashworth] told me you were the smartest lawyer I could hire."

I asked him if he would come down to my office with me for a minute. He had built this lovely office for me, which was amazing. When we got there I thanked him again for the office, and I pointed at the shelves and said, "Now see all these books here? That's what we lawyers use every day because we can't remember everything that's ever happened in the legal profession."

He thought for a minute and said, "Well then you better get busy looking it up because we need this solved right away."

After that, he would accept it when I told him I would have to do research.

One time we were in a discussion and I said, "You've been surrounded by people who tell you things that sometimes aren't right, but you make 'em give you an answer. I just refuse to do that unless I know I'm giving you correct information."

When I got there, Don Ashworth, whose background was in probate work, was trying to do SEC work because Bennett didn't want to pay another attorney to do that.

I told him I wouldn't do that because it was walking malpractice.

I said, "You know, if I go to jail, you're going with me, because you're the chairman of the board. Let's not do that. Let's hire people who know what they're doing."

He was a good listener that way. Actually, he was at times too good a listener. He would often ask you a question and be dead silent. And you would keep talking and talking to fill the voids, and you'd wind up wishing you hadn't said some of the things you said. He was a great inquisitor in that sense, because he'd let people talk themselves into a corner.

He'd often call me in my office and say, "Let's go to lunch." And we'd eat at the Pink Pony downstairs with the hotel customers. We'd start eating and he wouldn't say anything. So this one time I decided to wait him out. I think eighteen minutes went by without either of us saying a word, and he finally said, "I never thought you could be quiet that long."

Glenn Schaeffer

IF YOU WANTED TO GET IN TROUBLE WITH BILL BENNETT, THE SURE WAY WAS TO TELL HIM something you weren't certain of. This guy had a sniffer like a beagle. If you didn't have the answer he wanted at the moment — because he was very impatient — the worst thing you could do was come back with something off the cuff. If I answered honestly and said, "I don't know," he would say to me, "Well, that's what I get for having a poet as a CFO."

I'd then say, "Yeah, but I know who can get that answer for us."

And he'd say something like, "Okay, have the answer by end of the day. Now get to it."

Mr. Bennett possessed a skill that some people never learn: He was a world-class listener. He would listen until he'd let you talk yourself out. You'd have to learn to hold your tongue.

If you kept talking after you'd made your point, he would find the inconsistencies in your position or find what was illogical in what you just said. He had amazing aural recall. If you said it, he could repeat it back to you in exact words. And if you didn't believe it, he'd do it in your voice. He was an excellent mimic.

One time he was having me defend something that I was never going to convince him of anyway, but I was determined to get my way, so I argued, and then he argued, and then he just got quiet. And then I spoke again.

He said, "Glenn, you're a born salesman. You should remember the rule that he who speaks last loses. You won the argument. Just be quiet."

Tony Alamo

MR. BENNETT WAS A GREAT ADMINISTRATOR, BUT HE HAD HIS OWN WAY OF DOING THINGS. He was very detail oriented, and when he would bring you into his office, you never knew what kind of seemingly insignificant question he might ask you. He might ask you the sale price of something in the gift shop or the RV park. You never quite knew where he was coming from.

He'd ask you whether we were using real bacon for breakfast, or did we serve fresh orange juice or fresh-*squeezed* orange juice.

You always hated to say "I don't know," because that was not an answer he wanted to hear. I got pretty good at guessing when he'd ask me things.

I was having breakfast or lunch with him one day and he says, "What is the temperature of the steam tables in the buffet?"

I told him I wasn't positive, but I thought it was between 140 and 160 degrees.

Mr. Bennett said, "I think you're just pissing into the wind."

I saw the chef behind us in the kitchen, so I called him over. I said, "Chef, what is the temperature of the steam tables in the back of the line?"

He says, "One hundred fifty degrees."

I said to Bennett, "I hit that one right down the middle, didn't I?"

"You just got lucky," he said.

Another time we were walking through the casino, and Mr. Bennett said, "What is the hold on that bank of slot machines over there?"

I said, "That's gotta be a 96 percent payout bank of machines, so it's a 4 percent hold."

Mr. Bennett goes to his office, and ten minutes later I get a call from the slot manager, and he says, "You should know that Mr. Bennett just called me and asked me what the hold is on that bank of slot machines in front of the gift shop. You know the ones?"

"Of course," I said. "So what did you tell him?

"I told him 4 percent," he said.

"Son of a bitch," I said. "I got lucky again."

Billy Conn

MR. BENNETT WANTED THINGS DONE A CERTAIN WAY, AND WHEN SOMETHING WASN'T BEING done right, he was very direct in how he would explain it.

One day he called me in and said, "Billy, I just had an omelet downstairs. You know you have some of the greatest omelet cooks. They make them just perfect, light and fluffy with plenty of air in them. So this morning I had a cold omelet, and I have to wonder how many of our customers had cold omelets. How did that happen?"

I said, "I don't know, Mr. Bennett, but I'll go downstairs right now and make sure that it never happens again."

"Would you do that for me?" he said.

So I went downstairs and called our chefs together and went through the whole routine of making omelets . . . how many times I wanted the eggs whipped, the way I wanted the cheese sliced, how I wanted it put in the salamander [*the flaming device that heats the omelet*], and I got the message across very directly that Mr. Bennett was served a cold omelet that morning and that could never happen again. The whip cracks down the line, you know.

About a week later Mr. Bennett came into the hotel early, with his newspaper that he liked to read with breakfast, and his little waitress Carol serving him, and he ordered a cheese omelet. Now he wasn't a dainty eater. He always ate in big bites. So he's reading the paper and he takes a big bite of his omelet without looking at it. Well, he threw that newspaper down and jumped up and spit that omelet out. The cheese was burning hot and it scorched the roof of his mouth and gave him blisters on his lips like cold sores.

He guzzled some ice water, and actually went home that day and didn't return to work. I thought for sure I was fired, but he never said a word about it to me because he knew I'd followed his orders to make sure he never got a cold omelet again.

Mel Larson

One day near the end of the week, it was either a Friday or Saturday, Mr. Bennett came into my office and said, "C'mon, Mel, we're going for a ride."

We drove out to an old motorcycle shop on West Sahara. It was a pretty ratty-looking place. We walked through the aisles and out into the back yard, where there was a bunch of junk and old motorcycle parts piled up. It was pretty rundown. We probably spent thirty minutes there.

We drove back to the hotel, and he didn't say another word about it. Then later that day or evening, he called me in and said, "Mel, that old motorcycle shop we visited . . . I bought it. Make me proud of it by next Friday."

Well, that gave me just six days to get that shop into the kind of shape that would make him proud. I probably hired six or seven different companies to go to work. We repaved the lot in front, repainted the building, put in new carpets and shelves, had an old motorcycle restored and chromed and put on display, and put a rotating sign out front. We really did all we could to make it look good.

So that next Friday Mr. Bennett came back to my office and said, "We're going for a ride."

I knew where we were going. We drove out to his newly remodeled motorcycle shop. He walked around the front and back and went through the aisles of the store, and he didn't say a word. We got back in the car and drove back to the hotel. Obviously, he was pleased with our restoration of the store, but he didn't say a word. He paid you enough that he expected a job to be done right, and he didn't feel the need to pay compliments. And he was exactly right about that.

Al Hummel

I HAD WORKED ODD JOBS FOR MR. BENNETT IN THE FURNITURE BUSINESS IN PHOENIX, AND then spent eighteen years with the Otis Elevator Company. My sister Lynn had married him in 1963, when she was twenty-one and I was nineteen, and so I stayed in touch with them all through the years. While I had a good career at Otis, I think Mr. Bennett kept me in the back of his mind as someone who would be a loyal employee if the right situation came up.

Out of the blue one day in 1978 he called me and asked me if I wanted to come to work for him. I was getting a little disappointed with the elevator company, because Otis had been bought out by United Technologies and all of a sudden I had all these different bosses. Seems like every month I was meeting the new district manager or the new area manager, and they all had a different vision for the company, so I felt it was a good time to make a change.

Mr. Bennett had always told me that a key ingredient in finding good employees was loyalty, and he knew I would be loyal to him. I had been a good worker as a teenager with him in Arizona, and the fact I was his wife's brother gave him some assurance as well.

He had gotten the idea to build an RV park at Circus Circus because he knew that many of the people who patronized Circus had motorhomes, and he had only so many rooms in the hotel. He liked the idea of people driving in that would have their own place to stay, and he would just have to supply the casino and the food for them. He had started the project when I came onboard, but it was really going awry. They'd already changed contractors, so he put me in charge of the operation to finish the park, and once it was built he asked me to run it.

I wasn't a big RV fan. If I was out hunting or fishing, I'd either sleep in the back of my truck or rent a motel room. But I figured this was just another business and I knew I could run it.

I came up with a marketing plan with the help of one of the women who worked in Mel Larson's PR office at Circus. He kind of loaned me this girl as we were putting this thing together. She and I went out on I-15 and started counting the motorhomes coming into Las Vegas and it was quite a

Betty Lee Bennett and Billy Bennett, 1923.   *Navy bomber pilot Bill Bennett, circa 1945.*

Bill and his father Jack Bennett, circa 1943.

Bill and Bobbi Bennett near the time of their marriage in 1947.

Bennett (third from left) at Phoenix Country Club in mid 1950s. Bill became a good enough golfer to win the club championship, but later quit the game cold as his business career developed.

Bennett with his daughter Diana and stepdaughter Lynn, circa 1953.

Bill and Lynn ("Sam") Bennett on their wedding day, April 3, 1963.

Bill and Lynn Bennett on one of their date nights.

An early shot of Circus Circus. (R-J photo)

Bill Bennett's 50th birthday party, just after the purchase of Circus Circus. (l. to r.) Lynn Bennett, Bill Allen Bennett, Diana Bennett, and Bill Bennett.

Jay Sarno, the original mastermind and builder of Circus Circus, often called "a modern-day P.T. Barnum. (R-J photo)

Bill Paulos, seen at the Colorado Belle in Laughlin, NV, in 1987, a project for which he oversaw construction and operated for Circus Circus.

Mel Larson and his helicopter. He says his job description was very simple: keep the hotel rooms full. (R-J photo by Ralph Fountain)

Dr. Elias Ghanem, pictured in 1974 shortly after arriving in Las Vegas, was Bill Bennett's physician, friend, and traveling companion. (R-J photo)

Diana Bennett in her late teens.

"Sam" and Bill Bennett shortly after their purchase of Circus Circus in 1974.

Bennett with his mother Majorie and granddaughter Marlee.

Investment banker Mike Milken was the brains behind taking Circus Circus public in 1983. (R-J photo by W. C. Kodey)

Mike Sloan was the chief legal counsel and political brain trust for Bill Bennett at Circus Circus. (R-J photo by Jim Laurie)

When Steve Wynn opened The Mirage in 1989, it marked the first major resort opening on the Las Vegas Strip in 16 years. (R-J photo by Jim Laurie)

Circus Circus President Glenn Schaeffer, referred to by some as "Bill Bennett's surrogate son," was the face of the company to Wall Street in the 1990s. (R-J photo by Jeff Scheid)

Diana Bennett, casino executive.

Pulling "Excalibur" from the stone at the opening of the hotel in 1990.

Bennett loved tinkering with his remote control airplanes.

Bennett with hydroplane world champion and Miss Circus Circus pilot Chip Hanauer, Nevada first lady Kathy List, Governor Bob List, and Bill Pennington.

Chip Hanauer piloting the Miss Circus Circus to another unlimited hydroplane victory.

Bill Bennett (center) with Clyde Turner and Bill Paulos.

Bill and Lynn at the dedication of the William G. Bennett Elementary School in Laughlin, Nevada.

Joking around at home. Lynn Bennett could always make her husband laugh.

Bill and his favorite dog Scooter.

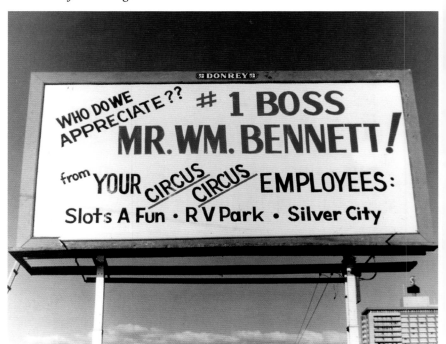

Bennett was a much appreciated boss to his employees, who paid for this sign.

Honorary doctorates were presented to Las Vegas attorney Robert Faiss and Bill Bennett, pictured with UNLV President Dr. Carol Harter.

In 1998, at his Sahara Hotel, Bill Bennett was honored by Culinary 226 for his help during the Frontier Hotel strike. (R-J photo by Jeff Scheid)

Diana Bennett and Scott Menke of Paragon Gaming discuss proposed Vancouver, B.C. resort-casino in 2010. (R-J photo by Gary Thompson)

The two Bills, Pennington and Bennett, who bought Circus Circus in 1974 and made it all the way to the Forbes 400 wealthiest Americans.

number. And I said to her, "How in the heck are we gonna get these people to stop and stay at Circus Circus?"

And having been well-trained by Mel, she said, "They'll stay for free." Now Mel's M.O. was that he couldn't sell anything, but he could sure give it away free to drive traffic to our place, so that's the concept we started with. I presented to Mr. Bennett that we would offer the first night free in our RV park, and we'd build a convenience store where we would sell propane. We'd make money on that. So even if they stayed just one night, they would get that first night free, but we knew many of them would stay a week or more. And they would eat and gamble in the hotel. Boy, did that take off. Mel helped with the billboards and the radio advertising on the highway and we packed that RV lot. The first month we made something over a hundred thousand dollars with that free one-night promotion, just from the RV park and the convenience store that sold liquor and propane.

It wasn't long after that Mr. Bennett called me in and said, "How would you like to get into the gaming business?"

I answered right away, "That's the reason I'm here. That's why I wanted to come to Las Vegas."

He was about to buy Slots-A-Fun, which had been taken over by the Gaming Control Board after there'd been some skimming problems there. Carl Thomas was in charge and he eventually ended up in the Black Book of guys banned from casinos.

[In 1978, Bill Bennett got heavily involved in the world of unlimited hydroplane racing, a sport he would stay competitive in until 1993. His boats carried the company colors, and were named Miss Circus Circus. The success of the racing team greatly helped market the Circus Circus brand around the country. In 1979, Bennett unveiled a new Rolls-Royce Merlin-powered state-of-the-art hull, which he co-designed with Dave Knowlen and was built by Norm Berg. The new boat finished second in National High Points for the unlimiteds, scored a victory at San Diego, and established a world lap speed record of 133.136 miles per hour. The boat's first driver, Steve Reynolds, had eight second-place finishes in 1979 and 1980, and two thirds. With Chip Hanauer in the cockpit, Miss Circus Circus dominated the unlimited hydroplane world between 1988 and 1990, winning ten races, with three seconds and a third.]

Ben Speidel
I GREW UP IN LAS VEGAS AND ONE OF MY FIRST JOBS WAS AT THE MINT HOTEL AS A BUSBOY in 1968. I was just fifteen, and Mr. Bennett was the general manager of the hotel. My mom was a cocktail waitress at the Mint, and that's where she met my stepdad, Norm Johnson, who was the inventor of the Mint 400 race.

I first saw Mel Larson racing at the Daytona International Speedway in 1972, and later on I formed a great friendship with him that has lasted to this day. We still meet for lunch once a week.

Mel is the one who first hired me to work for Circus Circus. He offered me a choice between working in the mailroom or working with Rodger Ward, a two-time Indianapolis 500 winner, on marketing items for the hotel and in particular for the Miss Circus Circus hydroplane team. The pay for both jobs was terrible. The starting wage was six hundred dollars a month, but the decision was easy. I chose to work with Rodger Ward. The racing team was formed in 1978, and they started racing that summer. My first day on the job was March 6, 1979. Our products business was called Jackets, Shirts, and Things, and I traveled to all the races.

Within two years, I was named manager of the Circus Circus RV Park, but I still stayed with the racing team for no extra salary. I was working sixteen hours a day, seven days a week then, but I loved it. Working with Mel and Rodger was just the best, and there were always celebrities and important people around because our racing team was winning like crazy.

I remember spending a weekend with Dennis Wilson of the Beach Boys. He was having a fling on the sly with Christine McVie, of Fleetwood Mac, and she was with him. They were staying in the RV park in a GMC motor coach. I remember when I introduced Dennis to Rodger Ward he was just blown away. Rodger was his hero.

That first year, Steve Reynolds was the driver of the boat, and he did really well, but then when Chip Hanauer became the driver, he won everything in sight.

Chip Hanauer
MR. BENNETT WAS THE BEST OWNER A DRIVER COULD POSSIBLY HAVE, BECAUSE HE GAVE YOU everything you needed to be successful, but I never felt any pressure from him. He wanted to win badly, but he also understood when things didn't go as well as expected.

When I was first hired to pilot Miss Circus Circus, I checked into the hotel and I asked one of the desk clerks what the owner of the hotel was like. She didn't know who I was. She just assumed I was another guest checking in. I remember she said, "Oh, we all love Mr. Bennett. He's just the greatest boss anyone could ever have. I can't imagine working at this hotel without him here."

That was good to hear, that I would be working for someone so well respected by the rank-and-file employees.

Over time I learned how important Mr. Bennett was to Las Vegas, but he never boasted or tried to elevate himself.

Another time I remember there were some serious negotiations with the labor union, and one of his top executives was saying he thought Circus Circus could get the union to fold under their demands, and accept lower wages. Mr. Bennett said, "No, let's give 'em what they want. I park my car here every morning, walk past all these hard-working people, we say hello to one another, and they all know full well how much money we're making. I want to be able to look them in the eye when we're talking."

I thought that was a pretty classy thing to say.

My fondest memory was being able to win the national championship with Miss Circus Circus in 1990 on Lake Mead, right in Mr. Bennett's back yard. I have never been more nervous, or put more pressure on myself, than I felt that day.

I didn't sleep well the night before, but I told myself I had to get some food in my stomach the morning of the race. I went to the coffee shop and ordered plain toast. I took one bite and realized I couldn't swallow it, so I just spit it out on the plate. I was that worked up.

Anyway, although we'd had problems earlier in the day, it all came together for us in that last heat. We beat our big rivals, Bernie Little's Miss Budweiser, and we had won it all for Mr. Bennett in his hometown. I remember after the race jumping in the truck with the crew, which was a tremendous group of guys, and riding back to the hotel feeling totally excited and proud of what we'd done. And I remember the look on Mr. Bennett's face when we pulled into the lot at Circus Circus, with the boat right behind us.

I don't know that I ever had a more joyful moment as a driver.

Glenn Schaffer

I GOT A CALL FROM MIKE MILKEN IN 1983 AND HE SAID I WAS GOING TO GET A PROMOtion. He said I should call Bill Bennett at Circus Circus. I knew what Circus Circus was, but I didn't know who Bill Bennett was and I didn't know much about the company.

I had met Mike about five years before, even before he did the subordinated debenture for Steve Wynn at the Golden Nugget in Atlantic City. Milken did the first nine-figure original issue of non-rated debt, what they call junk bonds. He had a market in Fallen Angels, and he had developed a network of buyers who rightly came to value his expertise and understand that they could receive extra return relative to the risk they undertook when they purchased.

Remember, in the 1970s the stock market was dead, and so all of a sudden Mike Milken said, "Well, gee, there are businesses out there that don't have access to rated debt, they can't do IPOs, and they can't grow, even though their returns would suggest that they should attract capital all day long."

And he zeroed in on the gaming business.

I was with Ramada when I met Mike Milken, and the company had gone into a tailspin because of cost overruns on the Tropicana Atlantic City. Ramada also owned the Tropicana Las Vegas, which it had bought in 1979, and that has its own story. Anyway, I met Milken in my office in Phoenix and we chatted and struck up a friendship.

After that I would occasionally go to his Drexel Burnham Lambert office in Beverly Hills and talk about the company and various financial issues. I saw like anyone else who knew him what a brilliant business mind he had.

So I started doing research about Circus Circus and Bill Bennett and it turned out there was about one degree of separation. Bennett was originally from the Phoenix area, and there were people at Ramada who had known him back in the day. They knew he had owned a chain of furniture stores. And I was friends with the Madison family, and Grey Madison had been Bill Bennett's running buddy in the early and middle '60s. I knew the Goldwater family as well, who Mr. Bennett knew from the Phoenix Country Club.

So I had some pretty good background on Bennett before I came up to Las Vegas and met him.

The company was just going public when I met him, and Mike Milken had told him about me and that I had a pretty good following on Wall Street and that I could help the credibility of the company. Still, in the early 1980s gaming stocks were not on the approved list. So I had become a student of entertainment stocks, and looking at 13F filings. I could see which institutions bought movie studio stocks, and who bought Disney, which was not in favor in those days. At Ramada we were pitching a turnaround play, and I thought movie stocks were more of a dice-roll than what we had.

I was barely thirty years old when Mr. Bennett made me the offer, which came in November 1983. Circus Circus went public on October 25, 1983, so I hit the ground running. I was looking for a growth platform. I thought, What if you had a company that actually made the margins that you're supposed to make in this business, and then some, and could generate the capital to grow with? I knew that if you had a unit growth company in this category, that you could create a very valuable entity very quickly. And you would stand out for doing it.

Gaming was not like the movie business, which would go from a hit movie to a bust, from feast to famine and back. Once these gaming properties achieve their identity in the marketplace, they spit out a lot of cash and then you can build another one, and another one.

When I got to Las Vegas I knew who to pick up the phone and call and say, 'You gotta buy some of this.' It didn't happen right away. I mean, three months after its Initial Public Offering was fifteen dollars, the stock was still at fifteen dollars. A year later, I had it at thirty, and it just kept going. When I say, "I had it," I mean I had the right team of people, which is what it always comes down to. I had people with the skills to operate, and the skills to open new places, which is how you make money in this business.

Michael Milken

I INTERACTED WITH BILL BENNETT AND BILL PENNINGTON FROM THE LATE 1970S FORWARD with the idea of financing the company, helping it grow, etc. Circus Circus was actually the very first casino company that we [*Drexel Burnham Lambert*] took public. It was quite a contrast in the sense that my firm did not want us to be an underwriter of gaming companies.

I felt very strongly about the gaming industry, but while my firm in the mid-'70s thought it was okay that we were a major trader of gaming debt, it didn't really want us to be the major underwriter. Eventually we did a deal for Steve Wynn to add all those luxury suites at the Golden Nugget, but the first gaming company we ever took public was Circus Circus.

It was an interesting interaction. Bill Bennett and Bill Pennington in 1983 were substantially different as individuals than they would have been in the mid-'70s. I'm not sure either of them really wanted the responsibilities of what it meant to be a public company.

I remember one night, in April of '84, when we had our big institutional research conference. By that time Glenn Schaeffer had come over from Ramada to Circus Circus, so we could have someone who could communicate with potential investors and knew Wall Street. There were six or seven hundred people in attendance and both Bills decided about an hour before the meeting started that they didn't want to go. So I remember I had to go up and speak, and Glenn took a major role in it.

I recall that we had also worked with the Tropicana Hotel when Ramada bought it. I think Glenn was with Ramada when they bought the Tropicana, which provided another bridge in bringing Schaeffer to Circus Circus.

That worked out well for everyone involved. When I was trying to convince Glenn to go to work with the people at Circus, I told him that they had a big future, that they understood a part of the Las Vegas market that not everyone else was interested in, and that he would have substantial opportunities there because Bennett didn't want to do things that a normal COO or CEO would do, like speak to institutional investors.

Glenn served them very well, and he benefited from that experience.

Bill Paulos

I CAN'T THINK ABOUT MR. BENNETT WITHOUT MENTIONING SOME OF HIS UNUSUAL EATING habits. I thought it was very strange that he liked mayonnaise with his caviar. I thought, man, if that don't kill ya, nothing will.

Anyway, to give you an idea about how picky Mr. Bennett was, I remember it was in 1989, I think, and although we had the Edgewater Casino and had just completed the Colorado Belle, and I'd been running both places for a couple of years, he had hardly ever been to Laughlin. And we're making money like you can't believe down there, and the place is booming. And we get word that Mr. Bennett's coming down to visit, with some of his family. This was just before he offered me the job to build the Excalibur.

So we get all excited and everybody's hustling to spiff the place up. And we're shining the doorknobs and polishing the floors and putting on our best face. Bob Gaudioso is the food and beverage manager and we're talking about getting all the foods Mr. Bennett likes, and making sure we have Donald Duck orange juice for his screwdrivers. And we knew he liked oysters, so Bob is picking through these oysters and trying to get the best ones for him. None of us knew exactly what kind of oysters he liked, but we're doing what we can to get good ones.

So Mr. Bennett is there and all this food is laid out, and the chefs are standing tall and feeling good about their presentation, and Bennett walks over and picks up an oyster, and says, "Where did you get these fuckin' oysters?"

Now this is a guy who rarely used profanity. And he picks one up and kind of sneers at it and says, "I've got boogers bigger than these oysters."

That's exactly what he said. Well, Bob Gaudioso was crushed. I mean it just hammered him. Bam! Right between the eyes.

And we figured, we're dead.

He left the next morning, not over the oysters, but without saying much more. Now it's very possible he enjoyed his stay, but we were all shell-shocked and we all figured the visit was a total disaster because the oysters weren't big enough. I tasted a few, and they were darn good, but obviously they weren't big enough to please The Man.

Ben Speidel
ON FEBRUARY 1, 1993, I WAS MADE THE GENERAL MANAGER OF THE COLORADO BELLE IN Laughlin. I remember the date because it was my fortieth birthday.

The promotion came out of the blue. Mr. Bennett called me up and said, "Ben, do you think you could run the Colorado Belle?"

I said "Absolutely."

I've always been a confident person and I knew I could learn whatever it took to do the job, and I'd work on it day and night.

He said, "Good, because you have a staff meeting in two hours."

It's a two-hour drive down there, but I had a souped-up Mitsubishi and I made it in a little over an hour.

I was replacing Arie Barendech, who had been running it, and by all accounts doing a great job. He was a well-loved man. But there was a problem
with too much noise coming out of the showroom, and some other issues.
Bob Gaudioso was also fired then. I do remember hearing that there was
something wrong with the oysters in the buffet.

Glenn Schaeffer

BILL BENNETT DID NOT HAVE THE LONG-TERM VISION FOR GROWTH THAT I DID WHEN I FIRST
went to work for him, but he put the right people in place to make it happen.
He was learning from me just as I was learning from him.

Early on I asked him, "What is your goal in this company?"

He said, "I want to see the stock at one hundred dollars a share."

I think he was just throwing out a number, but I said, "We'll beat it."

Now this conversation took place early on, in the first year. There's different ways of calculating the growth, but by the time MGM Mirage bought
Mandalay Bay [which emerged out of the original Circus Circus], the stock
was, you know, twenty-five to thirty times the value of its opening IPO, and
the biggest part of that growth occurred in the first ten years, between 1983
and '93. If Circus had had just one owner instead of two, I would have been
a billionaire. I would have been the first billionaire made in the business.

Of all the gaming companies, it was Circus Circus that led that way, that
taught Wall Street that gaming companies could be big, liquid growing
companies and that forever dismissed the stigmas that had previously been
attached to our industry. And Bill Bennett is central to that story. He was
modern in comparison to some others. He ushered in the modern era of
gaming with his team and the authority he gave us.

Bill Harrah was basically doing his thing as a Reno company, and Caesars was very respectable, but Caesars did not pursue a unit growth strategy
as we did, and they had many changes in leadership through those years.

Our comp for four of those ten years [between 1989-93] would be Golden
Nugget/Mirage, but you can look at the numbers and see that Circus Circus
was the true leader. And the leader of that company was Bill Bennett. None
of us did anything that wasn't embedded somewhere in that old man's mind.

Michael Milken

I'LL NEVER FORGET THAT YEARS AFTER WE TOOK CIRCUS CIRCUS PUBLIC, IF WE VISITED
Bennett or Pennington, or we visited the executive offices of the company,

there was not a computer to be seen. The only person who had a computer was Glenn Schaeffer. It was clearly the changing of an era, from older school executives who managed by the seat of their pants, totally understanding their business because they had grown up with it and knew what the customer wanted, compared to methods of today, where people are looking at so much data because they publish their numbers every month with the Gaming Control Board and so you know every month what everyone else is winning and what their occupancy is.

I know that Circus Circus's occupancy rate was running over a hundred percent every day because they would sell rooms twice if someone checked out early, and so by the early '80s the company was no longer boot-strapping. They were making a lot of money. A lot of people who are entrepreneurial didn't understand then what it meant to be a public company and have to communicate with shareholders about everything you want to do.

Glenn Schaeffer served them very well in that capacity.

Glenn Schaeffer

LET ME ADD THAT BILL BENNETT WAS A GAMBLER. HE WAS WILLING TO LET A THIRTY-YEAR-old kid become the chief financial officer in the first year of his company's going public. That's a big gamble. He just said, "Do it!"

He would say this: "I'm not going to tell you how to do it, but I will reserve bitching rights, and I will tell you when I think you're doing something wrong. But I'm not going to tell you to fix it, either. Because if I do that, you're not getting it done."

The lessons that he passed on were autobiographical. He told me when he started in the furniture business in Phoenix it was because someone saw something in him, and that person probably gave him too much responsibility. But he didn't blow that opportunity and he made a lot more money than anyone thought he'd make.

Bennett said he would rather take young men who were ambitious, who needed money and recognition, and who would handle the reins but that he couldn't run as fast as the young guys could.

If they didn't perform, they would get killed. He said it was the same thing in war: If you don't get killed, you're more valuable in the next battle. He said the money he'd made in his life was earned by going toward youth and not relying on instilled practices.

So I was a beneficiary of that. When I was hired in 1983 you could have gone to five hundred other companies in the United States, and they were not going to let a thirty-year-old be a chief financial officer from the New York Stock Exchange. Debbie Coleman, who was then with Apple, and I were the only two thirty-and-under CFOs in the U.S. who weren't related to whoever owned the company.

Oddly, he was insecure about things he should have never been insecure about. There were a few times he told me, "God, I wish I had been born with your intelligence." I told him he was. I said that education and intelligence aren't the same thing. He was just naturally a very intelligent man. There were times when I would write the language for the annual reports, or papers and memos to the board. I would pass those to him, and he would edit them. He'd come back with just a few marks made in pencil, but his editing was always right on. He was a natural editor.

I think he was driven for recognition, and so he used his intellectual ability to achieve monetary stature, which in turn gave him that recognition.

He was deeply wounded by . . . and I'm not sure he ever got over . . . the belly-flop he took in business in the 1960s in Phoenix. He told me once that he had to leave Phoenix to create a new identity for himself, because they would never let him back there. He said he had to go to Nevada to reinvent himself because it wouldn't have been allowed in Arizona. "Phoenix is like death to me," he once said.

Mel Larson

MR. BENNETT DIDN'T LIKE DOING INTERVIEWS AND HE WOULDN'T TALK ON RADIO OR TV. They'd call him and he'd say, "Go see Mel. He'll give you an interview."

I knew I had to do it right and I always wanted to make the company look good, you know. The hotel colors were pink and white, so I just carried that theme into my clothing and cars. I had a pink Cadillac, and I had a pink tuxedo and a pink sport jacket, and people would say, "How come you wear that silly gay pink stuff?"

And I'd say, "Listen, you silly son of a bitch, if you made as much money wearing pink as I do, you'd wear it, too."

I remember a time when Bill was snowed in, down in Kingman, Arizona, and he couldn't find his motorcycle, which he'd driven down there. The snow was so high in the parking lot it had covered his bike. He called me and asked me to fly down in the helicopter and pick him up. We had quite a discussion about where I could land, with the snow being so deep.

Anyway, on the flight back, the fuel was a little low, and I asked him whether we should land in Bullhead City or Laughlin to get fuel.

Bill said, "I think we can make it, Mel. Don't stop."

We went back and forth on that, and I finally said, "Bill, I'm stopping for fuel. The only decision you have to make is whether you think we should stop in Bullhead City or Laughlin."

After we'd fueled up, he told me he was proud that I wouldn't be bullied about such a decision, no matter who was giving the orders. He said that if I hadn't stopped for fuel, it would tell him something about my poor decision-making and he would have fired me.

Ben Speidel

EMPLOYEES WERE NEVER SUPPOSED TO GIVE INTERVIEWS WITHOUT MR. BENNETT'S PERMISSION, but I did once. It was when a car drove into Slots-A-Fun and a lot of people were injured. One woman lost an eye. It was terrible. I was called out at Lake Mead and told about it, and I arrived at the property and this good-looking woman in a white dress came up and asked me questions about the accident and the property. I put a really good spin on everything, and an article appeared in the *Review-Journal* the next morning with quotes from me.

There was a typo and they misspelled my first name B-E-E-N. I was in the coffee shop that day and Mr. Bennett walked over to my table and showed me the article, and he wrote the word "has," H-A-S, in front of the B-E-E-N. So it read like I was a "has been." That was a pretty strong warning that I better not give any more interviews without clearing it with him first.

Bill Paulos

WHEN I FIRST WENT TO LAUGHLIN, IN 1983, CASINO DRIVE WAS STILL A DIRT ROAD. I bought from the company a two-year-old white Corvette, so I'm gonna be cool when I roll into Laughlin, What a dumb fuck I am, right? So I go and nobody knows who I am. I'm going to check out the joint incognito and see what I'm getting myself into. And the Edgewater is a small casino, with only 219 slot machines, eleven table games, and one bar with a stage. There's no occupancy. The place is a disaster. I'm thinking, What have I done? I'd accepted the job before I saw the place. Bright fellow, huh?

So I'm going to stay there the weekend without anybody knowing who I am. First night there a band is playing, a giant fight breaks out, and one guy grabs an ax and is going after another guy trying to kill him. I'm thinking, This is insane. This is the last frontier.

I go outside to get in my car and there's brown dots all over my white Corvette. I ask the valet parker what's going on. He points next door at a tiny little place called the Colorado Belle. It's a little casino not much bigger than a house. And there's this spray out front, spewing water. I ask the valet guy what it is, and he says "It's their septic."

"Pardon me?" I say. "Are you telling me that this is shit splattered all over my car?"

"Yup," he says.

So I go back and tell Bennett that it's insanity down in Laughlin. He's calm and says, "Son, don't worry. We're gonna do things down there."

"Okay," I said. "I'm in your hands. Whatever you want me to do down there, I'll do it and we'll make money, okay?"

Within that first year we started building manor-type rooms at the Edgewater. In the blink of an eye we had four hundred rooms. A big problem right away was that we needed housing for employees and there was no housing down there. There were eighty-five residents in Laughlin when I got there. Bill Bennett partnered up with a guy named Bob Jones to build apartment buildings on our side of the river. Bullhead City, Arizona, is across the river, and I was living there, but we needed something on our side.

That first year, Bill Bennett never came down to Laughlin. I always had to go to Vegas to see him. Mel Larson would come down occasionally in his helicopter, because he was good buddies with Don Laughlin, who they named the town for. Don had the biggest place down there, but after we built those rooms at the Edgewater we were close in size. We also expanded the casino, so at that point we have fifteen hundred slot machines, we have thirty table games, and we've got a business that's really starting to move. And Bill Bennett and Mike Ensign are calling the shots all the way.

When we started that building down there, we were building everything for less than anyone else could build it. Starting out I knew nothing about construction, but I oversaw the construction, and the experience from that was invaluable. The guy in charge of construction for our company was Joe

Hulsey. He had started with Bennett at Circus Circus, I think working on the midway in the hotel. He ran the midway before they leased it out. He just fell into construction and he learned it and was very good at it. So between him and me, we built the Edgewater.

Laughlin really got on the national map after we built the Colorado Belle, which was actually a riverboat. Stories popped up in magazines and newspapers and television news reports everywhere.

The *Wall Street Journal* had assigned a bright Asian woman, Pauline Yoshihashi, to the casino beat. She was terrific. And one day I was walking her around the construction of the Colorado Belle — and Tony Marnell actually built that one — and she said, "This is really something. How did this ever come about?"

I said, "Our architect, Veldon Simpson, has got great ideas, but you know, it was Mr. Bennett. He just decided he wanted to build the biggest boat in the desert since Noah."

Well, I'll be damned if she didn't quote that directly the next day in the *Journal*. "Circus Circus is building the biggest boat in the desert since Noah."

That line had some staying power, let me tell you. So Laughlin was just getting bigger and bigger, and I think in our heyday with both joints open we were doing sixty million dollars bottom line down there. That was big bread. I don't think if you added everything together in Laughlin today it's doing sixty million.

Oh, there's another part to this story that's classic. Right before we built the Colorado Belle, sitting right between the two properties was this one house. It was owned by a lady named Mrs. Lafferty. We made her an offer, but she wouldn't sell. She absolutely refused to budge.

She had lived there nearly her whole life and she loved the river. She was really a lovely old lady, in her seventies at the time. She was widowed, and her kids would come to visit her from time to time, and she used every excuse in the book not to sell.

We brought Joe Hulsey over to talk to her because he was a soft-talkin' Cajun guy, and he would say, "Oh baby, oh baby, we just have to have this property."

Her silence said it all: Fuck you. I ain't movin'.

So one day she says to me, "I want to speak to Mr. Bennett himself."

I explained to her that Mr. Bennett never came down to Laughlin.

"Well, if he wants to buy my place, he will," she says.

So Mr. Bennett comes down. He's dressed casually wearing a nice short-sleeved shirt, the kind I like to wear. And he had on Sans-A-Belt slacks, which were big with him. He would call down to the store at Circus Circus and say, "Give me a pair of Sans-A-Belts in every color."

I remember he had on a light blue sports jacket and some light pants. He was dressed nice but casual. So he comes down to Laughlin and meets Mrs. Lafferty and she doesn't believe it's him. We're sitting in her place and she says, "You're not Mr. Bennett."

I mean you had to give her credit. She wasn't going to let anybody pull one on her, but he was very charming and you know Bill Bennett was a tall, good-looking guy, okay. And he could be as charming as he wanted to be. They finally started to see eye to eye, and this negotiating is over a house that's maybe fifteen hundred square feet, but it just happens to be smack in the middle of where we want to develop.

The final deal — I'm almost positive on these numbers — was that he gave her two million dollars and a lifetime room in the Colorado Belle, on the top floor. We even agreed to help her carry her groceries and provide bell service, the whole deal.

Mr. Bennett came out of her house when the deal had been agreed to, and he put his arm around me. I said, with some disbelief in my voice, "I'm gonna have this lady as a tenant for life?"

He says, "Billy, she's 72. What do you think the actuarial tables would say her life expectancy is? I mean how long can she last?"

Well, she made it more than a dozen years, to about 85. But she was a lovely lady, and she wasn't much trouble at all. But that's how we finally got the go-ahead to build the Colorado Belle. It all came down to sweet-talking Mrs. Lafferty.

Dr. Doug Thomas

I DIDN'T KNOW MR. BENNETT PERSONALLY, BUT MY FATHER ART THOMAS DID. HE OWNED a candy store in Circus Circus, called Henry's, and he had a long-term lease on the space.

Well, at the time of this story there were just two stores in Circus that had outside ownership. There was Henry's, and there was a ladies' dress shop. Bennett asked his hotel president, Tony Alamo, to buy out these leases because they were planning a build-out and remodel at the hotel. Tony was having a heckuva time striking a deal with the lady who owned the dress shop, so Bill Bennett said he'd negotiate with my father.

Bennett simply asked my father what it would take to buy out his lease, and my dad, who was a pretty sharp businessman, threw out an extremely high number, something like one or two million dollars. Bennett said, "Fine," and wrote him a check immediately for that amount and the deal was done.

Tony Alamo was still negotiating with the lady when he asked Mr. Bennett what had happened with the candy store. When Bennett told him how much he'd paid to my father, Alamo said, "Jeez, if you'd given me that much leeway, I could be done by now, too."

[According to the book Super Casino, *by Pete Earley, Bill Bennett got reputed mob hitman Anthony, "Tony the Ant" Spilotro to give up his jewelry store lease in Circus Circus by giving him a promissory note for $400,000. Years later, Spilotro and his gang would operate other jewelry outlets. Several of Spilotro's henchmen were busted breaking into Bertha's home furnishing store on East Sahara Avenue in the middle of the night, and were thereafter known as the Hole-in-the-Wall Gang.]*

Mike Sloan

LOOKING BACK, IT WAS INCREDIBLE HOW MUCH LATITUDE MR. BENNETT GAVE ME IN MAKING decisions. He probably gave me more freedom than any other person doing my job in the gaming industry. You could never explain failure by saying that Bill Bennett didn't give you the tools to do your job.

Early on I remember Don Mello, who was in the Nevada State Legislature and was a Democrat and the head of the Ways and Means Committee, had been talking about putting an initiative on the ballot to raise gaming taxes. So Barron Hilton had several top hotel executives down to a meeting in his office in Beverly Hills.

I was teasing Bennett, saying, "I hope no one from the Legislature is taking pictures of all these private jets down here."

Steve Wynn was there, and Mead Dixon, the attorney from Harrah's, and several other top guys, and Mead is making his presentation and he turns to Mr. Hilton and says, "Barron, what do you have to say?"

And Barron says, "Well, I'm wondering what Bill Bennett thinks."

Mr. Bennett and I were sitting at the opposite end of the table, and Mr. Bennett says, "Well, I don't know . . . that's why I brought my legal counsel here with me. Mike, What do you think?"

Now everyone else in the room was a senior person or an owner, and he was deferring to me on this. He asked one of the other guys to give me a ride back on their plane and he left early. But before he left he said, "Whatever Mike says we want to commit to this, we'll go by."

He didn't like going to these big meetings of other owners. It used to drive the owners crazy, but he preferred to send me and I could go and commit two million dollars, or five million, and he was all right with that. That's unbelievable to me, looking back on it.

When Mr. Bennett rose through the ranks at Del Webb, he was pals with a lot of guys, but he saw that as fortunes rose and fell, some of these people would drop him like a hot potato. I believe he gradually saw that too many people weren't true friends, that they were opportunists or were just there to take advantage.

I remember one year when Mr. and Mrs. Bennett were having their wedding anniversary, and in the group were just Elias and Jody Ghanem, and Mike and Nancy Sloan. Just the six of us. And on his big trips, sometimes it was just Elias and Jody. He was not one to reach outside a small community of friends. I think he just perceived a lot of phoniness in people.

The bankruptcy of his furniture company in Phoenix taught him a lot. He was very successful, and then suddenly he was not. And people reacted accordingly.

I think if you talk to almost any woman in Las Vegas who's been divorced from a successful man, you'll see how few people are loyal to the woman after the divorce is final. People will go with the guy who can help them in business.

Glenn Schaeffer

SOMEHOW THE TERM THE "YOUNG TURKS" BECAME A TAGLINE FOR ME AND RICK BANIS AND Bill Paulos and one or two other people. And Bennett liked that term. He liked having a young group of guys with energy and watching what would come out of that. He told me once that business isn't that much different from professional sports. He said you make money off of athletes. Good athletes know how to win. So you go out and draft or buy the very best athletes you can get, and they'll figure out how to play, and you help them figure it out.

Bill Bennett was our coach. He wanted specialists in various areas who would go out and work hard and learn by doing. Bennett understood apprenticeship, which he actually had to learn to be a top executive. He said that you learn by doing, and if you're not taking on enough challenges, then you're not learning enough and you won't earn enough money.

Once he understood what he had underneath him, he said that we were going to become the premier gaming company in the business. And we did just that. I mean, this was a much bigger thing than he'd ever done before, but he had the team and the players to do it.

Bill Paulos

HERE'S A STORY YOU WON'T HEAR EVERY DAY. PROBABLY THE MOST UNCOMFORTABLE MOMENT I ever had with Mr. Bennett. I'm in Laughlin running the Colorado Belle and the Edgewater, and I get a phone call from him and he says, "Come to my office in Las Vegas right away."

Well, I'm an animal in Laughlin, and my mind starts racing because the only thing to do in Laughlin is drink and fuck. That's it. When you're not working there's nothing else to do. I like golf and they were building a course there, but it was horrible. You hit the ball in the middle of the fairway and it wound up in the river. So, golf there was no fun.

So every Thursday night my race and sports book guy and my casino manager and I go out drinkin', gamblin', fuckin' around, raising a ruckus. And I can drink with the best of them, so I figured something bad happened maybe while I was drinking, because he sounded serious on the phone.

When I get to his office at Circus Circus, Mr. Bennett is sittin' at his desk, and the corporate chief of security is standing there beside him. Bennett pulls out a piss cup from under his desk. He says straight out, "Piss in that."

I say, "What?"

He says, "Piss in that!"

I say, "What the fuck?"

Now I'm hot. And I had never before gotten confrontational with him, but this has really rocked me.

Bennett hands me a letter that was written anonymously to the Gaming Control Board saying that I was the biggest drug dealer on the Colorado River. And that I used my own product.

Now I understood where this was coming from, because we were the biggest drug *busters* down there. I had used hidden cameras to catch some valet guys sellin' dope. So, we were cooperating with the cops, and this was obviously someone getting back at me. But nobody had asked me about it. Bennett just calls me in and tells me to piss in a cup.

I pointed to the security guy and said, "What the fuck is *he* here for?"

Bennett said, "He's gonna watch you piss."

Now I could tell Mr. Bennett is getting really uncomfortable, very uneasy, with this whole situation. He's not happy with what he's doing.

"Maybe he should hold my dick," I say, nodding towards the security guy. That's a direct quote.

So Mr. Bennett doesn't know quite how to respond, but he says, "Uh . . . ummm . . . uh . . . uh, I guess we can let you go and piss in the cup alone."

So I go and piss in the cup and I'm fuckin' steamin'. And before I handed it back to the security guy I put the lid on it and I put some drops of water on the lid so it'd look like I pissed on it. Oh, yeah.

After thinking long and hard about who sent this letter, we concluded that it was somebody from Don Laughlin's organization. His people would have staff meetings just about me and how much business we were doing because we were kickin' their asses down there and we were proud of it.

I gotta say when I went into that restroom to piss in that cup I was so angry that the thought went through my mind to quit the company. But the thing about working for Bill Bennett was that he paid you so much money that in a way he owned you. You actually felt like you were owned, okay? Not in a bad way, but you hesitated to go on vacation. And I knew if I went anyplace else on the Strip, I wouldn't make half the money I was making with him.

I know that Bill Bennett knew that this incident was devastating to me. So after everything was cleared up and back in check, he sat me down and said, "I'm sorry I had to do that, but you know we always do what the Gaming Control Board wants. We never go against any of their wishes and this happened to be a situation where I had to do this. It hurt me very deeply to have to do this. You're very much like I was when I was your age."

Then he said, "I like you very much."

Damn, he almost had me crying when I left after that meeting. But it's like I've always said: He could cut you to ribbons over some issue, but before you left his office he would usually say something to build you back up again.

Mike Sloan

BILL BENNETT WAS VERY SENSITIVE ABOUT CERTAIN THINGS. ONE YEAR, LIKE ON CHRISTMAS Eve, I think it was around 1991, he invited a whole bunch of us to his house for a holiday gathering. Now I had just gotten married for the second time . . . last time, I think. And my parents were coming to town, and my son had just been born, so that was eighteen years ago. And I said, "We gotta go to Mr. Bennett's house."

So we went over there, and I assumed it was just a drop-by situation. He was sitting in a chair, very relaxed, watching TV. And there's food, the kind you would offer for a Christmas dinner. Several of his top executives and his family were there.

Anyway, with my parents in town, I didn't stay long and said I had to go. I'd assumed it was just a situation to drop by and wish Merry Christmas to Mr. and Mrs. Bennett.

I could tell Mr. Bennett wasn't real happy when I left, and the next day Rick Banis said he and the other executives were stuck there all day. So I guess that was the expectation.

The next year I'm working on Christmas Eve and I haven't been told anything about a party the next day. So I come to work the day after Christmas, and Banis says, "How come you didn't show up at Bennett's house?"

I said, "Because he didn't invite me."

So I thought I should address it head-on and I went to Bennett and said, "So I must be on the shit list, because I didn't get invited to your Christmas party."

He says, "Well, didn't I call you on Christmas Eve?"

I said, "Yes you did, and you talked about such and such but you never said anything about the party."

He felt bad. "You're right," he said. "I forgot to mention it. I'm really sorry."

But little things like that were sometimes of great importance to him.

Bill Paulos

What Mr. Bennett got most concerned about was expenses. There would be meetings and he'd ask, "Why are you doing this, or why are we spending this money on that?"

Those never bothered me. It was just a man watching over his business. I'll never forget I was in a meeting in Bennett's office with Tony Alamo, and something had been done at Circus Circus that he wasn't pleased with. We walked out of the meeting and Tony said, "Wow, did we just get killed!"

"I said, "Ah, that wasn't so bad."

Sometimes in business things get blown out of proportion because you can press a button on somebody that sets them off. It just might be one of *their* buttons, not one of your own, but it gets them going.

Despite that one moment of pissing in a cup, I always felt like Mr. Bennett thought of me as more than just an operator of his.

I'm comfortable saying that I thought of him as a father figure in a way. I certainly never felt like I was his equal. Never. And I wouldn't today. For instance, down in Laughlin, he sent me his nephew Scott Menke when he was going to college and asked me to teach him the business. So I became sort of a father figure to Scott. I think Scott still calls me Dad today. And we became very close. Scott worked for me right straight through all the joints. It was like raising another kid. Mr. Bennett also wanted me to help his son, Bill, when he was over at Slots-A-Fun, and in the food and beverage. When he trusted me with his relatives like that, I took that very personally.

Scott Menke

I'VE REALLY PATTERNED MY WHOLE LIFE AND CAREER AFTER MR. BENNETT. HE WAS MY GREAT uncle, the brother of my grandmother, Betty Spitler.

Coming from Glendale, Arizona, from a wonderful family, but nobody necessarily of my uncle's prominence, early in my education I tried to find people that I could relate to, and look up to, and who would pay attention to me. And I was very fortunate in that I was at the right place at the right time when I was close to graduating high school and was looking for a college.

I went to UNLV at Mr. Bennett's suggestion and with his financial help, and he said he would share his knowledge of the hotel business with me. How lucky can you get, to have the benefit of all that knowledge from a man who was helping shape the entire industry in Las Vegas?

After I was in college, one of the biggest breaks I got during that whole time frame was when we flew down to Laughlin, where Mr. Bennett had just purchased the Edgewater, and Bill Paulos was down there running it. So we flew down from Las Vegas, and Bill takes us to lunch. He hears that I'm in the hotel department at UNLV, and Bill graduated in that department's first graduating class, so he takes a great interest in me, no doubt primarily because I'm the owner's nephew, but still, his interest was genuine.

He started me in a training program at Circus Circus and for three years the deal was that I had to do every job in each department as good as the standard employee before I could move on. So I had to clean seventeen rooms in a day before I could become an inspector, and so on. I did everything. I got killed for three years. I literally went through all the housekeeping jobs. I worked the casino cage, dealing 21, dealing craps, you name it. I could never go to valet parking or the bell desk, because that's where all the cool guys worked. I would work after school and during the summertime, but it was invaluable experience, obviously.

Al Hummel

WHEN I GOT OFFERED THE CHANCE TO RUN SLOTS-A-FUN, I IMMEDIATELY SAID I WOULD take it. I didn't really know much about playing 21, but I started going out with a friend and learning how to shoot craps, and we played blackjack and I taught myself a lot about gaming. But what I really learned from Mr. Bennett was the business part of gaming. And I take pride in how fast I learned it and how well we did. I turned that place around, and I like to think we paid for it in a year.

This was in 1980, and I know because the place had some problems that Mr. Bennett got a super good deal when he bought it. Because it was small and did so well, Slots-A-Fun actually became the best casino in Nevada in terms of the money it generated. We even beat Caesars Palace per square foot. I borrowed the idea of inexpensive shrimp cocktails from the Golden Gate, and we sold those big hot dogs for next to nothing, and we offered fifty-cent Heineken and Corona. It wasn't rocket science, but we had a super-friendly and relaxed environment that offered good value and we packed the place.

A few years after that Mr. Bennett calls me in again and says, "Do you want to go to Reno? I've got a problem up there."

He was having problems with his partner, Bill Pennington, who lived in Reno and was of course his co-owner of the Circus Circus Reno. They had gotten in an argument over something. It was over Easter weekend, I remember. He told me about it on Thursday, the day before Good Friday, and he said I had to be up there on Monday. Mr. Bennett flies me up there on that Monday, in a Lear jet. I remember he had to lower the ramp by hand with a rope. So I get off the jet and I assume he's going to take me to the hotel and show me around, but he wouldn't even go with me. He didn't want to set foot on the property, I guess.

Here I am going to run Circus Circus Reno and I don't even know where it is. I get in a cab and tell the driver where I'm going, and he says, "You can play there, but don't eat there. They just poisoned seven people with their food." I thought, Jeez, Louise! What am I getting myself into here?

We're now up to 1985 or '86. I immediately started having a battle with Bill Pennington over the running of the place. To put this in context, Pennington had that horrible boating accident in 1984. It was an absolute miracle that he survived it. He was underwater for something like eight minutes when this young kid, about eighteen years old, dove down onto the wrecked boat, pulled him out, and did whatever to revive him.

He was in a coma for several days, and nobody thought he'd survive it, but he did. The story has a bad ending because when Pennington got better he bought the kid who'd saved him a 930 Turbo Porsche. And in a matter of weeks the kid was killed in that very car. Unbelievably sad story.

Diana Bennett
EVERYONE SAID IT WAS A MIRACLE THAT MR. PENNINGTON SURVIVED BECAUSE NO ONE STAYS underwater as long as he did and lives. I think the fact that Lake Tahoe is such a cold lake was a factor in his survival.

My dad went up to visit him in the hospital and he was in a coma and he came to with Dad standing at his bedside. The first words out of Mr. Pennington's mouth were, "What did we hold in slots last night?"

Glenn Schaeffer
THE COMPANY THAT WENT FROM A MARKET CAP OF $240 MILLION WHEN I JOINED IT AND was in the billions when I left ten years later — that was Bill Bennett's company. I'll tell you why. Willie P. [Pennington] didn't pick me. Bennett decided who was going to play, what roles they were going to play, what we

were going to build, how much we were going to spend to build it, and who was going to open it. All of those decisions came from Bill Bennett's desk.

Pennington was certainly apprised of what was happening when we had board meetings, but he was not in the room when all the big decisions were being made.

Al Hummel

Anyway, once Pennington was back working after his accident he was undercutting me in everything I was trying to do in getting the place running right. I had fired a lot of people and put my own people in there to make it work, and whatever I would do, he would come right behind me and call a meeting and say, "Don't listen to Hummel! Do what I tell you to do. I own the place."

Oh man, I was going nuts. It was about eight months of misery. Pennington would come in each day and sit in his office, but he didn't really have any function as far as managing the property.

Mr. Bennett had told me he was going to get Pennington out of the hotel, but he never came up there to really check things out, so it was rough going there for a while.

Mike Sloan

Here's another example of how much freedom Mr. Bennett gave me to address problems. I used to go down every summer to Del Mar, outside San Diego, and I noticed that there was often this huge backup of traffic headed to Las Vegas at Barstow, where I-40 and I-15 meet. There was one time it was backed up fifteen to twenty miles.

Mr. Bennett had a house in Newport, but he always flew down there on his plane, so this traffic never became a problem for him. But when I told him about it, he said, "That's not good. I want you to look into this and see what can be done."

I got helicopters to take pictures of the congestion and all the cars backed up, and Bennett said, "You better get this fixed." I realized I had brought this to his attention, but I didn't know how to fix it, and I told him that. He said, "Well, you better figure it out."

Circus Circus spent several million dollars on this, and we finally convinced the Nevada Resort Association to get involved, and in 1991 Congress passed the first interstate transportation bill, or whatever it's officially called. That was the result of Bill Bennett recognizing that problem and letting me go ahead on it. There were a lot of hurdles along the way. We formed an organization called the Tri-State Compact, which was California, Arizona, and Nevada. I don't think Arizona and California really knew what our long-range plans were at that point, but it gave us more political punch to have them involved.

A political consultant named Ken Reitz helped me with the project. He was Chic Hecht's campaign manager when he upset Howard Cannon and was elected to the U.S. Senate. Ken helped me get the support of Republicans in Washington.

I had talked to a friend of mine named Bob Miller, who went to Las Vegas High School, who was in a big law firm in Sacramento, and he'd been the leader of the Republican Party in the California state Legislature. He hooked me up with a guy in Washington, who asked me how much money we'd need for the project. I told him something like forty or sixty million dollars.

He said, "You can't ask Congress for forty million dollars."

I showed him all our research, and our papers. My intention was to fix just that one little place where those two highways merge down in Barstow."

"You can't ask Congress for a piddling sum like that," he says. "That's ridiculous. How much is it gonna cost to fix the whole thing, so there's no traffic delays from California to Las Vegas?"

I told him I'd make some calls and get an answer. He told me we had until tomorrow. So we came up with something like $1.6 billion.

He said, "Now we're talking."

To shorten the story, some weeks later I'm down in North Carolina, at a Fourth of July party at Dick Gephardt's house. We had made some significant political contributions to federal candidates, and we loaded up a little more on Democrats than Republicans. Bennett liked Gephardt, because he liked his policies on trade. And I'm down there trying to figure out how to get to somebody who is the chairman of the House committee that deals with transportation issues.

I eventually get introduced to Congressman Bob Toricelli, who later on became a U.S. senator. I explain to Toricelli what we're trying to do and he picks up the phone and calls the guy who's the chairman of that committee. And the next thing you know this guy says, "Yeah, we can work on that."

This all happened because Mr. Bennett trusted me to do that and let me have all the resources to solve the problem.

Scott Menke

MY DESTINY BEFORE THAT FIRST TRIP TO LAS VEGAS WAS TO WORK IN THE FUNERAL-HOME business. My dad owned funeral homes, so I was going to follow in his footsteps and become a mortician and work in those places, which I did in high school. I worked visitations, and had people sign the guest register, and even went on calls to pick up the deceased at the hospitals or wherever.

My parents had split up about the time I was turning sixteen, and so getting to see Las Vegas and that opportunity at that time, well, sometimes life works out great. It was a chance to get out of Glendale and get a fresh start. You know almost everyone in my family went to Glendale High School. Mr. Bennett went there, my grandparents went there, my mom and dad were the prom king and queen. He was a football player and she was a cheerleader. Mr. Bennett was even a classmate of the great singer Marty Robbins. So the roots go pretty deep there.

I started at UNLV in 1982, a year before Mr. Bennett took Circus Circus public, and we were studying some of the things he was doing on the Strip in my hotel classes. When someone like him starts to believe in you at that young age, and says he sees good things in you, you hang on every word he says.

I took my first trip to Las Vegas with my great-grandmother, Mr. Bennett's mother, Marjorie, when I was sixteen. She was about seventy-eight or eighty at the time. He had sent a plane to Arizona for us, and he wanted someone to accompany his mother on the trip.

I was expecting to see some sort of a single-engine piper cub at the airport to pick us up. But instead we got a repainted Gulfstream 2 with circus clowns on it. Once in Las Vegas, we were taken by a limousine to Circus Circus, where we checked into the Presidential Suite, and Mr. Bennett's secretary gives me midway passes. So my life was automatically transformed in about ninety minutes. I still think back to riding in the limousine and knowing that I had to tip the driver, and I thought I was a big spender when I gave him two dollars.

I think I stayed probably seven days on that trip, and my whole world changed that week. The possibilities I saw seemed endless.

I think my uncle saw me as a funny kid, because he'd give me something to do and my eyes would grow wide. I think he saw he could have a real influence on my life. We were staying at his house on one of these early trips and he said, "You're gonna go to work today."

We'd go down and have breakfast at the Pink Pony restaurant at Circus. Then I'd go up to his office and he'd have me help the secretaries out with some chores. He'd give me a car to drive around, and I had a choice between a Mercedes or a Rolls-Royce or a '56 Thunderbird, whatever was available, and this was at a time when I'd barely gotten my driver's license.

It might have been on the second trip I took with my great-grandmother to Las Vegas that Mr. Bennett asked me to buy her a house in Glendale. She was living down there in a trailer, and of course he was taking care of all her expenses. He didn't want her living in the trailer anymore because it was getting old and he was afraid of fires or break-ins. He gave me ten thousand in cash and told me to go back to Glendale and make a down payment on a house for her. I mean, I'm just seventeen, so like I know anything about buying houses [*laughing*].

I did some research and found an assisted living place and moved her into an apartment there. After I'd found that, Mr. Bennett had my Aunt Lynn (Sam) fly down and that's when my aunt and I became very close. She spent about a month down there with my family, and I would drive her around because she was decorating this apartment I'd found. He was always doing something for our family. His compassion and generosity really helped bring us all together and make us much closer.

Al Hummel

WE BECAME VERY SUCCESSFUL AT CIRCUS CIRCUS RENO, AND I'M REALLY PROUD OF WHAT we did up there. But Mr. Bennett never came up there. He called me one time when there was a snowstorm over a holiday weekend, and he said, "Looks like you're in for it up there."

I said, "Yeah, I hope it doesn't screw up business." But he wasn't about to come up there and see for himself. The one exception was when I got married up there in 1990. He came up because my sister made him come.

Scott Menke

I lived in a dorm my first year at UNLV, so there wasn't a great deal of excitement. But then I moved into a house with a bunch of football players, and that was definitely an animal house. But I want to tell a story about the prankster side of my uncle, because that side of him is sometimes overlooked.

I was graduating from UNLV in 1987, and everyone from the Arizona side of the family comes up to Vegas for graduation. My grandfather Clarence Spitler, who died early in 2009, was there, and he and Mr. Bennett, who was his brother-in-law, were good friends. They'd gone to high school together and basically had known each other their entire lives. So the night before graduation my Aunt Lynn throws a party back at the hotel for all my friends and family, and the tequila starts flowing.

After dinner we all come back to the room and my uncle and grandfather are trying to get me to do shots. I'm just a college kid, but of course I think I can do shots, and before you know it it's about six in the morning, we've emptied several bottles of tequila, and I'm supposed to be at UNLV for the ceremony at noon.

My uncle and grandfather are wrestling around, so I go upstairs to one of Circus's great old suites. They were built by Jay Sarno and they have saunas in them and they were two stories with hidden rooms and everything. Man, if those walls could talk, they'd have some stories from when Sarno stayed there. So I go up to this huge closet inside the master bedroom, and I take a pillow and I'm going to try and get three hours sleep before I have to go out in 110 degrees and walk through the graduation.

How Mr. Bennett and Clarence found me in this two-story bedroom closet all piss-drunk I'll never know, but they have buckets full of ice water and they are not going to let me sleep. And they douse me with these buckets. Then they make me down another shot of tequila.

I made it to the graduation, but boy was I wounded. The whole family was wounded along with me, so they split early from the graduation and took all the cars and limousines with them and left me stranded there.

Here's another story that gives you a side of Mr. Bennett that people didn't see. When Diana got divorced from Billy Conn, the father of her two sons, my uncle wanted to take her out and show her a good time to celebrate the divorce. I was still in college, so this was like 1986. We go to the Steak House at Circus Circus and we start to have some cocktails, and he eventually says, "Bullshit, let's go back to the house and play a board game."

So we started to play Trivial Pursuit, and he just hates to lose at anything. He and I were partners against Aunt Lynn and Diana.

Now every time we don't get an answer right he's pissed, and it's my fault. And if I didn't know an answer, he'd take off his shoe and beat me with it.

"You stupid fucker," he'd say, "What am I sending you to college for? Don't you learn *anything* over there?"

Of course we're all laughing this whole time, but he's hitting me pretty good with this shoe. Well, about the time we've gone through three bottles of Bailey's Irish Crème, he's pretty drunk, and we're continuing to lose, and he flips the entire table over. Game over.

He was the same way playing Monopoly. Here was a guy who knew something about real monopoly, buying properties and buying and building hotels, and he just couldn't stand to lose a game he thought he should win every time. I know one time he was on his boat with Elias and Jody Ghanem and they were playing Monopoly and drinking, and he was losing and flipped the whole game, with the dice and the symbols and the motels and hotels and everything on the board into the ocean. Once again, game over.

I guess the laughs made it all worth it, but the bottom line was that he couldn't stand to lose.

Billy Conn

OH, THERE WERE SEVERAL TIMES WHEN THE RASCAL SIDE WOULD COME OUT OF BILL BENNETT. One time we were at Twin Lakes messing around with one of his remote control boats, when all of a sudden, Poof! There were feathers flying up in the air out of the willows. The boat had hit a black swan and killed it deader than a wedge.

This boat was just racing across the water and it got back in the willows and killed that bird instantly. It was a protected bird, so we had to get out of there before a game warden showed up.

We packed up our stuff as quickly as we could, and started throwing everything into our van, but we had a problem. We had this little dinghy that we used to float out on the water, and it was all inflated and we couldn't get it in the van fast enough, so we took a knife and punctured it, and folded it up and high-tailed it out of there.

I know Mr. Bennett loved animals, and he certainly didn't feel good about that bird, but we hauled ass out of there like kids who just broke a window.

Jody Ghanem

MY HUSBAND ELIAS, WHO WAS MR. BENNETT'S DOCTOR FOR MANY YEARS UNTIL A FEW years before he died, and I were privileged to go on several great trips with the Bennetts. On their planes, and their yachts, we went up the East Coast of the U.S. a few times when the colors of the trees were changing, and we went to Alaska and to Australia, and those were just amazing times and amazing memories.

I know everyone called him Mr. Bennett, even longtime employees and family members, and that's what I called him for the first few years after we got to know them in the 1980s. After a while, when I would address him as Mr. Bennett, he would say, "No, Jody, you can call me Bill."

But it took me a couple of years before I was comfortable calling the Bennetts Bill and Sam. I just had such respect for them, especially him being significantly older than I was, and I knew so many people still called him Mr. Bennett.

I think the first time I really got to meet and begin to know the Bennetts was some time in the 1980s, when we were invited to their house for their annual Christmas party. The house was beautifully decorated by Sam, who was very talented as an interior designer. There were some key employees at the party and I knew it was an honor to be invited. It meant that Elias had become a friend and an important business partner. It was at the time that Elias was starting the process of establishing health care contracts with the hotels and bringing down their health-care costs. Mr. Bennett was one of the first ones to give Elias a contract, and it was for all the Circus properties.

The relationship started on a totally professional basis, and then became a friendship. Even though I think Mr. Bennett had health issues even at that time, Elias becoming his primary doctor was never discussed at that point in their relationship.

Mike Sloan

I FOUND MR. BENNETT TO BE VERY EVEN TEMPERED AROUND THE HOTEL. OH, THERE WERE moments when he would get worked up, but they were rare.

My starting date working for him was June 1, 1985. I'll never forget that, because when I accepted his offer I had forgotten to tell him that some months before I had scheduled a two-week vacation with my family to Europe. I had organized the first international gaming attorneys' conference in London, and obviously I had to be there. Bennett did not like his employees taking vacations. He did not like people to be gone. He wanted you to work, work, work.

When I explained it to him I said, "Mr. Bennett, I know this is going to sound horrible, but I was so excited about taking this job that I forgot to tell you I have to leave the country for two weeks."

I didn't know at that time how much he hated vacations. He was really taken aback by this. This is a man who rarely cursed, and he said, "Well, you better be a goddam good lawyer." He clearly was not happy.

In those times when he was unhappy, in fact, he wouldn't raise his voice. He'd lower his voice to where you could barely hear him.

I did hear him get into a real public argument once with Tony Alamo in the Pink Pony, because Tony would not be quiet about something and Mr. Bennett was tired of hearing about it. But rarely ever did I see him act rude, discourteous, or abusive. I've seen a lot of guys in the gaming world beat up on their subordinates, but that was not his nature at all.

Mel Larson

BILL BENNETT WAS JUST A TREMENDOUSLY TALENTED BUSINESSMAN. ONE OF THE BEST YOU'D ever find. He made a fortune in the furniture business in Phoenix, but suffered a turn of events, and then he started in a brand-new industry, hospitality and casino gambling, and made a fortune in that. He had that natural something that great business people have, where you could put them in almost any business and they'll learn what they need to know and work hard and become successful at it.

He could be all-business, but on occasion he could go out and be one of the boys, too. And when he was relaxed like that you could treat him like one of the boys, but there was always a line you didn't want to cross. If you did, he'd give you that look or let you know to watch yourself. He was all business around the hotel, and he somehow had his finger on top of everything.

He'd call me in every now and then and ask me something out of the blue, and I'd wonder how the hell he came up with that question. I tried to be prepared to answer anything that might come up, but if he hit me with one I didn't know I made sure to get the answer for him right away.

When he hired someone, he put a lot of trust in that person. He delegated a lot of issues to his employees, and if they were going to stay employed for a long time, they sure better figure out a way to handle those issues. At the end of the day he'd go home and play with his remote-control airplanes and he'd have a few cocktails, and I think he was able to get his mind off work, but there were times when I'd get a call at home and he needed an answer right away.

One time I got a call real early on a Sunday morning, like five or six o'clock, and Mr. Bennett said he wanted to go in the helicopter with me. I forget where we were going, just to check out something, and he would do all sorts of tricky things to see how good I was at the controls. So even though it's early, he's got a cocktail and he sets it on my instrument panel, which wasn't perfectly level in the first place. He sets it there and says, "Now let's see how good you can land."

This drink is still half full and it's sitting there where it could easily spill and short out some of the instruments and cost thousands of dollars to repair . . . which of course he would have paid for.

Bennett just crosses his arms and watches me, and of course I'm really bearing down to land that thing perfectly. I took pride in my landings, and he knew that. So anyway I set that thing down without spilling a drop, and he picks up his drink and says, "That was very good, Mel."

Billy Conn

Mr. Bennett was always super attentive to the bottom line of costs, how much we paid for things, whether we were getting a good deal, why it made sense to buy in large volume.

He loved French fries with ketchup, and as food and beverage manager at Circus Circus I had recently found a good deal on ketchup. I bought like half a semi-truck full, maybe twenty-five or fifty thousand bottles, and I had saved thirty-four cents a bottle on what we'd previously been paying.

It was not the same brand of ketchup he was used to, and he told me one day he didn't like it and wanted an explanation. If he liked Heinz, I had purchased Hunt's or vice versa. So we had a conversation about it, asking why I had done that. I explained that he had talked to me in his office the previous week, and had scolded me about food costs and how we were spending too much.

I said, "I'm trying to save money on food, and I found a good deal. How about if I go and buy you your favorite kind and bring it to your table, so the next time you call me in about food costs it will be a pleasant meeting."

"That sounds good to me," he said.

So I did.

Clyde Turner

I THINK THE FIRST OCCASION I SPENT TIME WITH BILL BENNETT WAS WHEN HE WAS WORKING with the guys at Drexel Burnham Lambert, when he was going public with Circus Circus. The Golden Nugget was also getting financing from them around the same time. This would be in the early 1980s. There were occasions when we'd both be in Los Angeles and I was always invited to join Bill. And many times he and Bill Pennington would be together at lunch or dinner and we somehow got together.

There was another occasion when I was asked to come over and play some tennis at Bill's house. He had a nice tennis court at the house on Desert Inn street. I heard there were some wild times in L.A. and some food fights with the guys at Drexel. One of them was a principal of the company, but I forget his name. But those stories were kind of surprising when you consider the guys involved.

So my relationship with Bill Bennett was just social, until years later I got a call from him in 1993, but that's another story.

One thing that was different about him was that he would occasionally give people jobs who maybe didn't have the credentials to get those jobs, okay? Or should I say they didn't have the standard credentials that would have allowed them to come up in a normal organization where people are checking all the paperwork and comparing them statistically with other candidates for the position. He'd give them a job and basically leave them to do that job until they screwed up. And I think in the early days, even when they screwed up, he would admonish them in a very polite way. I mean, generally speaking Bill Bennett was a gentleman.

Bill Allen Bennett

IN THE 1980S, WHEN CIRCUS CIRCUS WAS THE PLACE THAT EVERYONE IN GAMING WAS watching with admiration, because the earnings were so strong, my dad was teaching Las Vegas how to be better at running casinos. He taught so many executives how to go after a different market, and how to stop thinking in old traditional ways.

He understood why so many of the old-timers and mob guys would cater to the high-rollers, but he also knew that the low-rollers who enjoyed coming to town greatly outnumbered the big players. There was just a huge market that the town was missing and that was being overlooked. So Circus Circus became kind of the Walmart of casinos.

He wanted the customers that Caesars Palace and the Dunes and even Benny Binion were not catering to. Binion liked it known that he would take any size bet, and he catered to those type gamblers, but my father stressed that the way you make your money in the gaming business is through volume. You do not make it by bringing in rich oil sheiks who can ruin your whole year with a hot run of cards over a couple days. You do it by grinding that percentage. The more those slot machines get pulled, the closer you come to the theoretical percentage that those machines will hold.

Scott Menke

MR. BENNETT LOVED LOOKING AT THE NUMBERS OF PEOPLE WHO HAD GONE THROUGH THE buffet each day at Circus Circus, and he studied the slot revenues. Those two numbers, buffets and slots, were really important to him because those were our key customers. If something was off with those, then there was a problem.

There were times where he would give me five hundred dollars and have me go over to the Riviera or the Stardust, which were big competitors of ours, and play the slots and talk to the women at the other machines to find out the reasons they patronized those hotels. He wanted to know what those places were doing that we weren't, so we could figure out a way to capture those customers.

He'd also have me drive through parking lots of competitive hotels and write down how many license plates were from other states. He would find jobs like that for me that helped him understand the market. It made me feel useful, and I was learning a lot about how the industry worked.

Bill Paulos

OKAY, I'VE TOLD THE STORY ABOUT PISSING IN A CUP, AND HOW THAT WAS A LOW MOMENT for me and an occasion where I thought Mr. Bennett was out of line. Here's a story to illustrate how classy he could be, and why he could be such a great guy to work for.

Sometime around 1990, after we'd built and opened the Excalibur, and done it for a fraction of the cost of the Mirage, and we were making great profits there, I get a call from the Global Gaming Exposition people. And the person on the line said, "We've nominated you for our Gaming Executive of the Year."

My first reaction is that it's a nice honor, and I'm flattered, and then I ask who else is nominated. I'm told the other two nominees are Bill Bennett and Steve Wynn.

I'm thinking, Holy shit. How the fuck can they do that?

"You can't make me run against my boss, for Chrissake," I said. "That's a can't-win proposition. I'm dead."

So now I've got to call Mr. Bennett, and I tell him, "Mr. Bennett, this is not right. I mean, I'm certainly not worthy. You're the one who makes all the decisions around here. I don't know why they did this. I'm sorry."

And what do you think he says? He says, "Billy, this is fine. We've got two out of three chances to beat Wynn."

So I end up winning this award as Casino Executive of the Year in 1990, and I'm uncomfortable about it. I mean, I'm only doing Mr. Bennett's bidding every time I make a move, and I'm put in this competition against him. But Bennett calls me and says, "Congratulations, you deserved it."

I say, "What do I fucking deserve? I'm only doing a job you're allowing me to do." And he says, "Yes, but you're doing it right. It's an honor for the company."

That's pretty classy, by anyone's definition.

Billy Conn

THERE'S ONE WORD THAT STILL RINGS IN MY HEAD WHENEVER I THINK OF BILL BENNETT, and that word is "procrastination."

One time Mr. Bennett called a bunch of us executives into his office. I got a call from his secretary, Nancy Lee, to come up for a meeting starting in ten minutes. I didn't know if the call was just me alone, or what. It was an unscheduled meeting, so that kind always kept you on your toes because you had no idea what he might ask you, or what type of job he wanted you to do. Any questions he might ask you were always felony questions, as far as importance. He didn't have time for misdemeanors. He also never minced words. He was a "cut to the chase" guy. You also knew it wasn't going to be a long meeting, because he thought any meeting that lasted over an hour was wasted time.

As I'm walking down the hall to this meeting, I see Mel Larson and Joe Hulsey and Mike Ensign, and I'm thinking, This is going to be a heavy meeting, especially since it was called on such short notice.

So he starts with some comments about the importance of getting things done on time and the challenge of running a large operation, and the kind of executives he thought he had. Then he said, "There have been some failings with this team, and they are unacceptable."

That pretty much sucked all the air out of the room. Man, it got real tense in there and it looked like heads might roll. He said he wasn't going to mention any names, nor was he going to single out any department, but he said, almost verbatim, "I want you all to train your eyes on me, every one of you. I'm very unhappy with what's going on in this company. I think I pay you all well to do your jobs. I *know* I pay you all well. But there are some failings in performance, and the key word is 'procrastination.' If any of you ever procrastinate again when I tell you to do something, the next time you get a bonus envelope, you're going to open it up and there will be nothing in it. And you'll know you procrastinated when I asked you to do something."

He then called Nancy Lee on the intercom, and she came in carrying a Budweiser beer box. Inside were a bunch of plaques, and on each of them, in bold letters, was the word "PROCRASTINATION," and the Webster's Dictionary definition underneath it, something like "to willfully put off something you should have done."

Mr. Bennett said, "From now on, I want this plaque sitting on everyone's desk. This is my gift to you. It may be my last. I want you to look at it every day, and don't ever procrastinate again when I tell you to do something. Meeting dismissed."

Of course all of us left the room wondering who started this fire, and whether individually we were the one to cause this meeting. Suffice it to say, this guy really knew how to light a bomb under your ass.

Michael Milken

WHEN BILL BENNETT OPENED THE HIGH-END STEAKHOUSE AT CIRCUS CIRCUS, I WENT TO the hotel to see where it was located. And I didn't ask anyone for directions to it. I wanted to find out on my own where it was located, and see whether I would have chosen the same location.

I was wandering around by myself, and I went first to the locations I thought the steakhouse might be, and it wasn't there. Then I noticed a place where if you've won prizes at the games arcade, you'd go to collect your prizes. It's where they kept the stuffed animals or whatever. And right across from there was the new steakhouse.

I remember thinking, Who would put a fancy steakhouse there, right where all the kids go to pick up their prizes? And my thinking was that I sure wouldn't have put it there. Then I realized only Bill Bennett would do that. Now they might have moved the steakhouse later, but that's where it was when it first opened.

I went inside the restaurant and it was beautiful, much nicer than anything else they had done in the hotels. It's stuck with me even today, years later, that Bill was oblivious somewhat to the contrast of where that steakhouse was, right there next to the rewards area for people who won at arcade games. He felt the world of the steakhouse was inside, when you opened the door and walked in. How different brilliant people can be. Steve Wynn has built beautiful restaurants, and if the environment isn't just right, he's ripped them out and started all over.

One thing is certain. Bill Bennett knew who his customers were and what they liked. He had a sense about things that was right on the money.

CHAPTER 4

Painful Split

Bill Paulos

IT WAS AROUND 1990 AND '91 THAT BILL BENNETT STARTED TO GET INCREASINGLY paranoid and impaired. I had a lot of meetings with him around that time because I was the general manager of Circus Circus, and we had opened Excalibur and we were in the early stages of planning Luxor. So we did a lot of brainstorming, and oftentimes there would be other people in the meetings, and Mr. Bennett would nod off. Right in the middle of a discussion he would fall asleep.

I felt bad for him when this would happen because he was my guy. I mean, this was the man who made me. No question about it: He *made* me. Between him and Mike Ensign, they were the mentors who taught me everything I knew.

I would sit really close to Mr. Bennett's desk in these meetings so I could give him a little kick under the desk and he would snap out of it. But I just hated to see what was happening to him, because I had so much respect for him, and it got progressively worse over the next couple of years.

I knew he was in pain, and there were a lot of problems, and it seemed like he was always fighting a new malady. I knew there were serious circulation problems in his legs and feet. And then there was his back, and this and that. You never knew exactly what was troubling him on any given day, but I always felt he was overmedicated.

Glenn Schaeffer

I REMEMBER MR. BENNETT TELLING ME ABOUT THE AIRPLANE GLUE, AND HOW IT HAD MESSED him up. He said it at an annual meeting in 1990 or '91. He apologized at that meeting and said that he had not had a very good year and that he was going to give himself a pay cut. He said he shouldn't have sniffed all that glue when he was younger. He made a joke out of it, but obviously there was nothing funny about it.

So my feeling is that for whatever reason he had neuropathy, and that it was probably substance induced.

Scott Menke

AT HIS WORST MR. BENNETT WAS TAKING TWENTY PERCOCETS A DAY, PLUS COUMADIN, THE blood thinner. And he was drinking a lot. It's true that he would fall asleep at his desk, but I remember times when you would think he was sleeping and he'd suddenly pop out with a comment that told you he was listening all along.

Bill Paulos

ALCOHOL PLAYED A PART IN BENNETT'S DECLINE WHEN HE WAS STRUGGLING WITH ALL THE physical problems, and the pills.

In the 1990s I did a lot of flying with him. All business. These weren't pleasure trips. And I realized after a while that he liked me going with him on these trips because I was the only one of his key people willing to drink in the morning.

And that's when I found out about the importance of Donald Duck orange juice to Mr. Bennett. We'd get up in the air on these trips, in the company plane, and he'd say, "All right, you want an Old Grandad?"

I drank bourbon and he would drink screwdrivers — vodka and Donald Duck orange juice — because the viscosity of that brand kept it from being obvious how much vodka was in the glass.

"Never use Tropicana orange juice," he'd say, "because it gets lighter when the drink is stronger. Donald Duck holds its color."

It was clear he considered it no one's business but his own how strong his screwdrivers were.

Scott Menke

ONE OF MY JOBS IF I WENT SOMEWHERE WITH MR. BENNETT WAS TO MAKE CERTAIN WE HAD a good supply of Donald Duck orange juice and menthol Ultra-Light cigarettes. If I forgot either of those, it was big trouble.

Bill Paulos

THE SITUATION WITH GLENN SCHAEFFER WAS VERY REVEALING AND ILLUSTRATES HOW MR. Bennett was slipping.

Until he had Schaeffer in the company, he'd never had an out-front guy. Glenn was great with the quotes and extremely bright, and during those years he became the face of the company for Wall Street. He had all sorts of great descriptions for what we were doing in the early '90s, like building "megastores" and "super casinos." He was a literature major, a creative writing guy from the University of Iowa's famous Writers' Workshop, and so when the *Wall Street Journal* or other national media were looking for stories on Circus Circus back when the stock was going berserk at fifty and sixty bucks a share, Glenn was the guy they would call.

[*Several people interviewed for this book mentioned a front-cover story that appeared in a gaming journal in the 1990s that featured Steve Wynn and Glenn Schaeffer as the most important faces on the Las Vegas Strip. By all accounts, the issue of that magazine sat on Bill Bennett's desk for several weeks. It was uncharacteristic of him ever to keep materials that didn't involve current business on his desk, and it delivered an omen to everyone who saw it there.*]

Mike Sloan

I TOLD GLENN THAT HE WAS GOING TO GET FIRED WHEN I SAW THAT MAGAZINE ON MR. Bennett's desk, and it stayed there for weeks. I said, "Glenn, you know that's not good. Nothing sits on his desk for very long."

It was shortly after that that Schaeffer got fired. It didn't take a rocket scientist to see that coming.

Glenn Schaeffer

MY RELATIONSHIP WITH MR. BENNETT STARTED TO SOUR SOMETIME AROUND EARLY 1992. Bill Pennington was exiled in 1988, and Rick Banis was fired in '91. I became the president. I was next in line. I think that Bennett, driven for recognition, didn't like sharing it. Or he decided that a man had served his term, whatever it was.

I don't think it can be overemphasized how much impact that magazine had that featured me and Steve Wynn on the cover. It think it was *Casino Journal*, or something like that. It was a gaming magazine. And the caption over the picture said, "Idea Men of the Year, 1992."

I certainly didn't pose with Steve for the cover, nor did I have any idea that it was in the works. As soon as the magazine came out, I thought, Uh-oh!

Most journalists don't understand the autocracy under which many corporations operate. That doesn't apply just to gaming companies. There's no gain for a number-two man getting that kind of recognition. Bill Bennett probably knew better, but it made him so angry he didn't reflect on the fact that I would never have set up something like that. That picture on the cover just crossed the line in his mind, no matter how it had come about.

Look, I got to be Glenn Schaeffer, I got to be this so-called *wunderkind*, because Mr. Bennett enabled it to happen. I got to go to Wall Street, I got to do all of that stuff, and I was a millionaire because of him. He'd given me those opportunities and now I was one-upping him. In his mind, and rightly so, if you're going to have a magazine cover featuring idea men, then you put Bill Bennett with Steve Wynn because Glenn Schaeffer's not going to do anything that Bill Bennett doesn't want done. From the time that magazine came out until I left the company, it never left the top of his desk. It was always showing up somewhere. Maybe he pulled it out when he knew I was coming in. I'm not sure. I just know that from the time it appeared, somewhere in the middle of 1992, maybe near the end of that year, I couldn't do anything right.

Clyde Turner

BILL BENNETT CALLED ME ONE DAY AND SAID THAT HE WAS ABOUT TO FIRE GLENN SCHAEFFER, that he'd been disloyal and that there were a lot of other things he was upset about. Schaeffer's title was president and chief financial officer. He said that he wanted to hire me to take Schaeffer's place, that the world didn't understand that he [*Bennett*] didn't want to retire. He made that point to me repeatedly, and he said if I would consider coming in and taking Schaeffer's position that I'd be the chief executive officer in six months, and that he himself would retire and leave within a year. I would then become chairman of the board. That was the deal, clean and simple.

Let me say that our agreement wasn't actually written down anywhere, but it was generally agreed to by both of us and known by others that that was our deal. I think Bennett talked to some of the other guys about it. The first part of it happened. I was made the CEO within that time frame, but the chairman part was a different story.

I had just launched a construction business at the time Bennett contacted me, building homes in Las Vegas, and I had assumed my long career in gaming was behind me. I struggled with how I could juggle the two roles, but then I realized that the opportunity with Circus Circus was so tremendous that I couldn't pass it up. I decided to take Bennett's offer.

Apparently the split with Schaeffer was imminent because shortly after I'd spoken with Bennett I came into Circus Circus to start work. Schaeffer was just finishing clearing out his desk. I walked into Glenn's office, we shook hands, and he walked out. I sat down and started taking calls from Wall Street, which I did nonstop for at least two days straight, from six in the morning until six or seven at night.

It was interesting because I learned at that point that Wall Street thought Schaeffer was running the company, not Bennett. I was being asked by everyone which direction Circus Circus was going to go under my leadership, as compared to Schaeffer's.

Let me say that Schaeffer was a world-class interface to Wall Street. He was really good and he's still really good. He's a really smart guy, very quick on his feet, and he understood the jargon and had developed a lot of relationships with the Wall Street guys. And I think that's what Bill was so upset about, that he was at least perceived to have relinquished the leadership of the company to Schaeffer. That would further explain why that magazine with Glenn and Steve Wynn on the cover would be upsetting to him.

Jody Ghanem

ELIAS AND I HAD BEEN ON THESE AMAZING TRIPS ON THE BENNETT YACHT, UP THE EAST Coast when the leaves were changing color, and Bill was such a gentleman and a perfect host. I remember on the first two trips he was so fun and enjoyable. I think it was the third trip we were on that you could start to see him change, and this was when this breakup was going to happen with Glenn Schaeffer.

He talked more about business on that trip, and it was clear he had a lot on his mind. He would drink, and then he would get quiet, and it was clear that he was troubled.

His wife, Sam, started to share some things, how there was some tension in the company. I tried to stay out of all that. I didn't like hearing it and I felt bad that all that stress was there while we were on a wonderful trip. I could see Bill was drinking more, and maybe on more medication. He also seemed to be getting paranoid. I could tell a split was coming, and he was dwelling on how it was going to happen.

The pattern was the same on that trip. We would get up in the morning and he was fine and making sure our plans were in place for that day and that everyone was having a great time. Mr. Bennett made you feel so comfortable, and both he and Sam were very giving and loving with their guests. Then at night he would drink and you could tell the worries would start to creep in.

Scott Menke

I'm not sure just how much Mr. Bennett worried about Steve Wynn and others getting all the media attention during those years. I don't think it was all that big a deal to him. It was important to him that stockholders and people on Wall Street could see that he was running one of the most successful companies in America. He wanted the respect of corporate America, and he wanted the respect of his employees and customers. That's what mattered the most to him.

Bill Paulos

I think there was a time when all the attention Steve was getting might have bothered Mr. Bennett. We opened Excalibur in 1990, and it was the biggest hotel in the world when we threw the doors open, with four thousand rooms. The next biggest was the Las Vegas Hilton with thirty-two hundred. And Wynn had opened The Mirage a few months before Excalibur and he got all the press, in part because he had spent $750 million and we had built our place for just $300 million. The Excalibur is still the best return on capital ever in the history of the gambling business, I think. I mean, the place was paid for in two-and-a-half years, which was spectacular.

[For six years during the 1990s, the Culinary Workers Union staged a strike at the Frontier Hotel on the Strip. During that time, Bill Bennett donated more than three million dollars in free meals to workers who walked the picket line. It was a gesture they never forgot, and later they erected a billboard thanking Bennett, and feted him at a tribute dinner.]

Diana Bennett

IT'S KIND OF FUNNY TO LOOK AT WHY MY FATHER WAS SO GENEROUS TO THOSE STRIKERS, because in another instance — Laughlin, Nevada — he fought against unionization. Laughlin was not a union town, and with our properties down there we did everything we could to make sure it didn't become a union town.

Our employees in Laughlin were paid very well, and my father deliberately paid them more than he might have in order to avoid their going with the union.

But on the Strip, unionization wasn't to go away, so my dad felt that everyone needed to be on a level playing field. As long as unionization was best for the city, strikes were not going to be good for anybody. If Circus Circus and every other property had to abide by the union, then so should the Frontier. And so for Margaret Elardi [*the Frontier owner*] to take that stand was doing an injustice.

I'm sure my dad spoke to Margaret, but nobody could change her mind. So he did what he thought was right in that case, and that was to support the workers and feed them meals for spending all those hours on the picket line. He felt very strongly that they were being treated unjustly.

Jody Ghanem

WHEN WE FIRST TOOK TRIPS WITH MR. BENNETT AND SAM IT WAS ON A YACHT CALLED THE Circus Circus II. Then when he broke up with Mr. Pennington, he built a yacht called the Picante, and we started to travel on that with him. He always took his sister Betty and her husband, Clarence Spitler, with us. And there were like five years of heavy traveling during that time.

Bill wouldn't let you pick up the tab on anything, and I just felt he loved his planes, he loved his boats, and he really loved sharing that time with us. I have the fondest memories of traveling with the Bennetts. They were the perfect hosts.

I remember having conversations with Mr. Bennett about airplanes, because he was such an expert about them. They weren't really conversations so much as a matter of him teaching us things.

When this near disaster happened in the Hudson River, when those birds got in the plane's engines [*January 2009*] and the pilot did such a miraculous job landing in the river, I clearly recalled Bill talking years before about how dangerous birds were for airplanes. He knew what caused any sound on an airplane, and he could talk about how dangerous it was to fly through certain clouds, and how turbulence would affect a plane.

I remember thinking that must have been what it was like to talk with Howard Hughes early in his life, when he was in love with aviation and setting flying records. I felt privileged when Mr. Bennett would discuss these things with us because I appreciated that I was learning about stuff I never would have known about otherwise.

It was about the time he was planning the split with Glenn Schaeffer that I saw him change. We were on a boat trip and he didn't like the captain, and so he had someone else captain the boat and we ended up running aground in the Martha's Vineyard area. We had to fly home early on that trip. We thought, How could he have a man captaining this boat that really didn't have enough experience? But that's when he was really preoccupied with all the problems back in Las Vegas.

But even after that we took a great trip to Alaska, and then, I think we went to Australia, right after the Luxor opened in 1993. But it was clear Bill's health was deteriorating, and he was drinking a lot. I don't know about the medications he was taking, but there was some paranoia creeping in. And he was complaining a lot about his legs and the lack of circulation.

Elias never discussed with me particular medical issues of his patients, but of course in the medical field you do have to be careful about prescriptions. It has to be controlled. And you've got boards watching you. I know there were many conversations about this, and Sam Bennett did talk to Elias a lot about the medications and trying to get Bill to stop drinking. He really did try.

Scott Menke

MR. BENNETT LOVED HAVING ELIAS AND JODY GHANEM AROUND ON TRIPS. ELIAS WAS ONE of the funnest guys to travel with. It was clearly both a business and personal relationship and friendship. All through my uncle's life he always would have a doctor around and he would manipulate that doctor. So he could have any prescription he wanted, whenever he wanted it.

He just felt more comfortable traveling with a doctor because if anything were to go wrong, a doctor was right there.

Mr. Bennett would find a way to have doctors become indebted to him. There was a doctor at a Pittsburgh hospital that he loaned the Challenger to for a month to fly all over Israel, so that doctor became indebted to him.

I'm not sure how my uncle and Elias first met, but they probably found each other. I don't think anybody had to sell either one on what they could do for each other.

Over the twenty-year relationship, I think they probably benefited equally. Elias got the Circus Circus business for his medical practice, and Mr. Bennett got attentive medical care.

A lot of people have accused Elias of getting him hooked on pills and all that other stuff, and that's so far from the truth. Elias took a lot of risks to try and get my uncle out of all these issues. My uncle had issues with medication going all the way back to around 1976, when he had some sort of medication overdose at Circus Circus.

Mr. Bennett was a mixologist, and a very Elvis Presley-style mixologist. He would take blood thinners and uppers and downers, but mostly painkillers. It was not a recreational thing. It was a significant problem.

I don't think his physical ailments were caused by diabetes. I don't know if anybody would have known the truth but Elias, to be honest with you, and Mr. Bennett had a way of making his own health decisions. He certainly didn't want to be unhealthy, but he also didn't want anybody knowing too much about his condition. He was a very strategic power player. He didn't want the wives and the daughters and me talking and sharing information with each other. He kept everybody at bay so he could do what he was going to do, which had a lot to do with his later firing Diana and myself at the Sahara. We knew too much, and he wanted to keep all his self-medicating more private.

It was very sad.

Ben Speidel

MR. BENNETT CALLED ME INTO HIS OFFICE IN THE MIDDLE OF MAY 1991. I KNOW THE dates because I hung onto the receipts for the hotel room at the Dunes.

He wanted me to take a close look at the Dunes as a possible purchase. I was told to do it on the sly, so I checked in with Heidi, who was then my girlfriend and is now my wife, and over the next two days I took hundreds of pictures of the place. I acted like a typical tourist, just flashing away with my camera, but I did it in a way that I could piece the pictures together and really give him a good look at the property. It was on the sale block at the time, and was eventually sold to Steve Wynn for seventy-five million. He then imploded it so he could build Bellagio.

When I reported back to Mr. Bennett, it was May 25 of '91. I checked that date against the hotel receipts. I showed him all the pictures and when he asked my opinion I told him if he bought the place, he could probably keep the old hotel tower, but the rest had to be torn down. But the golf course, which sat on 175 acres right behind the hotel, I felt was worth the price of the whole place. I thought it had great value.

Later on, he asked me to check out Bally's [*the original MGM Grand, which was the site of the tragic hotel fire in November 1980 that took eighty-four lives*], and I told him that I absolutely would not consider that as a place to buy.

Anyway, that same day in May, as I was leaving Mr. Bennett's office, Rick Banis saw me and quietly motioned me to come into his office. Glenn Schaeffer was sitting there with him.

Banis said, "What was the old man talking to you about?"

"It was between me and him," I said.

"Well, I'm the fucking president," Banis said. "Was it about the Dunes?"

I was in a tough spot, so I told him, "Yes, it was."

"What exactly did you tell him?" Banis asked.

"I told him it was a dump, but if I had the money, I'd buy it," I said.

Banis was clearly upset, and so was Schaeffer.

"Do you know what you did?" Banis said. "We're trying to buy the property where the Hacienda was."

It was clear to me at that point that not everyone was on the same page with where the company was going in the future.

Dick Rizzo

OUR INVOLVEMENT AT PERINI BUILDING COMPANY BEGAN WITH BILL BENNETT, WHEN HE took on a project that moved him from being sort of a secondary character on the Strip, in terms of identity, to a major player who oversaw the building of an iconic landmark property, the Luxor.

For us it was a very interesting time in Perini's growth as well, because up to that point we had not been involved in much of the major construction work in Las Vegas, and that was intentional on our part. We came here first in the early 1980s to build the Thomas & Mack Center, and at the same time we did the major expansion on McCarran Airport, the first original phase, and Cashman Field. We were a public company, and having the Perini name with its Italian heritage, our board was very concerned about forming a relationship with the gaming industry, and whether that might be a negative influence on the name of Perini.

It was the perception of having a connection to the Mafia, and the rumors that swirled around Las Vegas, and so the board was generally very "anti" our getting into gaming. But we had established a presence here, and I recognized the huge potential for the company in that industry, and I had formed relationships with many wonderful people that I trusted. The board in time realized that it made sense to give us a shot at working with the hotel-casinos.

The first Strip project we did was the remodel of the Tropicana Hotel, because we had a good relationship with Dick Snell, who was then the president of the Trop's parent company, Ramada. At the time Luxor was announced, MGM Grand was under construction across the street, and there was nobody in town that had the capacity, other than ourselves and Tony Marnell, to do the Luxor. We were excited to get that chance because it was our first ground-up opportunity to do something on the Strip.

It was a real challenge for somebody to take on. The Luxor is a unique structure that few companies would not be intimidated by. The sheer magnitude of it and the way it needed to be done in concrete was a real challenge.

Veldon Simpson was the architect, and he ended up being Bennett's buddy and confidant on the project. Bill gave him great credit for developing this totally original hook and theme of the Luxor. He was trying to create a unique and easily identifiable structure that he felt Circus needed to upgrade their image, and the Luxor accomplished that. It was even featured on the cover of *Time* magazine in 1994.

Bill Bennett had already established his talent in appealing to middle America with his other hotels, but with what Steve Wynn was doing on the Strip, I think he was motivated to upgrade what Circus was doing and create a hook on the Strip that would cause people when they got to Las

Vegas to say, "I have to go see this pyramid." And he really did that. The Luxor became a must-see location from the day it opened.

It was very gutsy on Bill Bennett's part to take this on because structurally and architecturally nothing had ever been attempted in the United States as large as that. It's the largest open-air clerestory structure in the country, and the codes that were written for fire, life safety, exhaust, etc., didn't even apply to such a massive building.

[*Clerestory is an architectural term denoting an upper level of a Roman basilica or of the nave of a Romanesque or Gothic church, the walls of which rise above the rooflines of the lower aisles and are pierced with windows. The purpose of the clerestory is to give light to the inner space of a large building.*]

The challenge for us structurally was, How do you do it? How do you build it? If you walk in there and just look, you have a twenty-eight-story clerestructure in which all of the floors are cantilevered in. So we had to figure out how to build a concrete frame that would accommodate that kind of a structure.

We did it with the help and cooperation of Bill Bennett's vision, the architects' talent, the structural engineer, John Pappas, who actually got put in jail as a result of other problems, and Bill Paulos, who was our go-to guy for the actual physical construction while we were building it and while we were doing the value engineering, the initial design and budgeting, and all that kind of stuff. Paulos was really the key to the cohesiveness of that. He was extremely good at his job. A super guy, too. Fabulous guy.

Sam Sabin

I WAS THE PROJECT MANAGER FOR LUXOR WHEN WE STARTED CONSTRUCTION EARLY IN 1992.

We considered Mr. Bennett to be a giant in the industry and a legend in Las Vegas, so it was a big deal when we got that job, because prior to that Tony Marnell's company had done most of his work.

R.C. White was the director of construction for Circus Circus at that time, and I remember when we were shown the boundaries and put up the fence around the acreage we were going to be working on, we felt we needed more space to the north of the property, into the Excalibur parking area.

R.C. said he didn't think that would be a problem, but that we should check with Mr. Bennett. So one of the first meetings I had with him was to request more space for our crews to work. Instead, Mr. Bennett gave us less than R.C. had promised. He said Excalibur needed that space and that maybe after Memorial Day, when things slowed down a little, we could expand our perimeter. I felt R.C. kind of set us up on that one.

Most of our discussions with Mr. Bennett were filtered through R.C. and Bill Paulos. Mr. Bennett would come on a site inspection every two weeks or so, and it was the damnedest thing, because every time he'd find something that wasn't quite right. He really had an eye for detail. From the ground up, he had a lot of insight towards what he wanted with the Luxor.

In doing some of the budgeting and planning, it was clear from the beginning that Luxor was going to be a clear step above other Circus properties in quality, but Mr. Bennett was still watching every penny. I know that when we were under way we realized that the inclinators, which were in each of the building's four corners, did not go down into the basement and the service area, so that meant the room service attendants and such would have to use a vertical elevator up from the service area to the main floor, and then transfer to the inclinators to get to the rooms. To fix this was going to cost around four to six hundred thousand dollars for each inclinator. That was at least a $1.6 million problem to fix.

Paulos said he sure as hell didn't want to go to Bennett with that request. I'm not sure what the situation is now at the Luxor, but I know that request was turned down.

Glenn Schaeffer

WE HAD ASSIGNED A WOMAN WHO WORKED UNDER MEL LARSON TO DO SOME RESEARCH regarding names for the new property. One day in a meeting she mentioned "Luxor," which was an ancient Egyptian city. That name was listed along with mythical towns and the Seven Wonders of the World. It's in there somewhere. And of course that was a perfect name, because it was authentic and it implied luxury.

We visited Egypt. I've been to the tomb of the kings and queens. I've seen King Tut. I've been in Nefertiti's tomb, up and down the Nile. I've been at Luxor.

I did say — and it was picked up repeatedly by the media — that the Luxor was the first pyramid built in a desert in more than six thousand years, and that phrase got a lot of play in the media.

Clyde Turner

IN MY VERY EARLY DAYS AT CIRCUS CIRCUS, WHEN I REPLACED SCHAEFFER, BILL BENNETT was lucid most of the time. He was sharp and on his game the majority of the time. But he had occasions — and I don't know whether it was the pills or the pain or whatever — where he had issues which would cause behavior that was different than when he was in control.

Prior to my arrival, I heard many stories where a number of executives were fired under unusual circumstances, usually when Bennett would become obsessed with some particular aspect of their actions. The one I heard a lot about was Rick Banis, and how he was fired because Bill had some issues with the landscaping at Excalibur.

Jody Ghanem

ON OUR BOAT TRIPS IN THE EARLY '90S, ELIAS'S RELATIONSHIP WITH MR. BENNETT WAS growing stronger, but I could see Mr. Bennett becoming more agitated on the trips. Often at dinner, he would start talking about people in the company and who he was going to fire. I felt bad listening to that.

This one trip back East, the timing of it was to see the colors change, and Mr. Bennett loved the planning of these trips, like how we were going to fly over certain areas at peak times, and how it would look like a valley of fire down below, with all the brilliant colors. He was an avid photographer and took some beautiful pictures, I remember. I think it might have been the third time we made that trip that he acted different. He was drinking more, and was more open about the things in business that were troubling him. He was getting increasingly paranoid on that trip, and instead of enjoying it like he had before, I could tell he was very bothered by issues happening in Las Vegas.

I knew that Glenn Schaeffer was like a son to him, so before the split happened and afterwards, he was just not the same to travel with.

Glenn Schaeffer

WE HAD A REPORT SYSTEM IN THE HOTEL. SOMEONE WOULD COME OUT AND SAY, "DON'T GO down to his office today."

Mr. Bennett's decline was gradual, but from the late 1980s on it was pretty steep. There was an incident where somebody played some of my words back to Bennett, and he called me into his office.

"You told [*so and so*] that I was irrational," he said, visibly upset.

"No, I didn't," I said. "I said you were erratic. There's a big difference. And you are. Some days you're better than other days, and I work with you on the good days."

I didn't know what else to say.

Mike Sloan

I REMEMBER MR. BENNETT CAME BACK FROM SOME TRIP, I THINK IT WAS TO AUSTRALIA, and when he got to Las Vegas he fired Rick Banis because the trees he planted at Excalibur weren't tall enough. It was like *The Caine Mutiny*. With all the homes and boats and planes and lifestyle he could enjoy whenever he chose, I don't think he particularly liked being just another rich guy that people fawned over. That was boring to him. He loved being at work. That was his passion. That was his life.

Dick Rizzo

BILL BENNETT WAS REALLY A HANDS-ON GUY WHEN WE WERE BUILDING THE LUXOR. HE HAD a very autocratic management style, and nothing happened on that job without his personal involvement. It would be nothing for him to go onsite at three in the morning and express his concerns. Or he might be there at six a.m. when our guys got there, and he'd tell them that he'd been there a few hours earlier and he had questions about something.

Now Bennett wasn't a construction guy, but he certainly knew how to build things in the sense of what he needed to be concerned about, how the flow of people through the building would work, and how to deal with the numbers of people that would be staying there and where certain venues should be placed and all that kind of stuff. He really was a person that was so hands-on that he allowed very few people to do anything without his total involvement and control. It surprised me how he could take on all that. With all he had to do, and with his health not being very good, I was amazed that he found the time personally to get involved in so many things during the construction of Luxor.

By the way, Steve Wynn is very much the same way. There is nothing that Steve doesn't personally touch as far as what goes into his casino, from the color of the walls, to the drapes, to the carpeting. The only difference, in my opinion, between the two was that Mr. Bennett never had the sophisticated taste that Mr. Wynn did, and so as a result he never got the recognition he probably deserved as being a visionary for Las Vegas. But they both perfectly understood their markets, and how to capture their particular patrons.

While I think Wynn's presence in Las Vegas, and all that he was doing, probably pushed Bennett to go farther, I do think Mr. Bennett would have built the Luxor anyway. Particularly at that point in time, he was trying to improve the image of Circus Circus as a company and a presence on Wall Street.

I don't think, as some people did, that the Luxor was a knee-jerk response to Mirage, because Bennett's client base was not anything close to what Steve was attracting at his places. They weren't competitors in any sense in the kind of clientele they were marketing to. They just weren't.

Sam Sabin

AT THE GRAND OPENING OF THE LUXOR, MR. BENNETT CAUGHT ALL OF US PERINI PEOPLE by surprise by making a comment that slammed the county building inspectors.

We had gotten invites to the VIP opening for some of the inspectors who had been especially helpful and had been great to work with. We had to do a fire test about two months before the opening, to show how smoke filtered through the atrium in the event of a fire, and about seventy-five people from the building code department helped us with that. Those guys had worked hand in hand with us, and then Mr. Bennett in his remarks something like, "We got this hotel open *in spite of* the building inspectors."

That was a little awkward for us.

Jody Ghanem

IT WAS WHEN THE LUXOR WAS OPENING THAT THINGS WERE GETTING WORSE. I KNOW SAM talked to Elias a lot and said that Bill's mind was slipping. They were trying to come up with a plan. He was going to start doing some tests at UCLA.

Mr. Bennett kept telling us, "I have a surprise for you two. I have a surprise," and he was so excited about it.

So we're at the opening of the Luxor and we walk in and at the entrance there are these two large camels. And draped around their necks are the names "Jody" and "Elias."

When we walked in and saw that, I thought, Oh my God. I was embarrassed. For Mr. Bennett it was a glorious moment, and the two camels were talking to each other like they were on *Gilligan's Island*.

Elias and I were both kind of taken aback. I mean he was doing this in honor of us, and the gesture was heartfelt, and wouldn't you know the next day on *Good Morning America* they have these two camels, and one of the show's hosts is interviewing Jody and Elias, the camels.

I was then thinking, something is really wrong here, because if this is the main attraction coming into the Luxor, with what Steve Wynn is doing with his properties, something is not right.

I know Sam Bennett was talking to Elias a lot, and they were trying to come up with a treatment plan. Bill started doing some tests at UCLA, because it seemed there were so many things wrong with him and they were struggling to find answers.

Early in our traveling with him, I think Rick Banis was on one trip, but I don't think executives wanted to be along because they worked for him and that wasn't a relaxing situation. So it was usually just Clarence and Betty Spitler and Elias and me and the Bennetts.

Mr. Bennett on the later trips would talk about firing someone when we got back to Las Vegas, and it got worse, and then he would tell stories about how if somebody was ever late coming to the airplane, he would just take off and that would mark the end of their relationship.

The last trip we took was first to Hawaii and then from there to Australia. And as soon as we arrived there, Mr. Bennett was very agitated and he had heard something about the other executives wanting him off the Circus Circus board back in Las Vegas. So he wanted to leave right away. Sam and I were having a great time so we begged him to stay two more days, because we had just arrived there, and he agreed, but he was mad on the plane home because something was happening and he was really anxious to get home.

Elias was scheduling more tests at UCLA, and these were expensive tests, and Elias would have to pull favors to schedule these, and then Bill would cancel. And it was difficult because Elias was jeopardizing himself and some of these relationships to set up these exams. Finally Bill decides to go down for one, and as I recall it was for a brain scan. Elias was running late getting to the airport, and Bill instructed the pilot to take off.

My husband came home and there was dejection on his face. He said, "Bill took off without me."

I was like, Oh my God. Like my heart just dropped because we knew that was the end of the relationship. Bill had told us that's what he would do to people when he was through with them, he'd leave them at the airport.

After that Dr. Ken Landau started traveling with the Bennetts, and it was sad for us because we had shared all these unbelievable memories with Bill and Sam Bennett.

Later on I know Elias put Bill together with Paul and Sue Lowden when they wanted to sell the Sahara. Elias didn't function as his doctor anymore, but he knew Bill's goal was to stay in the hotel business after he was forced off the board at Circus Circus. We all thought he was crazy to get back into the business. I think Mr. Pennington would tell him, "Bill, go enjoy yourself. Have some fun."

But he was determined to get back to work and prove to people that he could still run a company.

Glenn Schaeffer

THE YEARS OF THE EARLY 1990S WERE A REAL BOOM IN THE GAMING INDUSTRY. IF YOU wanted to be one of the companies that looked like they were in the fore-front of the industry, then you had to be going after new gaming jurisdictions. That's when you had Iowa, Illinois, and Missouri in play.

This was a boom that Bill Bennett did not want to participate in, because I think he felt it was threatening to his control, which he already felt was diminishing over the company.

That had also been a point of contention between the two of us, in particular pushing for the Chicago casino. I felt we should be competitive with Harrah's in running around the United States exporting our version of the gospel. And that was a direction for the company that Mr. Bennett didn't want to see.

For ten years prior to that, with anything we did in terms of growth, we were certainly serving the latent notions of his own mind. But what we were doing in 1992 and '93, Bennett wanted no part of.

So how did I feel at that point? Well, I knew that I was eminently hirable by another company, and that I might earn even more money in my next run than I had before.

As to how I felt having a break with Bill Bennett, a mentor and someone who felt like a father to me, a man that I knew had warm feelings towards me, well, it was just extraordinarily painful. It was a divorce. It was just as painful as my divorce from my wife.

Clyde Turner

It's probably been explained that Bennett made some unusual hires in key positions. There was the famous story of the boat captain that was brought in to run the slot department [*Craig Hodgkins*]. Then there was another guy who was his insurance writer. He hired him as executive vice president of something while I was there. This guy came in and built himself a big office, a very fancy office, and was paid lots of money, but he never did anything. So he finally went away.

Oh, there was a pilot from South Africa. Can't remember his name either. Bennett had to pull a lot of strings to get him over here and get him a green card so he could work for Circus Circus. He put him down in Laughlin, then brought him back to Las Vegas and I think he was the GM of Circus for a while.

But in the early days even when those people screwed up, he would admonish them in a very polite way, and give them an opportunity to do better, because he was a gentleman. In later years, when he was having these issues with the pain medicine, I think it affected his moods and he'd become obsessive. There were occasions where he fired people for what seemed like small issues, or something would happen which would just push him over the edge.

Craig Hodgkins

I started working for Mr. Bennett in 1983, as the chief engineer on his boats, and I became the captain six or eight months later. That boat was called the Circus II. I was captain for him from 1983 to 1991, and I captained three different yachts, the Circus II, Calliope, and Picante.

Around 1990 I got engaged to be married. I told Mr. Bennett about it and that we maybe wanted to start a family and that I wouldn't be captaining the boats forever. He said, "Well, let me think about that."

Maybe a month later he said, "I'd like you to think about coming to live in Las Vegas to work in the casino industry. What do you think about that?"

"I don't think I'd be cut out to live in the desert," I said, without any hesitation. "I just don't think that's something I'd be interested in."

He said, "I think you ought to think about that for a while. You've given me a quick answer, and it may be shallow and short-term thinking to let this opportunity go by."

So I went back to my cabin and thought about it for a while, and I realized that if someone like Bill Bennett, with all his success, was telling me that I had responded too quickly, then I definitely should take it to heart.

I must have spent the next year talking with Mr. Bennett about different things. Finally, I accepted his offer. Diana Bennett had been slot director for Mike Ensign at the Gold Strike and had just come into the fold at Excalibur. She was my first boss, right when it opened. Al Hummel was the general manager. I was married by then.

I know Mr. Bennett brought people in from other careers to work for him. He brought Richard Brand in from the aviation business. He was general manager of the Excalibur and Circus Circus for a short while. I believe I went the highest in the company, to general manager and then president at the Sahara, before, like nearly everyone else, I was fired.

Diana Bennett

CRAIG HODGKINS TURNED OUT TO BE ONE OF THE MOST LOYAL AND TALENTED PEOPLE WHO worked for my dad. My father recognized Craig's talent for management, and like in his own case starting out with the Del Webb Corporation, he knew that the gaming business could be learned later on.

Craig is still an offshore gaming executive with a charter company, so he's been able to combine his two talents.

Bill Paulos

I'VE NEVER TALKED ABOUT THIS BEFORE, BUT IT'S PROBABLY GOOD TO GET THIS ON THE RECORD, although I don't like talking about it. Around 1992 and '93, Mr. Bennett was getting more and more paranoid, depressed, disconnected, forgetful, and ornery. He had all of the traits that you would associate with a guy who was losing it. He would take people apart for no reason, which was something he would never do before. His character was totally changing. Every day he would do something out of character with the man we had known all those years.

MGM was about to open, and we were working like crazy on getting Luxor in shape for its opening. Schaeffer and Sloan and I and somebody else were sitting around talking, and we were all feeling that the company

was going to shit because, "the old man," as we called him in those latter
days, was losing it.

This was really difficult on all of us, but especially on Glenn Schaeffer,
because in my opinion Schaeffer clearly looked up to Mr. Bennett as a father.
And on those occasions when Bennett would be harsh on Glenn, he would
take it like a son being scolded by his father. At that time, in 1992 and '93,
Schaeffer was the face of the company, without question.

Somebody leaked, because somehow it got back to Bennett that we were
having these meetings. That's when Schaeffer left the company and eventually went with Mike Ensign, who had left to join the guys at Gold Strike.
And that's when Clyde Turner came in to replace Schaeffer as the president
of the company.

So now I'm getting calls from Wall Street, and stockholders are telling
me I've got to stay with the company. A guy named Rose urged me to stay,
and he had a tremendous amount of money tied up in Circus Circus. So
then I became the face of the company. I mean, there's a CEO and a president, and a this and a that, but they knew I was the one who had opened
Excalibur and was about to open Luxor so I was asked to stay and I told
them I wasn't going anywhere.

Glenn Schaffer

I'VE HEARD THE EXPRESSION "PALACE COUP," BUT THAT MISREPRESENTS WHAT HAPPENED
during the time when things were going downhill. These weren't group
meetings. These were one-on-one discussions. I never met with two of them
at the same time but once. I did tell the directors that I was going to quit the
company, and that I was going to quit on the following Monday morning,
and then they talked me out of it. They told me it would be wrong for me
to quit, and that the stock would go down considerably over personal issues
with Mr. Bennett, where he was in the wrong.

So I called a meeting on a Monday morning — I'm thinking it was in
January of 1993 — and suddenly Bennett was in a peace-making mood,
which I didn't expect. He said things like, "Look, we've got to stick together
around here."

There was this long back and forth between us over the next days. We
had a painful, searching conversation in his office. It was emotional. He

said, "What do we have to do to be closer?" He said, "Why don't you call me Bill . . . don't call me Mr. Bennett anymore."

First he wanted to fire me, then he didn't want to fire me. I said, "Do you want me to quit?"

He said no to that. But shortly after he did fire me, and when reporters would ask him about it, Bennett would say, "I didn't fire Glenn Schaeffer. He quit."

Bill Paulos

I WAS BROUGHT IN BY MR. BENNETT AND ASKED SOME QUESTIONS ABOUT WHAT I'LL CALL the "unholy alliance," and the private meetings that had been held. I just said that it was nothing, just some of us conducting business and discussing how we could improve our share price and stuff like that. I certainly didn't tell him that we were strategizing about how to get him out of there.

At the time Schaeffer left we were really rushing to get Luxor open. Bennett said we were going to open on this certain date in 1993. It's clear he was having a race with Steve Wynn to get it open before Treasure Island opened.

We had problems with the Luxor, obviously. It was a very controversial building. The inclinators were a major headache. We had to change wheels on the inclinators four times within a month, okay, until we got the right polyurethane. They actually were a great innovation, but they scared people. It was a bumpy ride because of the pressure on the wheels. Technically, the inclinator was a mine cart being pulled up the side of a building. That's what it was, nothin' else, but people were damn near having heart attacks riding them.

Everything about it was tough. I mean, it was certainly the toughest project I've ever done. Perini Construction did a masterful job building it. A masterful job. But very early on we had to make the decision on whether to spend two million dollars to blast some of the caliche at one of the corners underneath the building. The decision was made by Glenn Schaeffer, and I suspect Bill Bennett, not to do it. Over the course of the years that decision cost the company tens of millions of dollars because it completely fucked up the bottom floor of the hotel.

Dick Rizzo

THERE WAS A TIME, AND THERE WAS ACTUALLY SOME MEDIA COVERAGE OF THIS, WHERE THIS rumor mill was going on about the Luxor pyramid settling and turning and twisting. Bill Bennett was convinced that his competitors had come up with this story to bring him down. He had a paranoia about it. I would say it was to a point of obsession. One of the rumors that got a lot of play was that the gods were twisting the structure because of anger that another pyramid was being built that would replicate the original Pyramids.

Bennett was convinced that somebody in the community, some of his competitors, were actually feeding the media frenzy with this stuff, and it caused him to spend extraordinary amounts of money to quell those rumors. At Perini we had to take a whole bunch of testing labs and borings and instrumentations on the structure to make sure that it wasn't moving, it wasn't settling, and it wasn't turning. Bennett simply had to prove to himself and to whomever was listening that in fact all this talk was bullshit. It was at a time in his life when paranoia really took over.

Sam Sabin

OF ALL THE PROJECTS I'VE WORKED ON IN MY YEARS WITH PERINI, THE LUXOR WOULD RANK right at the top. We learned a lot about geometry during that time. It was a completely concrete structure, and concrete is always shrinking, so there were issues with the building settling and service cracks and such, but we didn't have time to wait for all this because we were on such tight deadlines. The initial suggestion was to build the structure and then wait for a year for everything to settle. Obviously, that doesn't work in Las Vegas. There were so many unique challenges that went with building that pyramid.

I will say that Mr. Bennett had great respect from everyone that worked around him, and he was involved in all the details, from the color of the carpet to the finish of the glass. He was well informed throughout and offered valuable input on nearly everything.

Mike Sloan

DURING THIS PERIOD OF TIME, BENNETT WOULD CALL ME AT HOME AT NIGHT, AND YOU COULD hear the ice cubes clanking in his drink as we talked. It was funny because if one of my kids answered the phone, Bennett would say "Hello," and then there might be a ten-second delay before he would identify himself. And so my kid would hang up the phone, and he'd have to call back.

I know he drank a fair amount in the evening, and I don't know the specifics of his pain medication, but I know he had a tremendous amount of leg pain. Over time, it just changed the nature of who he was. He was no longer the Bill Bennett I had first met.

Dick Rizzo

Mr. Bennett was never a personal-type guy. He'd never ask you questions about your wife or your kids or anything like that. He was strictly business, always business. Very blunt at times, and he'd try to catch you off guard. Actually, I guess unpredictable is a good word to describe him.

On his bad days, it was almost like he had early signs of Alzheimer's, to me. He would forget what he had told you. Or he would deviate in a conversation and go off in some odd direction and we'd all sit there and listen and leave the room and say, "What the hell was that all about?"

It was obvious that something was not right.

Diana Bennett

One of his secretaries, Betty Hanseen, and others around my father would try to protect him on those days when he wasn't feeling good. They could tell early in the day whether he was having a good or bad day, and if he wasn't himself, they would keep others from seeing him and come up with excuses to keep him out of meetings. They were loyal to him. That was just something that had to be done.

Dick Rizzo

Even during the latter days of construction on Luxor we all appreciated Mr. Bennett. We all recognized what his weaknesses and his shortcomings were and we worked around them. I think part of the abruptness he showed was because he would lose track of what he was trying to accomplish, and he'd just get angry and frustrated and take it out on somebody — whoever happened to be in the room at the time. And we'd sit there at attention and just shut up and listen and walk away and say, Okay, that's Mr. Bennett.

Now Bill Paulos is a very open guy. He was always very forthright in wherever he was coming from, and he was very much a part of those meetings. Paulos would say what we all knew, that Bennett was going through difficulties but that it was our responsibility to get him to the finish line on this hotel. I don't think anyone held Mr. Bennett's behavior against him or felt it was a sign of a weakness. He wasn't well, and we knew this was a gutsy guy that really was taking on much more than he had ever attempted before in his lifetime. I'm sure he had moments along the way where he thought, *Oh, shit. What have I got myself into here?*

Although there were things that were unfinished when the hotel opened, I think everybody pulled together so that Mr. Bennett got what he wanted out of the hotel's opening. That night created exactly the image and the impact that he hoped it would have. It was artful the way they opened the hotel without giving the public the impression that parts of it were unfinished. There were guided tours through several areas of the hotel, and it was all well managed.

Some of the room finishes weren't done, but more importantly, a lot of the venues that were a part of the second level — the entertainment venues which were kind of complicated and had last-minute technology issues — could not be opened. And water problems caused some parts of the boat ride not to open. That being said, I think opening night for Mr. Bennett was done with such skill and orchestration that it was one of his proudest moments. He had accomplished what he had set out to do, which was to open an iconic Las Vegas Strip property in fierce competition with his biggest competitors of the day.

Clyde Turner

THERE MIGHT BE SEVERAL DIFFERENT VERSIONS OF THE DAY OF THE STOCKHOLDER MEETING, where it became obvious to everyone that a change had to be made, but this is mine:

There was a stockholders' meeting at the Luxor. Now it was traditional at these meetings that Bill Bennett did not make presentations. For all the years that Glenn Schaeffer had been with Circus, he had made the presentations. And he was terrific at doing that. When I replaced Schaeffer, I assumed that responsibility. All the Circus board members would of course be sitting there. And they might get a question directed at them from time to time and have an answer they would contribute. The room was filled this day, with a couple hundred people.

I sensed that day that Bill was going through one of those cycles where he didn't feel good and was irritable. In the middle of my presentation to the stockholders he cut me off and whispered to me not to say any more, but to just call for questions.

And the questions started coming. And they started to come to him, and he couldn't answer most of them. It became unbelievably embarrassing to everybody on the stage. And then he said he couldn't hear the questions, and that the air-conditioning fans were too loud.

To the extent that I could, I would step up and answer the questions and help him through it or whisper in his ear, whatever it took to get the damn meeting over with. It was just so painful and awkward.

The reporter Pauline Yoshihashi was there from the *Wall Street Journal*, and everybody was anxious about her presence because we knew the next day's report wasn't going to be a good story.

It was in the board meeting that immediately followed the shareholders' meeting that Bill said he wanted to have only the outside directors in the room. Now I didn't think that was provided for legally. I was the only inside director except Mr. Bennett. Sloan was the general counsel, and so he was excluded from the meeting as well.

I'm told that Bill went in there and started the presentation by saying that he wanted to fire me and that he wanted to fire Sloan. I was told this by Sloan.

Mike Sloan

WHO COULD EVER FORGET THAT DIRECTORS' MEETING? AS IT WAS ABOUT TO START, BENNETT said, "Okay, Clyde, you and Mike stay out. I want to talk to the directors."

I told Clyde we couldn't do that. He was on the board of directors and I was the secretary. Anyway, Bennett went in and told the board that they needed to fire Clyde and me. That's what I was told by more than one person in the room.

What Mr. Bennett had lost sight of was that over the years I was with him I had suggested putting several of the directors on the board. One of them was Tony Coelho, who had been the number three guy in the U.S. House of Representatives. Another was Carl Dodge, who had served for a long time in the Nevada State Legislature and whom I had got appointed chairman of the Gaming Commission. Jimmy Cashman was on the board, and so was Fred Smith from the *Las Vegas Review-Journal* newspaper, men I had known and been friends with for years.

The board saw from that meeting and the stockholders' meeting that preceded it that Bennett was losing it a little bit, and as a consequence we didn't get fired. Instead, Bennett was encouraged to give up the title of CEO. He wasn't just encouraged; he was told to give it up.

Later on Mr. Bennett, as many recall, tried to buy the Hacienda after those of us at Circus had just had a board meeting seeking to do the same thing. It was my unpleasant duty to go out and see him and tell him I'd spoken to three different law firms, and because he was privy to our intention to do this — because he was in the meeting when this was discussed — he was legally forbidden to do this. I said I hated to be put in this situation, but I had to tell him that the board was going to have to sue him. And we did sue him.

I think he made the move for the Hacienda because he was bitter and angry. He eventually backed down because he knew we had a case against him, but it put me in a terrible position because he had been so incredibly good to me. Because of him, I didn't just have a job, I had a life. He was willing to let me do so many things. For many years I believe Circus Circus had the biggest influence on the workings of the Nevada Resort Association, partly because I had picked John Schreiber, who had been the former head of the Las Vegas FBI, to be the full-time guy. And then he was followed by Richard Bunker, who had worked at Circus.

Bennett let me become his instrument of power and he gave me unbelievable freedom to use it, as long as it was used for good causes.

Dick Rizzo

I didn't see Bill Bennett as being a guy who was hands-off regarding his executives, at least in our experience building the Luxor. I mean, I don't know how detailed he got into the day-to-day operations of guys like Sloan and Paulos. But I know that he really didn't allow his people to make any important decisions without his personally being involved in understanding the issues. He made it clear to us at Perini that in important matters he wanted to make all the final decisions. As far as the construction side of things, he was very autocratic, very non-delegating actually.

Clyde Turner

After Bennett said he wanted Sloan and me fired, the directors really hit the wall. They realized in that meeting that Bill was dangerous to them.

The guy that surprised everybody when he came out against Bill in that directors' meeting for what he was asking was Art Smith. Art had been one of Bill's best friends and the person who, when he spoke out, probably hurt Bill the most, because Bill had given Art a lot over time. He'd given him money, presents, lots of stuff, and he'd made sure that Art was his guy. Art was the ex-CEO of First National Bank and lived in Reno. You might compare it to Julius Caesar looking down and seeing that Brutus was part of the mob that was after him.

Bennett had made me CEO a few months before this meeting in 1994, but now it was past time when he had promised to step aside and make me chairman of the board. But with him acting so strange, I was frankly thinking about resigning on a personal basis. But the board assured me they would make this happen, and they asked if I could work this out with Bill so it didn't have to be so combative. But with Bill at that time you couldn't work it out. He just wasn't right.

Bill Paulos

IT WAS AFTER LUXOR HAD OPENED AND GONE THROUGH SOME TOUGH EARLY MONTHS WHEN out of the blue I get a phone call from this guy from Australia who wants me to come there and build and operate his casino. The company was Crown. The Packer family owned part of it, although they weren't the majority owners. Lloyd Williams was the guy who offered me the job. He offered me the world. It was an incredible offer. If I took the offer, I had all this Circus Circus stock that I was gonna lose, and he was willing to pay for all of it. It was a seven-figure signing bonus. It was one of those offers you can't refuse, and I could see the writing on the wall at Circus. Everything was coming apart and starting to get crazy.

Mr. Bennett didn't have the idea of stepping down anywhere on his radar at that point, and things were very weird. So I make the decision I'm going to Australia and I've gotta tell him. I drive down the Strip that morning and my stomach is absolutely shot. It felt like a thirty-hour drive, and I'm soaking wet with nervous sweat. I had every bad emotion you could have.

I go into his office and say, "Mr. Bennett, this is the hardest thing I've ever had to do in my life, but I've accepted this job" . . . and I'm rambling on nervously. And I was surprised because he did nothing but congratulate me. He was totally classy about it. He made me feel like he was proud that I'd gotten such a good offer.

The only other person of the top executives that left of their own volition was Mike Ensign. Everybody else was fired. Everybody else, in our terminology, got shot.

One of the phrases we'd use was, "Just remember, there's a bullet in the gun for each and every one of us. If you stay long enough, you will eventually get fired from your job."

So I'm proud that I was one of the only guys not to get fired.

Now here's something even more unbelievable. Mr. Bennett threw a party for me, a small dinner gathering with the other general managers, wishing me goodbye and good luck. And he gave me a Rolex with an inscription on the back. It was unheard of. Thus ended my career with Circus Circus.

Jody Ghanem

I WANT TO KEEP THIS BALANCED IN TALKING ABOUT THE TRIPS AND VACATIONS WE TOOK WITH the Bennetts. In those first years we had so much fun. Sam Bennett would tell me that having younger people with them kept the energy up, and so we had a ball on all those trips.

Sam was a beautiful woman, and she had a beautiful life, but as Bill got sicker she became the caregiver and she lost many of the things they had enjoyed so much. He sold his airplane, and he sold the home in La Jolla, and he sold the Picante, the yacht that she had enjoyed so much. It was almost like Mr. Bennett would get jealous to see her have a good time.

She would occasionally ask me, "Why does he need to sell these things that I love and that we've enjoyed together? It can't be for the money, because he doesn't need the money."

Then when he bought the Sahara he sold his airplane to Arthur Goldberg, who was running Park Place. Later, we took trips with Mr. Goldberg, and it was nostalgic and I would think, Oh my God, we're on Mr. Bennett's plane.

We heard that Bill wanted to buy back the plane, but there was no way Mr. Goldberg was going to sell it back to him. These are big egos we're dealing with here. All those top hotel executives wanted the biggest plane, the biggest boat, the best hotel.

In the late 1990s, Elias was diagnosed with cancer, and by that time Bill Bennett was already not really with it. As I said, Ken Landau was traveling with him because I think he just always wanted a doctor with him.

Bill came one time to visit Elias, and I'm sure Sam got him all dressed up for that. He still had that elegance and air about him, but he was bitter, and he was telling us how he was going to do better than Steve [*Wynn*]. The conversation was all pretty negative. Actually very negative. We got along with everybody, so it was hard to listen to, and I knew that this wasn't the Bill Bennett we had come to know and love.

Then Elias passed away in August of 2001. And Bill passed away just over a year later.

I prefer to remember all those great trips in the '80s, when everyone was healthy and we had such wonderful times. Those are memories I'll cherish forever.

Nancy Gambardella

I REFER TO THE YEAR THAT MR. BENNETT LEFT CIRCUS CIRCUS ENTERPRISES AS "THE YEAR from hell." Another employee, Melissa Jones, and I used to talk about how the company changed immediately when Mr. Bennett left. It just wasn't the same company.

Chapter 5
The Swan Song:
Buying the Sahara

Scott Menke

I HAD A LOT OF RESPONSIBILITIES THAT MR. BENNETT WOULD GIVE ME IN THE EARLY AND mid-'90s. I would have to take a lot of meetings for him. I took meetings with the mayor or the governor if Mr. Bennett didn't want to go, and he had me looking closely to determine which hotel he was going to buy after he left the company.

We looked at the Frontier and the Riviera and the Sahara, and then it was decided to buy the Sahara. Deadlines on down payments would pass, and I would have to get a check from him. And then when we had the check written, Mr. Bennett, depending on the medications he was taking, might forget which hotel we were buying.

Diana Bennett

THERE'S NO QUESTION DAD WANTED TO BUY THE HACIENDA, BUT WHEN HE REALIZED HE couldn't get that, the Sahara was the next best option. There might have been some nostalgia involved there, because the Sahara was the first property on the Strip that he managed, but the main thing is he thought he could do something with the place.

It had the great convention space, which was kind of funny because he hated conventions and thought they were a waste of time for Las Vegas, but at least there were bones in the construction that he could work with.

The truth was my dad was not physically or mentally in shape to buy a hotel when he made that purchase. We overpaid for it, and the previous owners had totally given up on taking care of the property. They stopped replacing light bulbs, they stopped putting in air-conditioning filters. When a filter was clogged it was just removed and no replacement filter was put in. The kitchens didn't work, there were ovens that didn't have doors on them, and the rooms were completely disgusting.

They saw an interested buyer with a lot of money, and they took advantage of the situation.

The Sahara had always featured big-name showroom entertainment. Johnny Carson performed there for years, and Don Rickles and names like that. That was different from what my father was used to having. Big names in a showroom just weren't his market. He never had the caliber of hotel and the big players that he felt justified the expense of hiring those headlining entertainers.

I've already talked about how Benny Binion was a great teacher for my father in the gaming business, and I know Benny never hired big-name entertainment in the Horseshoe. He once said, "I'll be damned if I'm gonna let some hotshot musician blow my bankroll out of the end of his trumpet."

With the King Arthur show at the Excalibur, there was a huge enough showroom that you could get a lot of people in there, with cheap tickets, and the show was there for the long term so you could get to where the show paid for itself.

Dad never wanted the volatility of high-rollers and all that went with that. You didn't want to attract just two high-rollers to your place, because they could kill you. If you were going to bring in whales, you needed a hundred of them to balance one another out. That was something that didn't interest him at all.

I've said many times, I wish my dad had just flipped the switch to turn on the big spotlight at the Luxor on opening night, and then resigned as chairman of the board. Because I think that was the brightest moment of his career, and everything was downhill from there.

Cameron Conn

THAT MIGHT HAVE BEEN A PERFECT SWAN SONG, BUT THAT JUST WASN'T MY GRANDFATHER. Had he quit after the Luxor opened, I think he would have died within a year. He needed that big challenge. He needed a reason to get up every morning.

He and I talked about his retiring, and I remember asking once what he would do, and he said, "Well, there's got to be a lot of small businesses that could use my expertise," and I told him that was an excellent idea. But he never chose to do that. He needed something that would challenge him more. And I guess buying a hotel that would compete against his old market was what turned him on.

Scott Menke

HE DIDN'T WANT FAMILY MEMBERS AROUND AFTER HE BOUGHT THE SAHARA, BECAUSE HE WAS in bad shape. We knew too much, and he still wanted to control his environment, and he didn't want anyone knowing how many pills he was taking or how much he was drinking.

Ben Speidel

I THINK WHEN MR. BENNETT BOUGHT THE SAHARA HIS CLEAR INTENTION WAS TO KICK Circus Circus' ass and take no prisoners. He was angry about everything that had happened to push him out of Circus Circus. But he was not well physically, and he had spent too much money already. I think he should have torn down the Sahara and built a new place. He owned the land across the street to the west and it was sitting there empty.

Diana Bennett

THERE'S NO QUESTION THAT HEALTH ISSUES TURNED MY FATHER INTO A DIFFERENT PERSON IN the last eight or nine years of his life. I used to go to the pharmacy to pick up the prescriptions, and there was only one pharmacy we could use, so you can draw your own conclusions from that.

I would tell anyone dealing with a strong personality late in life that the family needs to pull together and make certain first and foremost that you don't damage the person's pride. Someone as strong as my dad, if he wanted something done, we made sure it was done immediately. I sometimes wonder why our employees at Paragon Gaming don't jump when Scott [Menke] and I ask for something to be done. I guess Scott and I don't scare people as much as my father did.

Late in life he was still very vulnerable, but he never lost that strength. He expected things to be done, but his thinking was not logical, so the things he wanted done were not the right things to do. So those who stood up to him, like Scott and myself, who were always trying to protect his best interests, had to leave. Yet he was still running this huge business.

I had to go behind his back and meet with Nevada Gaming Control and tell them I was concerned about him, that we were trying to do the best we could to protect him, but if they sent an agent into the Sahara just to watch him operate, they were going to think there was a huge problem. Gaming Control was very understanding, and the people on that board were very good to us through that difficult period of time.

John McManus
I WAS WORKING AS AN ASSOCIATE IN FRANK SCHRECK'S LAW FIRM IN FEBRUARY OF 1996 when another associate in our firm responded to sort of a vague ad in the paper looking to hire an associate general counsel at a Strip hotel. He found out it was the Sahara, went in for an interview, and was told it was actually for the general counsel position. They were just being cheap and wanted to attract someone younger.

This person was offered the job, but he was not that much of a risk-taker and he declined it. I said, "You're out of your mind. Why wouldn't you take that job? Where do I send my resume?"

So I sent in my resume and got an interview with the general manager, who at the time was Al Hummel. I think Al liked me, thought I'd be a good candidate for the position, and was going to set up an interview for himself, me, and Mr. Bennett.

Whatever happened internally, I got a call from Mr. Bennett's office to come in and interview. When I got there, I was interviewed personally by Mr. Bennett for about half an hour, and I got offered the job right there. I don't exactly remember how it came down, but I remember Al being quite surprised that I had already met with Mr. Bennett and been given the job. That gave me my first insights on how things worked at the Sahara [*he laughs*]. You know, Mr. Bennett just did whatever the hell he wanted.

I was twenty-nine years old when I took that position.

Matt Smith
MR. BENNETT HAD BEEN A PATIENT OF DR. ELIAS GHANEM, AND I TOOK CARE OF GHANEM'S VIP patients, so Elias asked me if I would work on him. I was a physical therapist at the time and went on to become president and general manager of the Sahara. I actually succeeded Craig Hodgkins in that position, who

was his boat captain, so I guess both of us are examples of Mr. Bennett's quirkiness when it came to hiring executives later in his career.

Bill Bennett had been diagnosed with peripheral neuropathy, which is kind of a generic diagnosis. He had problems with weakness and balance and there were some safety issues we were concerned about. I wasn't doing anything to relieve the pain. He was taking massive doses of Percocet for that, and I don't think it's a secret that he had an addiction to pain killers. My job as his physical therapist was just to help him get back to function. His loss of balance and the weakness in his legs and back often left him in a wheelchair, and Bill wanted to be able to work on his feet while at the Sahara. I was asked to work on his strength, his proprioception [*the sense that allows us to know what position our body parts are in*], and his balance. Treating the pain with peripheral neuropathy is not something we do in therapy.

Marlee Palermo

I WAS WORKING AT THE SAHARA SOMETIME AROUND 1996, JUST SITTING IN FOR THE executive secretary Sally, who was Sam Bennett's cousin. When she would go to lunch I'd fill in for her for the hour.

This one day Grandpa walked in, and he looked right at me. I said, "Hi, Grandpa," and he just stared at me and walked away, like he didn't know who I was. It just didn't click that I was his granddaughter. I was so dumbfounded I started to cry. I don't know if he was just so medicated that he was out of it or what. I called my husband Chuck and said, "He didn't even recognize me!"

I have fibromyalgia, and I believe my grandfather had that as well. It's so painful that there are days I can't even get out of bed. I'm amazed that he had the strength and determination to work all those years when I know the pain he was in was excruciating. I don't know how in the world he did it.

Bill Allen Bennett

I HAVE A THEORY ABOUT WHAT CAUSED ALL OF MY FATHER'S CIRCULATION PROBLEMS, BUT it's only a theory. We built a lot of model aircraft when I was a kid. Dad became such a leader in the model aircraft field that he knew many of the manufacturers on a first-name basis. [*Bennett is an inductee in the model airplane hall of fame.*] We would occasionally build models that would be featured in the model aircraft magazines.

When we were still in Phoenix, in the early '60s, companies were always sending him free kits to assemble, and they'd send us paint samples to try. We were spraying these paints in enclosed areas with no ventilation, no masks, or anything. There just wasn't much awareness about the damage these paints and glues with their exotic chemicals could cause. I don't know what was in this stuff, but I do know that there was one we used and afterwards it made me feel really strange, and I had the taste of it in my mouth for a long time. It seemed to be sweating out of my pores.

I know there were days my father's feet and legs were hurting him even back then, and it could have been caused by those untested chemicals in the paints we were using. I'm not sure that some of my health problems didn't result from those chemicals as well.

Al Hummel

The last job I had for Mr. Bennett was at the Sahara Hotel. It was a horrible situation. I went there in 1996, when he fired Diana. When he brought me in I had no idea all this was going down. He just calls one day and says to come in, that he wants to talk to me. I had retired by then. I was out motorcycle riding, playing with my cars, having a ball. Plus, I had a house in California and was spending a lot of time there.

I don't know if this story belongs in the book or not, but here it is:

During the time I was retired I would visit him and my sister at their house, and I'd throw out a couple of ideas I thought might be helpful, but I certainly wasn't looking to go back to work. I had plenty of money, my houses were paid for, and I had all the toys I needed. But Mr. Bennett calls one day and says he needs help, and asks me to come to the Sahara and talk to him. As I'm taking the escalator up to see him, here comes Diana down the other escalator, and she's bawling.

She says to me, "You could have at least waited for the blood to get cold."

I'm pretty sure that's what she said. And I was thinking, What? I didn't know when Mr. Bennett called me that he was going to ask me to take over his daughter's job as the hotel general manager.

Bill Allen Bennett

I remember visiting Diana in November [1995] when she was running the Sahara Hotel for my father — she had become general manager — and she shows me the December forecast. I looked at what she was doing in November, and November is always a lot better month than December in Las Vegas, and he had her draw up this forecast that showed the hotel making a big profit in December.

I said, "Di, there's no way you're going to be able to do this."

She said, "I know. I can't do it. It's impossible."

That's when I knew Dad wanted her gone. He wanted her out of there.

But really he did her a favor, because she became very successful on her own. She's had a lot to do with the fact that the industry is now almost totally using coinless slot machines. She had a lot to do with that and with the development of those systems. She's really brilliant, and she would never have had the opportunity to show that under my dad.

I want it on the record that I love my sister very much, and always have.

Al Hummel

At the Sahara Mr. Bennett says, "I need you to help me out of this mess, Al. You know we're not making any money here, and we're not getting things done right."

I had no idea what had gone on between him and Diana, but this is a man who'd been so good to me all my life that I couldn't turn him down. I definitely did not want to un-retire, but I felt obligated even though I knew this was a bad situation.

I brought in some people I trusted and tried to get the property turned around, but Mr. Bennett was obviously not in good shape. He wasn't thinking clearly. We were going to remodel the hotel and casino and make changes on the grounds and other stuff, and it was going to be my job to oversee that.

Back in the Circus Circus days, when he would call me in to his office he would sometimes make a brief statement and my first reaction was to think it was the dumbest thing I'd ever heard. Then about two o'clock in the morning I'd wake up and realize what he said was a stroke of genius that I couldn't get my head around at the time he'd said it. He wasn't a man of a lot of words. He would say something and you had to think about it for a while.

But then at the Sahara he'd make a statement that didn't make sense, and it still wouldn't make sense after I kept thinking about it. I realized he had really slipped.

He was bringing in friends to work there that weren't qualified for the job. He brought in his boat captain that he wanted to make the slot guy. And there were other instances like that.

Then one day he started accusing me of forging his signature, which of course I never would have done. I finally said, "You know, Mr. Bennett, I don't need this bullshit." I packed up and left. I went back to my house in California.

I still visited him and my sister after that, and I let that whole experience go. I knew he wasn't right during that time, so I held no grudges. But I do hold a grudge against the top guys who forced him out after they built the Luxor. They exposed him and allowed him to look bad . . . all those bastards that he had made rich beyond their wildest dreams. They should have handled that situation so much better than they did. I still get angry thinking about it.

Nancy Gambardella

I HAD BEEN RETIRED FOR A YEAR, AND THEN ONE DAY I READ IN THE PAPER THAT MR. Bennett had bought the Sahara. I called him and he hired me back to work for him there.

He was a pistol, that's for sure, but he always treated me well and he had a good heart. People have no idea how many anonymous gifts he made to charities. Most people knew that he gave a lot of money to the animal shelter, and to UNLV, but there were many others. He was approached by Mona Silverman to give money to the new Jewish temple, Temple Beth Shalom, when they moved it from Sahara Avenue to Summerlin, and he wrote a check for $250,000. He gave that same amount when Mike Ensign approached him about helping Christ the King Catholic Church.

One time I'll never forget is when Steve Wynn called him about participating in a Republican fundraiser he was hosting at Shadow Creek golf course, and I overheard Mr. Bennett saying he was good for a quarter.

When he got off the phone, I said, "Is that a quarter million, Mr. Bennett?"

He said, "No, Nancy, it's one quarter. Twenty-five cents."

He actually wrote out a check for $.25.

Mr. Wynn sent it back with a note on it that said, "Not cashed. Insufficient funds." He included a note that said, "Bill, if you need a little financial help, let me know."

Marlee Palermo
I REMEMBER SOME OF THE SCREAMING MATCHES BETWEEN MY GRANDFATHER AND MY MOTHER at the Sahara when things weren't going well. That was going on right before he fired her. They weren't really arguments, because he was the one doing all the screaming. She never yelled back at him. I think Mom lost a good twenty pounds during that time. She went from about 140 pounds down to 120. When he fired her she was shocked, but I think part of her was relieved as well. After that she went to work for Casino Data Systems and started building her career again and showing how much talent she had in business.

Matt Smith
AT THE TIME MR. BENNETT HIRED ME AT THE SAHARA, I HAD BEEN THE REGIONAL VICE president of Health South, and the company had gone through a major acquisition. I had made a decision to leave the company and go back out on my own in the rehabilitation business. Because Bill knew I had a business background, and we had formed a strong friendship, he asked me to come into the gaming world with him. That was in 1998.

The deal when I started at the Sahara was to go in and mentor under Bill and the general manager, Craig Hodgkins. But on day one, my very first day on the job, he took me into this other office and said, "This is your new office. You're now the general manager."

He had moved Craig to casino manager, and gave me the GM job on my very first day at work. Now I heard right away about the history of GMs there. The over/under betting line for the other Sahara executives was that I'd be gone in five months, but I actually made it for eighteen months before I was fired. Needless to say, it was a rough crowd to break into because the other executives knew I had no experience in gaming at all, but I went on to become good friends with many of them.

A lot of crazy things went on during that time, and there were many days when the things he did were nonsensical, but I will say when Bill Bennett was operating at full capacity he was probably the best bottom-line operator in the gaming business. He was not the creative top-line revenue kind of guy, but he was very good at sharpening the pencil on expenses, and he was excellent at bottom-line operational efficiency. He could really squeeze money out of an operation.

The reason he bought the Sahara, in my opinion, was because he had cut his teeth on that hotel when he worked for Del Webb. So there was an element of nostalgia and he felt a strong connection with the property. But he hugely overpaid the Lowdens when he bought it.

I got the hotel appraised a year later and it was worth about half what he paid for it. Plus, it was a declining property, full of asbestos and other problems that cost a lot to fix. Even with all that, we were actually operating in the black six months before I left there. So as ill as he was, Bill still knew how to turn a business around.

John McManus

Al Hummel was gone from the Sahara about three months after I started. I heard the final conversation. Mr. Bennett was telling Al to fire Nancy Junis, and Al said no. He then said something like, "I've had enough of this shit," and he quit right there.

Although Mr. Bennett probably shouldn't have bought the Sahara, and in my opinion he never would have bought it earlier in his career when his health was good, it was sold at a tremendous profit later on and left his family in terrific shape financially. He also had purchased land to the west, which was eventually sold to Rick Hilton, Barron Hilton's son and maybe better known today as Paris Hilton's father, and that led to the Hilton timeshare project that is there now. Then MGM Mirage ultimately bought twenty-seven acres for well over $300 million. I'm not sure of the exact figure. This was after some other potential buyers would put down millions of dollars in deposits and then forfeit the money when the deal wouldn't close.

The way I looked at his buying of the Sahara was that he purchased it because he wanted to be relevant in the industry, and he wanted to be back in the game making decisions. There was a revolving door of general managers there, from Diana to Al Hummel to Craig Hodgkins and Matt Smith, and it was unbelievably frustrating, to Diana and Al in particular, because from the time I started there Mr. Bennett's health and mental state took a pretty sharp decline. Most days he was only there until about noon, and it wasn't like even on his good days you saw his old brilliance or a cohesive plan to fix the Sahara. That's because he wasn't in shape physically to walk around the property, and he didn't really know what to fix because he didn't really know what he had bought.

But I did admire his analytical way of thinking, and how he could analyze a problem and come up with a solution. When I would present an important issue to him, I would have studied the issue beforehand, talked to a number of people before I went in to talk to him, and then I might, for instance, give him option A, B, or C. And then he'd come back with D as a solution.

He didn't make things overly complex, and he would look at matters from different angles, and he was always thinking about how something would impact the bottom line. He was very black and white in that area. He was terrific in understanding expense and revenue. His wasn't a conventional approach, but even late in his career he frequently came up with the best answer to solving a problem, one that you hadn't considered. I enjoyed watching his mind work at those times.

Diana Bennett
LATE IN DAD'S CAREER, AND CERTAINLY WHEN HE WAS AT THE SAHARA, IF YOU TOLD HIM no on anything, you got fired. Early in his time at Circus Circus he would tell me that all his executives had nine lives. That if a person didn't screw up a few times, he or she wasn't doing the job, and wasn't trying new things. In the last ten years of his life, nobody had more than one life. If you did something wrong, even a little thing, you were gone.

Clyde Turner
IN THE EARLY DAYS AT CIRCUS CIRCUS, I WAS TOLD THAT BILL WOULD BASICALLY LEAVE HIS key employees alone to do a job until they screwed up. When they did, he would admonish them in a very polite way. I mean, Bill Bennett was a gentleman. Generally a gentleman, okay? But in the later periods, when he was in pain and using all the pain medication, his moods would change quickly. He'd become obsessive. Like obsessing about the magazine article with Schaeffer, and the landscaping with Rick Banis. He just wouldn't let go of things then, and heads would invariably roll.

Linda Christie
UNCLE BILL FIRED BOTH DIANA AND SCOTT WHEN HE OWNED THE SAHARA, BUT HIS THINKING processes weren't what they should have been. I don't know that it was any

specific thing that he did. It might have been nothing at all, but I know when it happened Scott was devastated because he idolized Uncle Bill, and that feeling was mutual for years.

Scott took my grandmother, Uncle Bill's mother, to Hawaii when she was in her eighties and they had a great time together. Scott was really good with her, and I know how much Uncle Bill appreciated that. So the way it ended was unfortunate, and the ending shouldn't reflect on how good their relationship was for all those prior years.

Clyde Turner

DIANA BENNETT ALREADY WORKED FOR THE COMPANY WHEN I SIGNED ON. I WAS AWARE OF Diana and of the good work she did. She became a big part of the restructuring we put in place after I took over for Bill Bennett. I basically went around and did an evaluation of every single property. With all the confusion and transitions that were taking place, and with all the hubbub on Wall Street, we were a company in trouble. Actually, trouble's not the right word. Let's just say we were challenged, and our stock price wasn't what it should be, or could be.

We weren't making the kind of money we should make and we had to figure out what we were going to do to reconstitute and take this company forward with what we had. And part of that was making some changes and allocating the best people we had to different properties. By the way, we elected to keep the same salary structure and bonus structure that Bill Bennett had put in place.

The main problem was that there had been inadequate replacement of furniture fixtures and equipment and carpeting, and the kitchens had to be upgraded in many of the properties.

When I did the one tour of hotel rooms at Circus Circus with Mr. Bennett after I first was hired, I thought the rooms were horrible and he thought they were fine. I had come from a different culture working with Steve Wynn, and there was a lot that had to be improved at Circus. The rooms in Reno were particularly shabby. There hadn't been one nickel spent on Reno since it had been opened.

I wanted the best people in place to oversee these improvements, and Diana was one of those people that was clearly a top choice. I believe she was running the slot department at Luxor at the time, but I promoted her to be the general manager of the Colorado Belle and the Riverside in Laughlin. She did a good job down there.

I don't know why Mr. Bennett hadn't given her a bigger job before. My feeling was that he was happy when I gave her that GM job. I do know he had issues with the guys she married. That was one of the things he obsessed about, and talked about a lot. He thought she should have done better with the men in her life.

Dr. Carol Harter

I WAS NEW TO THE PRESIDENCY OF UNLV IN 1996, WHEN I FIRST MET BILL BENNETT. All I knew about him previously was that he was an iconic figure in gaming in both Las Vegas and Reno and that he was a major influence in both places. I also knew, I don't remember how, that he had come up from the bottom, that he was a self-made man.

One of the major responsibilities of a university president is fundraising, and so I hadn't been at the university long before Mr. Bennett's name was on my radar. I had heard he was a fairly eccentric person, and that he hadn't done much for UNLV in previous years, and I was warned that if I was going to make an attempt to meet with him, I might be rejected. So I wasn't quite sure how to do it until it came to me in a very indirect way.

Scott Menke was close friends with Bill Bayno, our head Runnin' Rebels basketball coach at the time, and I had much interaction with Bill, of course, and he introduced me to Scott.

Scott's a UNLV alum and a great guy, and he said early on that I should meet his uncle. He arranged to set it up through John McManus, the in-house attorney at the Sahara. Scott was only about thirty at the time, and John was about the same age, and I thought it was interesting that this iconic older figure would have these young guys in key positions around him, you know. I think it's good for one's creative juices to surround yourself with much younger people, but at the time I was really quite surprised.

John McManus called on the day of our appointment and said he would meet me outside our Humanities Building, where my office was. I was shocked when this monster limousine pulled up to get me. I remember thinking, I hope some faculty members don't look out and get the wrong idea.

Once I got to know Bill Bennett I realized he was this sort of bigger-than-life guy, and when he agreed to meet with me he was going to make sure I was transported in style.

It was a lunch date in his office, nothing fancy there, just ordering sandwiches from the restaurant downstairs, and I clearly remember the first words out of Mr. Bennett's mouth were, "Well, young lady, are you coming here to ask me for money?"

I swear he said, "Hello," and that was the next thing he said.

I immediately responded with, "Oh, Mr. Bennett, I would never ask you for money on the first date."

I had to think of something to break the ice because I was thinking, Oh God, it can't start out any worse than this [*she laughs*].

He then told me that a previous president of the university, who shall remain unnamed, had asked him for money the first time they met, and he didn't like that, and he was testing me right off to see if I would do the same.

So I knew right then and there that unless he led me in that direction I wasn't going to mention anything about a gift to the university, and I would just hope that at some future point it might happen.

That's what fundraising is about. You make friends and you do it over time. It's a very slow process normally, but the irony was that Bill Bennett started to talk about it right off.

He was pretty direct and he said he knew that private fundraising was important, and I talked about my vision for the university. It was a nice conversation, but he was very, very direct. I wasn't sure how to take him, and I didn't know if he liked me or not. When the lunch ended, John McManus drove me back to the campus in the limousine.

I'm going to guess it was six months before I met with him again. In the meantime, Scott called and emphasized that I needed to have another meeting with his uncle, and that there was a lot of money in the family foundation, and that Mr. Bennett had recently sold a plane and put significantly more money into the foundation. I was impressed with how business savvy Scott was, but then I knew he had a lot of experience working at his uncle's hotels. At the time I hadn't yet met Diana, who was to become a good friend. I just knew Scott from his friendship with Bill Bayno, and he coached me beautifully through the process.

Scott's message was that I shouldn't let too much time go by before I met with his uncle again because he'd liked me and was disposed to giving something to UNLV. I know there are two other meetings that took place, one time with Scott and me and Mr. Bennett, and another time Governor Mike O'Callaghan was there. Mr. Bennett was friends with the former Nevada governor and valued his opinion. I believe these meetings took place in 1997. Mr. Bennett told me at the second meeting that he wanted to give something to the university and he said, directly as always, "What do you need?"

I had no idea what level of gift he wanted to give, so I knew I had to be careful about how this was presented. When large gifts come in, it's always out of sheer generosity, but the money is still usually directed to an activity that the donor is interested in.

I figured the natural area of interest for Mr. Bennett was the hotel school, right? But Scott had mentioned that he thought it might be towards the business school. He'd also told me that Mr. and Mrs. Bennett had given money to animal-related causes. But we didn't have a veterinarian school at UNLV, so that was going to be hard. He'd also given money to save wild burros in Nevada, I think anonymously.

Todd Conn

When I was a kid at my grandfather's house we'd talk a lot about animals. He loved his dogs. Scooter was one of them that was his favorite. He was just a little mutt. All of the animals that my grandfather and Sam had were pound puppies, rescue dogs. That was a big thing with the animal shelters. They'd call and say, "Oh, listen, we have this wonderful dog, but it's uglier than sin."

The shelter people knew that my grandfather had a big heart when it came to animals like that. He also had a cat that lived forever, called Stoly, named after the vodka, and I think that cat made it to about twenty years of age.

Dr. Carol Harter

I was told that Mr. Bennett had also given money to elementary schools to buy books and computers, again most of that anonymously.

Scott and I agreed that it might be attractive for him to do something for the College of Education. I went to the dean of education and talked with him about some needs his department might have, but again I had no idea of the size of the gift we might receive, and you can't be presumptuous. You have to have a range of potential projects to present to a donor. Scott kept emphasizing that Mr. Bennett had a great capacity to give, so there was nothing that might be too huge, but of course I didn't want to start too large.

I learned from the dean that they had a need for a small facility for professional development purposes, where students who are being trained to be teachers would be able to view through one-way glass small classes of students actually being taught. There was a lot of juggling that would have to take place because at the same time we were moving the Paradise School, which housed the law school classes, over to our campus.

It also was to be a very high-tech facility so that students could even do computer-related minutes of these meetings and sessions and talk about the stylistic things that the teacher was doing so they could fully analyze the activity.

We figured we could do the project back then for a little over two million dollars. Obviously, you can't build anything for two million today [*2009*], but that was the proposal we gave to Mr. Bennett.

When I showed it to him he right away said, "Oh, that doesn't turn me on that much."

You learn to develop a thick skin when you're raising money, and my skin was pretty thick after spending six years in New York. It was getting even thicker in Las Vegas.

But then he said, "Tell me again why you want to do that."

I said, "Because it gives young people who are learning to be teachers firsthand experience watching real teaching take place, and it greatly enriches their learning experience."

"Well, okay, if you really believe in that," he said, "I want to see good teachers in Las Vegas. How much will it cost?"

I told him the estimate was $2.2 million.

"Okay, you've got it," he said.

I was thinking this would be paid over time, but I had to delicately bring up the payment schedule to see how this would work.

"No, I'll write you a check tomorrow," he said.

The next day, John McManus came riding up to UNLV in the big limousine and handed me a check for $2.2 million.

Scott Menke

Bill Paulos was in the first graduating class from the hotel department at UNLV, and of course Mr. Bennett had everything to do with my going there. So he had a good awareness that UNLV was a school on the rise, and he knew how important the university was to the city. It was a natural cause for my uncle to be drawn to.

Dr. Carol Harter

We opened the building for the Department of Education and we named it the William Bennett Professional Development Building. Unfortunately, Mr. Bennett was fighting some illness at the time and he couldn't come to the opening. So I decided that we should present him with an honorary Ph.D. He had already received a Distinguished Nevadan Award before I came to UNLV, so that seemed like the appropriate thing to do.

I remember Scott Menke being a nervous wreck, because he knew that getting Mr. Bennett to the graduation ceremony was going to be a problem. That happened in 1999 or 2000, I think. Scott told me beforehand that there was no way Mr. Bennett was going to sit through a whole commencement. So we arranged to have a limousine drive him right to the door where we were going to have lunch between two commencements, and I was going to personally greet him there. He wasn't in a wheelchair, but he was a little infirmed. He wasn't about to be managed by anyone he didn't know. The ones who helped him were his wife, Lynn, Scott Menke, and me. We actually got him in his uniform — the cap and gown — and slipped him onstage for the awarding of the honorary degree. We then slipped him off stage immediately after it had been awarded so that he didn't have to sit through a never-ending commencement. That was the only way he was willing to do it.

I think the kind of personal contact he got from the person to whom he'd given the money was very important. I realized that I was the person he wanted to hand him that degree. It went well, because with these honorary degrees the recipient doesn't have to speak. I read the proclamation and the university provost put the robe around him and that was it.

I know Mr. Bennett was very pleased by the whole thing. Everyone in his family said there was no way he would ever have even thought of showing up if he wasn't flattered by the honor. Again, in its own curious way, that ceremony and the way it was handled sort of tied him to me. My sense is that there was a nice personal bond there. He valued that, I think.

My favorite Bill Bennett story revolves around the second major gift he gave the university. After we got that first building opened, you don't go right back for another big gift, right?

My agreement with Scott was that he could signal me when he thought there was another major contribution to the Bennett Family Foundation, which would happen when Bill sold another plane or something like that. So one day I get a call from Scott and he said he thought the foundation was well equipped to make another major gift, and that I should go and see Mr. Bennett.

This time I was more prepared and I had a really good project in mind. I even brought a little wooden model with me so he could visualize what I had in mind. It was for a preschool child development center, again for the College of Education, that would take children from infancy into school years. It was a unique design and won several prizes for the architect who created it. It had all open spaces, and the walls lifted like a garage door, so that when the weather was good, the kids could run right out into the garden areas or the teacher could hold a class out there.

At that time, we just had the model because no such thing had been done anywhere in the United States, or perhaps anywhere.

Again, the limousine came to pick me up and I brought this model with me, and I was very excited about it and couldn't wait to see his reaction to the idea.

So Mr. Bennett looks at the model, and the truth is he was really luke-warm to the idea. But the conversation shifted to some war stories he told me, and his wife Lynn came in and out of our meeting, and she looked at the model and said she liked it. So I said to him, "You could name this building for Lynn, you know."

She kind of preened when I said that, and I could tell she liked that idea. The meeting ended without any kind of commitment, and even Scott couldn't tell me later what he thought of the idea. So I thought maybe it was going nowhere.

Then one day Betty Hanseen, who had been Bill Bennett's former secretary and was now mine, called me in the office and said that Bill was on
the phone and he was furious.

I said, "Oh, shit! What does that mean, Betty?"

She said, "I don't know, but do you want to talk to him right away?"

I took the phone and said, "Hello, Mr. Bennett. How are you?"

"Goddamn it!" he yells. "Do you know what your institution has done
to me?

"No," I said,' trying to remain calm. "What have we done?"

"I got some of those guys over here from the hotel school to give us some
consulting, and they're charging me eighty thousand dollars. The first
$5,000 invoice just landed on my desk. Now what are you going to do
about it?"

I'm thinking a mile a minute at this point, so I started to explain that
our faculty had the right to do consulting work after their regular faculty
jobs. I said that this was something the university controlled, not something
I controlled.

"I don't give a damn," he said. "I've already given . . . how much have I
given to your university?"

"Well, by now about three million dollars," I said.

"So what are you going to do about it?" he said.

I had no idea at that point, but I said, "I'm going to fix it. Just move that
bill off your desk, and you will not get another bill from my faculty. We'll
figure it out."

"Well, that's good," he said. "That's why I like you. You know how to solve
a problem. So this $5,000 bill is going to disappear, right?"

"Yes," I said. "Just throw it away."

Then he said, "Oh, by the way. You know that thing you brought me a
while back, that project. What was it again?"

I told him it was the preschool, for students of the preschool and studying day-care activity.

"How much was that again?" he said.

"Five million dollars," I said.

"I'm going to send you a check tomorrow," he said.

I took a deep breath when I heard that.

"Mr. Bennett," I said. "Do you realize that this phone call has cost you four million nine hundred and ninety-five thousand dollars? [*she laughs*] "That's all right," he said. "It's the principle of the thing!"

John McManus

I CAN'T BEGIN TO TELL YOU HOW MANY LARGE CHECKS MR. BENNETT WROTE ANONYMOUSLY, to help out causes he heard about. Above everything else, he had a good heart.

The disappointment at the Sahara — although it turned out fine for his estate — was that Mr. Bennett had all this money, and he bought this aging dog of a property, and I think the main reason was to prove everybody wrong that he didn't have what it took anymore. His attitude was that he was going to turn this thing around and make it profitable. He had made promises to the people who left Circus Circus to come work for him, and he had every intention of keeping those promises, but they were all predicated on the property being successful. And he just wasn't the same person he'd been at age fifty, and he had purchased this terrible property, and with his health situation he just wasn't able to make it happen. So he left under very poor circumstances, and I'm sure that was a terrible blow to him because it had all been about proving them wrong, and he wasn't able to do it.

CHAPTER 6
His Rightful Place

Mike Sloan

Bill Bennett had an outstanding relationship with organized labor. He had a good relationship with Ed Hanley, who was the international president of the Culinary Union. He loved Dick Thomas of the Teachers' Union. He just liked talking to ordinary working guys.

He was never comfortable around blowhards. He didn't like people who tooted their own horn. You'd sit him down with Dick Thomas and they'd have a good talk at lunch. Bennett would eat most days downstairs at Circus Circus in the Pink Pony. He'd sit in the same booth, often eat just a hot dog, and that was his style.

He really listened to what his employees would tell him. He would observe the customers and their behavior, but he'd listen closely to his employees when they talked about the customers.

D. Taylor

I was an organizing director for the Culinary Union when the Frontier strike of 1991 started. [*Taylor is now the secretary-treasurer of Culinary Workers Union Local 226.*] I know that Mr. Bennett was close to our international leader Ed Hanley, and he also became friendly at that time with John Wilhelm, who later on became the general president of the national association [*and is currently the president of UNITE HERE, the international hotel and casino workers union*].

Mr. Wilhelm told me that Mr. Bennett felt those workers were right in striking and that he wanted to help them out in any way that he could, so he chose to feed them three times a day. What a great gesture.

Bennett was a unique individual in corporate America, and he obviously cared a great deal about his workers. He looked at his employees as partners in his success.

Todd Conn

MY GRANDFATHER DIDN'T MINGLE WITH THE CLIENTELE IN THE HOTEL, BUT HIS EMPLOYEES . . . that was another thing. He probably had more interaction with his employees than he did anyone else. He was always friendly to employees, but he was stern. If you messed up, you'd better be able to handle the mess and solve the problem.

When I worked at Circus Circus after he was no longer a part of it — I was a bellman there when I was nineteen and twenty years old — I'd hear from the employees who'd worked there for twenty-plus years. They'd tell me things like, "Oh, my God, your grandfather was the best. This place is crap now, but it was wonderful when he ran the place."

They would talk about how he would always say hi to them, and give them bonuses. They felt like their jobs were secure, and it wasn't like other places where every winter when the business slowed down people would get laid off. He didn't believe in doing that. He hired smart and lean, and he kept employees on the payroll. He would tell the staff that in order not to lay anybody off, he wasn't going to hire more people during the busy season, that they just had to work extra hard in slow times, and in some cases carry the weight of two people. But if you did your job right, you would always keep your job.

Mike Sloan

I DON'T THINK YOU'D GET MUCH ARGUMENT THAT THE TWO MOST IMPORTANT PEOPLE TO LAS Vegas from the early 1980s to the mid-'90s were Steve Wynn and Bill Bennett. I know Barron Hilton used to call Bennett all the time and ask his advice on things.

I think deep down Bill Bennett thought he was every bit as good a hotel man as Steve Wynn. He probably thought he was better than Steve. That's just the way really successful guys think, that they can do things better than the next guy. And I think over time all the media attention Steve got bothered him a good deal. Bennett shunned publicity, but he also wanted the recognition. I remember hearing that when Steve was making plans for Treasure Island he said to someone that he was doing it to show us what

Excalibur should look like. You can imagine what Mr. Bennett thought of that remark.

I don't know that for an absolute fact, but I heard that from several people. Of course, we built Excalibur for three hundred million dollars, and Steve could never build anything for only three hundred million.

Steve made a point of saying that most hotel developers, if they have a budget of four hundred million, they'll try to cut costs down to three hundred and seventy-five million. Wynn's attitude was that if the budget is four hundred million, he'll spend four hundred fifty million and that will make it that much more successful. And he's probably right.

Michael Milken

DON'T WE HAVE TO REGARD BILL BENNETT AS THE SAM WALTON OF LAS VEGAS? HE SHOWED the middle class and the blue-collar people that Las Vegas was open to them, too.

The Excalibur, when it opened in 1990, was classic Bill Bennett. It was an elaborate amusement park atmosphere. A whole floor for arcade games. He had the Knights of the Round Table in the showroom. And Excalibur was built for less money than anyone else could build it. As I recall, it cost something like three hundred million and was paid for in two years. And it was profitable from the minute it opened.

Today these hotels are lucky if they generate maybe fifteen percent on what they cost to build. I think the Excalibur generated forty percent, just a world of difference. Steve Wynn and Bill operated on different ends of the market, but they both made it work.

If you look at the west side of the Strip, with Circus Circus, and then Excalibur and Luxor and later on Mandalay Bay, which of course was under Bill Richardson and Mike Ensign, that world was created by Bill Bennett.

On that west side, nearly one in five falls under Bennett — by that I mean properties that he put in place. To think that a hotel like Circus Circus with thousands of rooms could run over one hundred percent occupancy year-round is unheard of. I believe they did a million room nights a year at that hotel. No other hotel can come close to that number. So he is responsible for a whole redefining of what is possible in the hospitality industry. Bennett was totally focused on return on capital, and his rate of return was higher than that of those focusing on the high end of the market.

You have to put him with Steve Wynn and Kirk Kerkorian as one of the three most important developers in Las Vegas history. He totally defined a market and showed people that you don't have to go to Bergdorf Goodman or Neiman Marcus or Nordstrom. He showed that Wal-Mart could do really well in the hotel-casino industry, too.

Mike Sloan

I DON'T KNOW HOW MUCH PEOPLE TALK ABOUT THE CHARITABLE SIDE OF BILL BENNETT, BUT it was impressive. When a policeman in Las Vegas would get killed, Bennett would write a big check to the family.

One night I was home late at night watching TV, and Mr. Bennett calls and says he's seen on the news where a boulder had come down a hill and hit a tour bus and badly injured a man. It didn't happen in Nevada. It happened in Colorado. And that state didn't have any more money to pay for the guy's medical costs. Bill Bennett tells me to get hold of the governor of Colorado, Roy Romer, because he wanted to send, I don't remember exactly, either twenty-five or fifty thousand dollars to Colorado to help this guy. He didn't want credit or recognition for any of this. He just wanted to do it. He definitely had a soft spot that would come out every now and then.

John McManus

YOU PROBABLY HEAR TEN TIMES MORE ABOUT STEVE WYNN THAN YOU DO OTHER POWERFUL gaming industry figures in modern Las Vegas because people like Wynn and Donald Trump are great self-promoters, but Mr. Bennett and some others just don't seek the limelight. And I think Bennett is often overlooked because of that, even though he really paved the way in terms of the independent guy taking the company public into the financial mainstream.

He didn't like public speaking, for instance. I can't tell you how many events I had to speak at for him. In fact, in the five-plus years I worked for him at the Sahara he never once spoke publicly at anything. That was his choice. But he clearly paved the way and helped bring the casino industry into the mainstream, in the Wall Street world.

I think operationally he also had a huge impact on the way things were done, and he provided a roadmap for other hotel-casino operators.

Tony Alamo

BILL BENNETT WAS NEVER GOOD AT PAYING COMPLIMENTS. I REMEMBER WHEN WE HAD THE ribbon cutting for the new sky-rise tower at Circus Circus, and the expansion of the casino. I was in charge of all that as the general manager. Several dignitaries were there, and Nevada Governor Richard Bryan and other politicians. It was about ten in the morning. When Bennett cut the ribbon, I was standing right next to him and he leaned over and said to me, "You did a great job."

He said it so softly that I was the only one who heard it. He was not the kind of man who would say that so everyone could hear. He did not have close friends. I know he was very close to his wife, Sam, but your relationship with him as an employee was business oriented.

Cameron Conn

I'M ONLY TWENTY-EIGHT, BUT I'VE STUDIED QUITE A BIT ABOUT MY GRANDFATHER AND HIS philosophy and how he made it work. When he and Bill Pennington bought Circus Circus it was failing, but it had a good location on the Strip and they saw the potential. They understood right away that this was their product and they needed to market it not just to one segment of the marketplace, but to everybody.

For a long time, during the 1950s and '60s, Vegas was segregated in terms of the people and clientele that were brought in. It almost had the mantra that it has now: Whatever happens in Vegas stays in Vegas, it's a boys' playground, it's adult oriented, it's an all-night party and all that.

My grandfather steered away from that and in effect said, Listen, I have a place called Circus Circus. I'm going to offer the Pink Pony, cheap buffets, I'm going to have free carnival acts, and I'm going to do all sorts of stuff that hasn't been done before in Las Vegas so that I can bring in not only those people who want to escape their everyday lives, but I also want to attract families. That's where he saw himself and his property becoming successful.

He knew he could have loss leaders with the rooms and the food, but that by packing the place with people he would generate gambling revenue. He couldn't make this go with the two hundred rooms they had starting out. He had to have two thousand rooms to service the profit for his place. He understood how to drive that high traffic, none of which would be big players, but he would make it work through the volume of small bets from middle-class tourists who appreciated that they were getting bargains in other parts of the hotel. That was the essence of his business model at Circus Circus.

With the current recession, we're kind of coming full circle with his thinking. Room rates in 2010 are cheaper than they've been in years, we're marketing to families as well as adults, and we need to open our doors to all segments of the market. There's only so many high-rollers, and those don't keep you going from year to year.

Mike Sloan

I THINK MR. BENNETT'S COMPLICATED RELATIONSHIP WITH HIS FATHER WAS A DRIVING FORCE in his success. He was constantly trying to prove that he was good enough. He was also proving it to himself. A lot of us have that kind of thing that drives us, but I just feel that was really important to Bennett.

When he was listed in the *Forbes* 400 wealthiest Americans, I believe it was important to him. He appreciated the recognition, but he didn't take it too seriously. He would look and see who else was on that list, but he was also not the kind of guy who would associate himself with others on that list. He always knew deep down who he was.

We did some work on putting a cap on the amount of punitive damages that could be given in civil lawsuits. I think when that issue went to the Supreme Court, Barron Hilton wanted to make the ruling retroactive because the Las Vegas Hilton had been hit pretty hard in the scandal where those girls were molested during the Tailhook convention.

[The Tailhook scandal refers to a series of incidents at the 35th annual Tailhook Association Symposium, held at the Las Vegas Hilton in September 1991, and the resulting investigations conducted by the U.S. Navy and the U.S. Department of Defense. At the symposium, numerous USN and U.S. Marine Corps aviation officers were alleged to have assaulted women or otherwise engaged in improper and indecent conduct. As a result of the subsequent investigations, a number of officers were formally disciplined or refused advancement in rank. Military officers and observers alleged that flag officers attending the symposium were not held accountable for knowingly allowing the behavior in question to occur. It was generally thought that the scandal highlighted the U.S. military's attitude and treatment toward women in the

areas of sexual harassment, sexual assault, and equal treatment of women in career advancement and opportunity.]

But although he greatly admired Barron Hilton, and understood his position on the punitive damages cap, Bennett said, "We're not going to go for that."

He would always look carefully at both sides of an issue and come up with a reasonable position.

We also took a major role in getting alternate dispute resolutions for lawsuits, to be able to go in and reach mediation and arbitration. During those good productive years before Bennett had all his health issues, what I saw at work from day to day was a very reasonable, far-sighted, greater-good thinking man.

Marlee Palermo

HAD MY GRANDFATHER NOT COME TO LAS VEGAS WHEN HE DID, VEGAS WOULD NOT BE WHAT it is today. It wouldn't have been nearly as accessible to the middle class. He understood that group of people so well, and he gave them what they wanted. It still amazes me, knowing the kind of pain he was in those last years, that he was able to show up and work at all.

Diana Bennett

EVEN AFTER BOTH HIS LEGS HAD BEEN AMPUTATED, SAM WOULD GET HIM UP IN THE MORNING and clean him up, and a car would take him to work. Dad went to the office every day he was able, up until about a month before he died. I think he was happier at work than anywhere else.

Todd Conn

I COULD HAVE FOLLOWED MY GRANDFATHER'S PATH INTO THE HOTEL INDUSTRY FOR A CAREER, but I didn't like the direction the big corporations were going. My long-term dream when I was working different lower-level jobs in the hotel industry was to some day walk through my casino like my grandfather did, pass all my employees walking up to my executive elevator, and if I saw a piece of trash on the ground, bend down like my grandfather would do and pick it up and put it in the trash can, so that they could see the kind of pride they all should take in their hotel.

And when it came to comps, they would be given only to the people who were gambling and putting in money, not to people who were complaining and not doing anything. As I studied the hotel business in the '90s, I saw more and more comps going to keep people happy who were complaining. These were people who bitched about their room, and then got a comp as consolation. At Circus Circus, the whole philosophy was about providing a cheap room and gaming and having fun, okay? If you were expecting that your room should be immaculate, you know, with 700-fiber-count Egyptian linen sheets, then you're in the wrong frickin' place.

I was very influenced and respectful of the way my grandfather ran his properties. And I despised the people that ousted him when the time came for them to make their move. Those were some low-life cheatin' sons of bitches in my opinion. They know who they are. They were just a bunch of cowards that knew they could make a financial gain by voting him off the board. They hadn't done any of the hard work. They basically came up with a little conspiracy to get my grandfather out. They played the game, and I'll tip my hat, they played it well, but they can't say that any of the genius behind the empire was theirs. They had to steal somebody else's idea.

You know, it's one thing to be the king who built the empire from nothing, and it's another to storm the castle and try to claim the credit for yourself.

E. Parry Thomas

I CAN THINK OF SOME REASONS WHY BILL BENNETT IS SOMETIMES OVERLOOKED AS FAR AS getting credit for the growth of the Las Vegas Strip. He was a private man, and he kept his inner thoughts to himself pretty well.

He didn't spend a lot of time with owners of other hotels. He kept to his knitting and did a great job turning things around at Circus Circus, because it was such a loser when he took over. At Valley Bank we were reluctant to get involved initially when he and Bill Pennington approached us, because the hotel was doing so poorly. But they had built that successful slot machine business and as it matured we could rely on the cash flow from that. They really had super cash flow from that, and we then felt more secure to give the loan for Circus. I think Kenny Sullivan handled that for us.

Bennett was a very capable man. I know that Jay Sarno had some loans from the Teamsters when he built Circus Circus, and there were people like Anthony Spilotro [*the Joe Pesci character in the movie* Casino] with shops in the hotel when Bennett and Pennington took over. That jewelry store of Spilotro's was nothing but a fence for stolen jewelry. I don't know how Bennett got them out of there as peacefully as he did, but he deserves credit for handling that problem without any violence.

I really liked Bennett's independence, and his thinking, which often didn't go along with everyone else. I remember when the hotel association in Las Vegas met about the importance of conventions, and that Bill took a lone stand against promoting them. He stood his ground against the others because he didn't feel conventions generated any significant business for his hotel.

Tony Alamo

I DON'T KNOW HOW ELSE TO PUT IT: BILL BENNETT HAD BALLS. HE WAS VERY AGGRESSIVE, he was a visionary, and he was charismatic. But most importantly, it should be recognized that his decision making was without hesitation, and time and again he had the balls to make very difficult decisions. Those were decisions that could have cost him his company every time he went forward opening these properties like he did. Opening the hotels in Laughlin and Reno, and the expansion of Circus and the Excalibur and Luxor, you know with each one of these he could have taken the company down if those properties would have failed.

For that reason, I would put him right at the top with Steve Wynn. He's in the top five in importance in the gaming history of Las Vegas, probably the top three.

Dr. David Schwartz

IN WRITING MY BIOGRAPHY OF JAY SARNO, I'VE COME TO LOOK AT BILL BENNETT SORT OF like the anti-Sarno. He wasn't a flashy guy. A very sensible guy in a lot of ways. However, the one thing he had in common with Sarno is that both were self-made men.

Bennett's brilliance came from focusing on value-oriented customers and figuring out how to exploit a niche that no one else in town was taking advantage of. I think a lot of the economic circumstances really favored Bennett in the late 1970s and early '80s. The bottom had dropped out of the economy, not nearly as bad as in 2008 and 2009, but similar. This was right after Caesars Palace had opened up its Fantasy Tower, which was Sarno's idea.

So Caesars opens that tower in '79, and I think it was the next year that Circus Circus opens up their Manor, which is the motel stuff and is as different from the Caesars suites — which, incidentally, is where they filmed a lot of the movie *Rain Man* — as you could possibly get. Well, here's Caesars, this extremely high-end place trying to draw customers as the economy tanks, and then in 1982 the Mexican peso gets devalued, and Caesars had a ton of markers from Mexican high-rollers that they had to totally write off. And other Strip properties, like the Riviera and the Tropicana, were also going after high-end play then, and they all took big losses.

Meanwhile, Bennett had just been building a lot of rooms, getting people in the hotel for less than twenty bucks a night, grinding them out, turning them over, and gradually other companies are looking at Bennett's success and starting to go that way. The Riviera changed its approach, and so did the Tropicana. They went from courting high-rollers to following more the Circus Circus model.

By the middle and late '80s, people were looking at Circus Circus as the most successful casino company in the world.

Then The Mirage opens in 1989 and suddenly Mirage Resorts is viewed as the most successful casino company in the world. Steve Wynn said, in effect, Hey, if they can make money at that end, I can make a lot more money up here by investing a lot more. And he did. Now how much of Circus' success was Bennett and how much was the work of other people in his company, I don't know. But he was the guy at the controls, so he has to get the credit.

Cameron Conn

I THINK MY GRANDFATHER CHANGED THE WHOLE WAY OF THINKING ABOUT GOING TO LAS Vegas for a vacation. In the 1950s and '60s someone saying they were heading for Vegas would conjure up images of a lot of cocktails, going to see a French revue, or maybe Sinatra or Sammy Davis Jr., and partying pretty hard.

But once Circus Circus became popular it made sense if someone said they were going to Las Vegas and taking the whole family. It didn't sound like such a taboo thing to do anymore.

He did the same thing at Excalibur. You take your kids there and they'll have a lot of midway games to choose from, and rides to take, and you can

include the whole family for an evening out at the King Arthur and the
Knights of the Roundtable show. The hotel became a playground for both
adults and children. He built large arcades there which you'd never really
seen before in Las Vegas. Later, at Luxor, there was a whole floor of games
on which there was no gambling at all.

Glenn Schaeffer

THE DEFINITION OF A HIGHLY SUCCESSFUL EXECUTIVE IS ABNORMALITY, AND BILL BENNETT
was Example A. He was an extremely difficult man to work for at times,
but he was also brilliant in his own way. He expected of you only what
he was willing to do himself. He said that it was a very competitive world
out there and everybody wants your money. And if you are going to beat
people in games for the highest possible stakes, you can't do it with a half-
way commitment.

I had given so much to the company that when the rupture came and I
left, it caused a bit of despondency on my part. It was as though I had been
thrown off the Starship Enterprise.

The last time I spoke to Bill Bennett was the day I left the company, some
nine years before he died. I did go to his funeral, however.

In regards to where he ranks in the pantheon of important figures in
the growth of modern Las Vegas, he's in the top five. What he did that
is so important was that he normalized professional management in the
gaming business.

I'm saying in terms of having a doctrine, no one was better. In business
today, I use Bill Bennett's daily operating report. All of us who worked
with him use it. That's because, as Bennett said, "Numbers have a way of
de-mystiquing everything. They allow you to get away from hope and want
and wish. It's a report card, and it's not hard to read."

He said it many times: Revenue minus cost equals profit. He said that's
how you make all the money you want in the world. It's not e=mc- squared.
That's all you gotta do, guys, he would say, and every time you try to make
it more complicated than that, you're going to fail. So we either do things
that increase revenues or that restrain or cut costs, and by doing that we
magnify and amplify profit. Those are the kinds of behaviors that get rewarded around here.

And so we had a bible, and that was those daily reports that did not miss the monthly numbers by one percent and that would go to the audit every quarter. And if an executive did miss the numbers, he was going to have a big problem.

Diana Bennett

MY FATHER HAD AN INNATE SKILL WITH NUMBERS, THE KIND OF ABILITY THAT CAN'T BE taught in a classroom. I don't know whether it's something that is just in the genes or what, but he passed that ability down to me, and my son Cameron has it as well. We can look at numbers on a spreadsheet and just make sense of them immediately.

My dad would look at a numbers report and he could work from the bottom up and figure out where they came from. He didn't need a calculator or a computer or anything else. He just knew if the bottom-line number was valid, he could work back up through the numbers above it and make sense of it, or find something that was wrong.

When I worked for him in slots he would ask me a number, like what did this particular machine on the floor do today. And if I made up a number, I'd be dead, because he usually knew the number before he asked me. You learned very quickly if you didn't have the exact answer, you should say, "I have no idea, but I will find out for you." Anything short of the exact answer would never work.

He was really good at researching subjects, or reading manuals to find out how something worked. When he started to study blackjack, we dealt the game at home, we played it for hours, and we practiced different strategies. He was intent on learning exactly how it worked, how gamblers could cheat at it, how they could count numbers, all of it.

When I was a child, the encyclopedias were kept close to the kitchen table because if a subject or question came up during dinner and you didn't know the answer, you got up from the table right then and looked it up in the encyclopedia so you'd have the answer immediately.

I did the same thing with my children. When they were young and asked a question, I'd tell them to go look it up in the encyclopedia. Now I tell them to look it up on the computer. You can Google anything these days.

Ben Speidel

IF YOU LOOK AT THOSE YEARS BETWEEN 1974 AND 1993, I BELIEVE BILL BENNETT WAS the most important figure on the Las Vegas Strip. Look what he did: He took Circus Circus from a big loser to the biggest winner of all; he built the Excalibur; he built the Luxor; he showed how it should be done in Laughlin, by remodeling the Edgewater and building the Colorado Belle; and he compensated his key employees better than anyone else. He also was loved by the Culinary Union for his steady support and for providing all the free meals during the Frontier strike.

Oh, there were a lot of other big players during those years: Morris Shenker at the Dunes, Wildcat Morris at the Holiday and later the Landmark, the Binions downtown, and Ralph Engelstad at the Imperial Palace. Those men were good operators as well. But I don't think anyone functioned at a higher level than Mr. Bennett during that time.

Of course, some time after The Mirage opened, Steve Wynn took over the number one role, but it was incredible what Bennett accomplished during the peak years of his career.

Al Hummel

A COUPLE OF WEEKS AFTER MR. BENNETT DIED, MY SISTER CALLED ME AND WANTED ME TO come over from California, where I was happily retired, and run the Sahara. It was losing serious money then, about nine million a year. And I know that for a fact because I studied the numbers.

So I walked out of the house in California, grabbed my dogs, turned the lock, and came to work the day after New Year's in 2003. I became the CEO of the Sahara until we sold it in 2006. Fortunately, we sold it at the height of the market.

I was a good businessman, but I wish I'd had the talent that Mr. Bennett had. He was just amazing. And the most fair and honest man you'd ever meet, as long as you worked hard for him and didn't screw up.

It's not widely known that he paid back all the people he owed money to in Arizona after he declared bankruptcy. He couldn't have that on his conscience, that he screwed all those people out of their money.

You really had to study Mr. Bennett to understand how his mind worked. If you said or did the wrong thing at the wrong time, you could get fired on the spot, especially near the end of his life.

I remember one time when I went to him for a request to purchase something. It could have been at Slots-A-Fun or maybe at Circus Circus. I made the request, I guess without a lot of urgency in my voice, and he said, "Come back when you really want it."

He felt I wasn't confident enough with my request.

Another time I came to him to buy something, and he turned around and pulled out the big numbers book he had handy, and he said, "We've got three hundred fifty million dollars. Why are you asking my permission to buy such a simple thing?"

He made you really think about things you were asking for, and gather your thoughts before you went to him.

Linda Christie

I REMEMBER UNCLE BILL TELLING ME ONCE, "THERE'S A LOT MORE PEOPLE IN THE WORLD with nickels than with hundred-dollar bills, and that's what we're trying to market — a place where the average Joe can come and have a good time."

He grew up lower middle class and he liked the people he grew up with. He had a humble beginning and he could relate well to people who were raised the same way.

Bill Allen Bennett

JUST LIKE THE JAPANESE TAUGHT US IN AMERICA HOW TO BUILD BETTER CARS, MY FATHER taught Las Vegas how to be better at running casinos. Through Circus Circus he taught the Strip how to stop thinking in old traditional ways and go after a different market.

He saw that there was a huge market that Las Vegas was missing, and from that he became kind of the Sam Walton of casino owners. He went after the customers that Caesars Palace didn't want, and that the Dunes and even Benny Binion at the Horseshoe didn't want. Those places didn't cater to the customers that my dad wanted. He fully understood that you made your money in the gaming business in volume, and not by bringing in rich oil sheiks that can ruin your whole year with a hot run of cards. He made it by grinding the percentage. The more those slot handles get pulled, the closer you come to the theoretical percentage that those machines will hold, and he fully understood how the slots were the most attractive games to the gamblers, and they offered the biggest profits to the casinos.

There were some lively arguments about which departments in a hotel should make money. Some of the bean counters today would say that every department in a hotel has to make money. My father didn't believe that. He believed that you had to know where to spend a buck in order to make two bucks.

Food and beverage and hotel rooms, all of it was a loss leader to him. Even though in some of those departments he made a profit, those profits were insignificant to what he made off the slot machines. The slots were where the real money was made.

When I was a general manager and saw what the slot departments were doing versus the pit, and what every department was doing, down to every single dot and dash, I saw it was the slots that made Las Vegas. And the trick to slots is volume. You don't mind Ma and Pa Kettle in your casino, you know? You really want those masses of people with small budgets that are going to spend a certain amount per day. And you don't mind at all their using their coupons and getting free popcorn and a cheap buffet and all that.

When other operators saw the profits that Circus Circus was making under my father it changed the entire way they looked at the gaming business. Suddenly, other casinos started putting in arcades. The impact was tremendous.

Dr. David Schwartz

JAY SARNO AND BILL BENNETT ARE CERTAINLY ON THE SHORT LIST WHEN YOU TALK ABOUT important figures in the development of Las Vegas. I think without Sarno, you'd still have dealers wearing string ties and that sort of thing.

With Bennett, if you stopped the clock in 1988, he would be acknowledged as the guy who reinvented Las Vegas. You know, if The Mirage had never been built, Excalibur would probably be the model for everything that happened. And Bennett would have a much more prominent place.

Bennett demonstrated how important playing to the low end of the market could be for Las Vegas. He understood how to fill up the rooms and keep the slots busy.

I think both Sarno and Bennett are hugely important in the big picture. But my guess is that if both Sarno and Bennett took a walk down the Strip in 2009, or drove a golf cart past all the hotels, Sarno would be happier than Bennett with what he saw. Especially when you look at City Center.

[*The last five to ten years of Bill Bennett's life were difficult. The pain from the circulation problems in his legs grew worse by the month, and there were several subsequent amputations of his lower extremities. It started with his losing toes, then a foot, then a leg. He became more and more reliant on pain medications and alcohol to alleviate the discomfort, but his inner circle of family members saw to it that he remained as comfortable as possible under the circumstances.*]

Diana Bennett

MANY PEOPLE THOUGHT MY FATHER SUFFERED FROM DIABETES, BUT THAT WAS NOT THE CASE. He clearly had a circulatory disease that caused him great discomfort. Like anyone who is experiencing a lot of pain, he wasn't himself a lot of the time when the pain was at its worst.

There is a theory that all of the thousands of hours he spent making model airplanes, and sniffing the glues that were required to make these planes, and which hadn't been carefully tested for safety, affected his nerve endings. I think that's very possibly the case.

But he was never diabetic, and he never took insulin. The veins and arteries in his extremities just weren't getting the blood flow that was necessary. There were five or six surgeries. They'd remove a toe, and the next time they'd removed more.

A year before he died they said they needed to amputate his left leg at the knee, and he refused. He was deathly ill. There was gangrene, and his whole body was toxic. They told Dad he was going to be dead in twenty-four hours if they didn't amputate that leg at the knee, and he refused.

We staged an intervention. We got the doctors to come, but more importantly we got former Nevada Governor Mike O'Callaghan to come. Mike was an amputee from the Korean War, where he won a Silver Star for valor, and I knew my dad respected him greatly.

I also called Ralph Engelstad, another good friend, but he was out of town.

At seven a.m. the following morning the doctors, Sam, Mike O'Callaghan, and I were in Dad's room at Sunrise Hospital.

One of the doctors repeated what he'd already told him: "Mr. Bennett, this procedure *has* to be done."

Dad looked at Mike and said, "What would you do?"

Mike said, "I can't tell you what to do, Bill, but I can tell you that I've lived a helluva life without a leg, and if somebody had given me a choice back then to lose a life or a leg, I would have done just what I did. And that was to give up a leg to have a life."

"I need time," Dad said. "I want to see my dog."

He didn't say that he wanted to see his grandchildren, just that he wanted to see his dog Sassie, which was a rescue dog like all of his and Sam's pets. Dad knew that dogs weren't allowed in hospitals, so that was just his way of letting us know that he wasn't going to get his leg amputated.

I told Dad that Sassy would be coming to his room. I got Sassy tranquilized, put her in a basket to hide her, and took her into his room.

He thought he was throwing us a wrench with the dog request, and he was pissed off when we were able to pull it off. The dog was in the room with him for about an hour . . . the nurses were aware of it but they were helpful and understood the situation . . . and Dad finally conceded that we could take the dog home and do the surgery.

So they took his leg off, and then later on part of his right leg. When that first leg was off, he would hoist the stub up on the arm of his chair at home, and then lean his elbow on it when he was talking with people. I think he did it for shock effect.

Dr. Carol Harter

I KNOW THAT MIKE O'CALLAGHAN WAS A CLOSE FRIEND OF BILL'S BECAUSE HE BROUGHT HIM into the room when we were having our early discussions about a gift he was considering to the university. I think he respected Mike so much he liked to get his opinion on things. I can tell you that Mike was not at the beginning friendly to the notion of a woman president at UNLV, and that was true of a lot of people here. I think when he saw that Bill Bennett and I got along, he eventually warmed up to me.

I just remember being a little uncomfortable when O'Callaghan was called into that early meeting because there was no explanation given for why he was there, and he was obviously a big-time player in Nevada.

Later on I really enjoyed listening to the two of them talk because they had so much shared history about Las Vegas, and they would have fascinating conversations about their military history. Bill was a flyer in the war, and of course Mike was wounded in Korea. They both were very patriotic, and they discussed the righteousness of the wars, and they completely agreed upon who the real heroes were.

I was glad to have met Governor O'Callaghan under those circumstances because afterwards Mike called me a few times for comments about something that was going on at the university, and he was much friendlier than he had been initially.

Bill Bennett was one of those men — those throwback characters — where his word was his bond. If he told me I'd have a seven-figure check in my hand the next morning, it was there. There was never any question about it.

In my eleven years at UNLV we raised about $550 million, and I have never once been told that a gift was coming that it failed to materialize. That's pretty remarkable, if you think about it. I'm from New York, and I don't think people in New York trust each other like that.

Back East, you'd want to get the promise down on a piece of paper, but that certainly hasn't been necessary in Las Vegas, and Mr. Bennett exemplified that.

Scott Menke

When I think of Mr. Bennett's legacy, and how he achieved such great success in the gaming industry, I think it all boils down to his simplicity. He grew up in a relatively small town in Arizona, in a middle-class family, and then he joined the Navy. He understood his blue-collar clientele because he was one of them growing up. He knew what those people wanted in a vacation, and he focused on their wants at both Circus Circus and Excalibur and that was his success.

Those same types of people were his employees, and he always got along beautifully with his employees. He would talk to them at length. For instance, he would hear from Carol, the waitress in the Pink Pony, about what the cocktail waitresses in the hotel thought of their uniforms. He would get involved in those types of issues with his employees.

When the Culinary Union was threatening to go on strike because they were bargaining for higher raises, and the town was doing great, Mr. Bennett would say, "How can I tell our employees that they can't have a two percent raise when we're doing well?"

He was always the first to settle with the unions, and everyone knows how he provided meals for the strikers during the big Culinary strike at the Frontier.

He was also brilliant at getting the right men in the right positions to run the company, and then paying them so well that they wouldn't be tempted to leave. Mr. Bennett was making all this money, and he understood the only way to keep his key people loyal was to have them making good money too.

Mel Larson

When you work for someone for twenty years, as I did for Bennett, you just develop a great trust, and when you've seen a guy have such great success as he did, your loyalty grows through the years. I didn't get a lot of offers to go to other hotels, because they knew how loyal I was to Circus Circus, what with my pink Cadillacs and pink sportcoats. Other executives knew they couldn't match what I was getting paid.

I had great belief in Bill Bennett. If he had told me to go up to the fifteenth floor and jump out a window, I'd go up there and jump out, figuring he was testing a safety net or some other damn thing.

After I retired and I heard that Bennett had bought the Sahara, I wasn't surprised. There was some sentiment there, because he had been general manager of the Mint, and then Del Webb gave him the Sahara, so I think he always had a soft spot for that hotel, which had been good to him as he was climbing his way up the corporate ladder.

Ben Speidel

I ran into Mr. Bennett out in front of the Sahara Hotel in about 1998 or '99. I think it was the last time I saw him. It was before the amputations, and he was standing in front, waiting for his car. I could tell he was in some pain.

I had a sense of guilt that I didn't go over to work with him when he bought the Sahara. It wasn't that he offered me a job, but as someone who'd worked for him all those years, I know he would have had a spot for me if I'd gone to see him. I was a little reluctant to walk over and talk to him, wondering if he might not be a little bitter, or angry that he hadn't seen me. But I couldn't resist visiting with him.

I held out my hand and to be polite said, "Hi, Mr. Bennett, I'm Ben Speidel."

I was thinking at that moment that I wished I still worked for him, because I loved the man and had so much respect for him.

He just looked at me and said, "I know who you are."

I don't think he said anything else. I could tell he was different.

Craig Hodgkins

MY TIME AS PRESIDENT AND GENERAL MANAGER AT THE SAHARA ENDED FOR A TERRIBLY stupid reason. Mr. Bennett called me on a Sunday and said, "Hey, I like the way that new casino layout is all changed around, with the craps tables in the front."

I was glad to hear that, but I thought it was odd that he was calling on a Sunday to tell me that. "But the next time you do something like that," he said, "you ought to call me and talk to me about it beforehand."

I should have just kept my mouth shut and rolled with it, but I was always totally honest with him. "Mr. Bennett," I said, "what are you talking about? We had meeting after meeting in your office about all the changes."

He obviously didn't remember any of it. "So who else was in these supposed meetings?" he said.

"We had architects and consultants in there with us," I said. "You were at all the important meetings."

I realized then that he was on so many painkillers and Percocet and with the drinking, he had totally forgotten all of it.

"I never thought you'd lie to me," he said, "and now you're lying to me."

So he fired me. That was in February of 2002. He died at the end of that year.

Matt Smith

WHEN I TOOK ON THE CASINO MANAGEMENT POSITION AT THE SAHARA, I STILL CONTINUED to work on Mr. Bennett's physical therapy, but I didn't do it as often. I probably still worked on him two to three nights a week.

I have great memories of coming over to his house on Desert Inn, doing his therapy, and then right after we'd have a big, tall screwdriver, his favorite drink.

He would sit and tell me stories of Moe Dalitz and the mob days in Las Vegas, and he made me assure him that I would never repeat those stories, which I haven't, but they were very interesting and educational.

He even talked about his battles with his management team and gave his side of the story on his exit from Circus Circus Inc. We had a lot of good sit-down social time, which was special because not a lot of people came over to visit Bill. Sam kept him very protected at home, and I think being his therapist and also an executive with him, we formed an intimacy that caused him to be comfortable to open up with me. He even talked about his businesses in Arizona, the furniture stores and restaurant and going bankrupt and all that.

It should be said that Bill was a guy who just never gave up. He showed his resilience when he came back and bought the Sahara, and he kept doing therapy after the point where a lot of people would just give up. He was physically as resilient as anybody I've met. I understand that his mental capacities diminished and there are many reasons for that, but his tenacity to continue to be as resourceful and active as he stayed was amazing to me. Having seen a lot of people his age, and in that kind of pain, I've watched so many make the choice to give up. And he never did.

Ben Speidel

THE RELATIONSHIP THAT MR. BENNETT HAD WITH HIS KIDS WAS PRETTY UNUSUAL. I KNOW he thought the world of Diana, and she was a terrific operator in her own right, but she didn't get any favors from him as his daughter.

I knew Bill Bennett the son pretty well because he'd worked for me at Slots-A-Fun. He was a food and beverage director for me and I thought he did an outstanding job. He was always very well organized.

[*Lynn Hummel Bennett, "Sam" to her husband, died unexpectedly at age sixty-four in December 2006. The teenage girl who had fallen in love with Bill Bennett, a man seventeen years her senior, stayed happily married to him for thirty-nine years, until his death in 2002.*

She was described by more than one interview subject as "the perfect high-powered executive's wife." She not only by all accounts did a wonderful job as surrogate mother to Bennett's children when she entered their lives, but she was a reliable partner to her husband through all the highs and lows of his business career. She also proved a loyal caretaker during the last years of her husband's life, when the pain of circulation problems overwhelmed nearly every aspect of their lives together.]

Diana Bennett

MY RELATIONSHIP WITH MY STEPMOTHER SAM WAS ALWAYS STRONG, BUT IT GREW STRONGER, and my respect for her grew even greater during the last part of my father's life.

Understand, she could have hired full-time people to take care of him, to do all the dirty work, but she never did that. Oh, there were times when nurses came in during the day to help care for him, but there was no full-time help. Sam was the one who got this man up, showered and dressed him every single day. And near the end he'd had both legs amputated, so you can imagine what kind of job that was.

He was angry, even physically abusive. There were times I know where he physically hurt her. He could be mean when the pain got bad, and yet she stood by him. You know what they say about the caretaker experiencing as much pain as the one they're caring for. He took it out on her because she was the one who was always there.

Cameron Conn

IF YOU BROUGHT ANYONE ELSE IN TO CARE FOR MY GRANDFATHER, IT WOULD BE LIKE THROW-ing them to the wolves. He would have been impossible for them to deal with. I think Sam understood that the job was hers, and hers alone.

Diana Bennett

I WOULD CALL AND GO OVER IN THE EVENINGS DURING THOSE LAST YEARS. YOU NEVER JUST dropped in. You always called and made an appointment.

I went to the house several nights a week and cooked for him, because if I made him something that I knew from my childhood that he liked, like homemade chicken and dumplings, he would eat it. Sam was frustrated because she would have trouble getting him to eat anything she cooked.

So I did it as much to give her a break from cooking as to get him to eat something.

She pretty much gave up her entire life to care for him during that time. She stopped getting her hair and nails done, which was not easy for a woman who looked terrific whenever she went out. But she was just afraid to leave him alone.

I used to tell her that she could just leave him, and then he would have to hire people to take care of him. If he was as mean to them as he was to her, we knew that they'd walk out and he'd realize how wonderful she was to him. I told her he acted this way with her because he knew he could get away with it.

Sam was really an angel. She reiterated over and over again that she had married my father for better or worse, in sickness and in health, and that he had given her the greatest life anyone could ever hope for. She used to say to me: What kind of a person would she be if she wasn't there to go through the bad times with him?

Of course he wasn't mean all the time. There were a lot of times when after bouts of being mean he would be sweet and funny and telling stories about how much he loved her. His moods would shift as the pain increased or decreased.

The two of them even during all the good years were reclusive. They kept a very narrow circle of friends. They were not comfortable around a lot of people; you might even say they were a bit paranoid. They were suspicious of people liking them for their money. That sort of goes with the territory when you have that kind of wealth.

I will tell you that my father and Sam loved each other deeply till the day both of them died. Even though my father had been dead for four years, and Sam was still a very attractive woman, it never occurred to her to ever think about having anybody else in her life but him. People would mention that possibility to her, that maybe she should date, but that never occurred to her.

Al Hummel

IT'S BEEN FOUR YEARS SINCE WE LOST MY SISTER. I WOULD SAY HER HEART JUST GAVE OUT. I had a problem with her smoking, and I had a problem with her using the inhalers.

One time she told me she had a hard time catching her breath, and I said, "Well, okay, here's what I'm going to do. I have all these emergency oxygen units at the hotel [*Sahara*] that security uses when someone passes out."

I had my chief of security come over and show her how to use it. All you had to do was open it, put the mask on, and pull the handle. It was just a light amount of oxygen, but I thought it might help. This was just a couple months before she died. In hindsight, I've thought many times, goddamn it, why didn't I do something more than that?

Because of her smoking and her problems breathing, I think it was probably heart issues that caused her death.

Maybe there was something genetic, but shortly after Lynn died I had a physical and the doctor found ninety percent blockage in an artery. I had to have emergency surgery, and my thought was that she had the same thing.

Dr. Carol Harter

WELL, WE HAD THE EDUCATION BUILDING ON CAMPUS THAT WAS NAMED IN LYNN'S HONOR, and there had been other gifts made to the school by the foundation after Mr. Bennett died, and Lynn and I had become good friends. She was continuing to be very supportive of the university, and was finding her own way after caring so well for him through his medical problems.

In February of 2006, less than a year before she died, she had invited my husband, Mike, and me to go with her and Diana and Scott Menke on her boat on a private cruise to the Bahamas. We had the most wonderful time. It was on her 125-foot boat, the *Aerie*, and it was just the five of us and the crew.

We hooked up at the Atlantis resort in the Bahamas, where we stayed for two days because of weather issues, and then we went sailing all the way down into these beautiful remote islands. We'd dock, then anchor out and go in on a little boat and explore the islands where there were no people. We fed the wild pigs on one island, and set up a barbecue on another. It was a totally memorable experience because we'd never done anything like that.

I had seen Lynn just a week or so before she died. She was adding a whole new room to her home that she showed me. I don't want to be the spokesman for her death, but I know she was having trouble breathing and she had ordered oxygen from the hotel which they brought to her. They found her dead with the tank still there. It was such a shock.

Diana called me the night of her death, but I didn't get her call. I read the news in the paper the next morning, and I called Diana and she confirmed it. I couldn't believe it. I thought that Lynn was pretty healthy. She was doing Pilates and had lost thirty pounds and looked beautiful.

Scott Menke

I DON'T THINK MR. BENNETT COULD HAVE FOUND A MORE PERFECT PARTNER FOR HIMSELF than Sam. I just know that she was a beautiful, classy woman, and whenever she would walk in the room he would light up. I learned a lot from her, because I did a lot of things with her. She became like a second mother to me.

Diana Bennett

I KNOW A LOT OF LAS VEGAS HISTORIANS MIGHT LOOK AT THE OUSTER OF THE MOB AND Allen Glick and Frank Rosenthal from the Stardust as a pivotal moment in the city going from being mob-controlled to a respected Wall Street corporate-darling town. But I think equally important was my father's and Bill Pennington's taking over Circus Circus from Jay Sarno. I saw people like [*Black Book figure*] Carl Thomas in the hotel every day. He was sharp-looking and as good a dresser as you'd ever find, but he was also a totally mobbed-up guy.

Thomas and guys like him were removed from the property within months after my dad took over, and that was no easy task. It required a lot of intelligence and a lot of finesse to turn that place from a good-old-boys hangout to a place were family entertainment was the main priority, and middle America was made to feel more than welcome.

I think my father belongs right up there at the top of the Las Vegas leaders' list with Steve Wynn. We hear a lot about how Steve changed the face of Las Vegas. That is true, but my dad opened the door for Steve to do that because he created the business model that created the current Las Vegas. That's where people actually looked at all segments of the hotel-casino business, from hotel rooms, to food and beverage to gaming and entertainment, and understanding how to mass market the entire package to get as many people in here as we could from the rest of the country and the world.

My dad's genius was basically putting the whole package together to make it all inclusive to the largest number of patrons. His ability to do that got Wall Street interested and got large national corporations interested.

Did Steve Wynn come in and take it up fifteen notches from there? Absolutely, and he deserves due credit for that. But if my dad hadn't done his part, Las Vegas would not have risen to where it is and where it has been for the last twenty-five years.

The last days of my father's life were a particularly difficult time. He was in the hospital at Sunrise, and I remember we were watching football games on television. Dad was in fantasyland, and he imagined he was making bets on the games with Ralph Engelstad. I was supposed to be leaving the room to make these bets.

One time a porter passed by our room and Dad yelled out to him, "Have you placed your bets?"

The porter gave me a quizzical look, and I motioned to him to just nod his head. He did, and my father nodded back.

More than once Dad said to me, "Let's get Ralph and get on the plane and fly out tonight." I know he was ready to go home, and my thought was that we would soon check him out of the hospital and go home, like we'd done so many times before.

I was monitoring him through the day and night, and checking his urine output in this basin he had on the bed. I had given him some Arizona iced tea, and once when I left the room so he could urinate, he didn't call me back in for about twenty minutes. When he did, I looked in the basin and it was very dark-colored, and I was afraid he was urinating blood. He'd actually just poured the tea into it to alarm me, I guess.

On the last day I remember Sam being in the room with us, with her head in his lap, and he was stroking her hair and saying how beautiful she was, and how he was sorry that he'd made her sad. He just kept saying he wanted to go home, and then suddenly he closed his eyes and he was gone.

I guess the toughest part about being Bill Bennett's daughter was going through all the highs and lows. It was being on a pedestal one minute, and then knocked off it the next. And I never knew for sure what put me up there, and what it was that knocked me down.

I hope my own children feel every minute of every day that I love them unconditionally, that it doesn't matter if they've screwed up or not. I want them to feel they can always come and talk to me and that the channels of communication are always open.

I hate to admit this, but my father's love was very inconsistent, and very conditional. But I retain the Bennett name to this day because I take a great deal of pride in his legacy and what he did for our industry and our community. It's a name I wear proudly.

Contributors
(in order of appearance)

Diana Bennett
Bill Bennett's daughter and a major contributor to this book. She is currently the owner and chief executive officer of Paragon Gaming.

Betty Spitler
Bill Bennett's sister. She currently resides in Glendale, Arizona, where she and her brother were raised.

Linda Christie
Bill Bennett's niece, and the daughter of Betty Spitler.

Lynn Lucia
Bill Bennett's stepdaughter. She currently resides in Texas.

Bill Allen Bennett
Bill Bennett's son. He worked in a variety of positions for Circus Circus Enterprises and resides in Las Vegas.

Al Hummel
Brother-in-law of Bill Bennett, he is the younger brother of Lynn (Sam) Bennett. He held a number of executive positions for Circus Circus.

Billy Conn
Former husband of Diana Bennett and father of their two sons, Todd and Cameron. He held a variety of positions under Bill Bennett.

Nancy Gambardella
Bill Bennett's executive secretary for eighteen years, at both Circus Circus and the Sahara Hotel.

Ben Speidel
A longtime employee and executive under Bill Bennett, he provided valuable information and photos for this book.

Glenn Schaeffer
Chief financial officer for years for Circus Circus Enterprises, who functioned as the face of the company to Wall Street during its glory years in the 1980s and early '90s.

E. Parry Thomas
Former president of Valley Bank, called by many the Most Important Person in Las Vegas for nearly three decades. Subject of the biography *Quiet Kingmaker of Las Vegas.*

Peter Thomas
Son of Parry Thomas and former president of Valley Bank of Nevada.

Mel Larson
Director of marketing and public relations for Circus Circus for twenty years, notable for his pink sportcoats, cars, and helicopters. He says his job was simply "to fill the hotel rooms."

Bill Paulos
A top executive with Circus Circus for many years, he was instrumental in building Excalibur, Luxor, and the Colorado Belle in Laughlin.

Mike Sloan
Chief legal counsel for Circus Circus, and invaluable in fostering important political relationships for Bill Bennett.

Dr. David Schwartz
A UNLV history professor and expert on gaming history in Las Vegas. He is currently writing a biography of Circus Circus creator Jay Sarno.

Michael Milken
Probably the most important behind-the-scenes player in modern Las Vegas history, Milken helped Bill Bennett and Bill Pennington take Circus Circus public and become the darlings of Wall Street in the 1980s. He is currently the chairman of the Milken Institute, a nonpartisan think tank.

Tony Alamo
A top executive for Circus Circus for many years and a close business ally with Mike Ensign, who many felt was the executive closest to Bill Bennett. Alamo is a central figure in the book *Super Casino.*

Chip Hanauer
A several time world championship unlimited hydroplane racer who brought Bill Bennett a world championship racing crown at the helm of Miss Circus Circus.

Dr. Doug Thomas
A prominent Las Vegas dermatologist whose father, Art Thomas, was a store owner in Circus Circus when Bennett and Pennington took over the hotel-casino.

Scott Menke
The great-nephew of Bill Bennett who learned the hotel casino business at a young age. He is currently the president of Paragon Gaming.

Jody Ghanem
Wife of Bill Bennett's late physician and business associate Dr. Elias Ghanem, she took many trips with the Bennetts and was a close personal friend.

Clyde Turner
Former top executive with Steve Wynn who later assumed a major leadership role with Circus Circus.

Dick Rizzo
The president of Perini Construction who worked closely with Bill Bennett on the construction of Luxor.

Sam Sabin
An executive with Perini Construction who served as project manager on the construction of Luxor.

Craig Hodgkins
A one-time boat captain for the Bennetts who later became president of the Sahara Hotel under Mr. Bennett.

Cameron Conn
Youngest grandson of Bill Bennett, and currently an executive with Paragon Gaming.

John McManus
General counsel for Bill Bennett during the Sahara Hotel years and beyond.

Matt Smith
One-time physical therapist for Bill Bennett, he later became president of the Sahara Hotel.

Marlee Palermo
Granddaughter of Bill Bennett and daughter of Diana Bennett, she worked at the Sahara Hotel.

Dr. Carol Harter
Former president of the University of Nevada, Las Vegas and current executive director of the Black Mountain Institute.

Todd Conn
Grandson of Bill Bennett and currently a police officer with the Las Vegas Metropolitan Police Department.

D. Taylor
Local Culinary Union secretary-treasurer and head of the international union's gaming division.